Y0-BFG-588

DEMOCRATIC SCHOOL ACCOUNTABILITY

A Model for School Improvement

Edited by
Ken Jones

Rowman & Littlefield Education
Lanham, Maryland • Toronto • Oxford
2006

Published in the United States of America
by Rowman & Littlefield Education
A Division of Rowman & Littlefield Publishers, Inc.
A wholly owned subsidiary of The Rowman & Littlefield Publishing Group, Inc.
4501 Forbes Boulevard, Suite 200, Lanham, Maryland 20706
www.rowmaneducation.com

PO Box 317
Oxford
OX2 9RU, UK

British Library Cataloguing in Publication Information Available

Library of Congress Cataloging-in-Publication Data
Democratic school accountability : a model for school improvement / edited by Ken Jones.
p. cm.
Includes bibliographical references.
ISBN-13: 978-1-57886-462-1 (hardcover : alk. paper)
ISBN-10: 1-57886-462-3 (hardcover : alk. paper)
ISBN-13: 978-1-57886-463-8 (pbk. : alk. paper)
ISBN-10: 1-57886-463-1 (pbk. : alk. paper)
1. Educational accountability. 2. Educational tests and measurements. 3. School improvement programs. 4. Teachers. I. Jones, Ken, 1949–
LB2806.22.D46 2006
379.1'58–dc22 2006002898

∞™ The paper used in this publication meets the minimum requirements of American National Standard for Information Sciences—Permanence of Paper for Printed Library Materials, ANSI/NISO Z39.48-1992.
Manufactured in the United States of America.

CONTENTS

FOREWORD

Monty Neill

For several decades, education in the U.S. has been increasingly under the sway of standards, tests, and sanctions policies that purport to improve public schools. States promulgate standards stating what students are to know and be able to do; "rigorous" assessments "aligned" to the standards are used to determine whether or how well students meet the standards; and students and teachers are rewarded or face sanctions for their test scores. The underlying idea is that schools will focus on what is most important ("laser-like" is a common term) and will change curriculum and instruction, leading to higher scores. Those rising scores will be proof that schools are improving.

Many states had moved quite a way down this road even before the No Child Left Behind law (NCLB) imposed a federally mandated structure of tests, "Adequate Yearly Progress," and sanctions. If the tests-and-sanctions theory were valid, we should already be seeing significant improvements in schools. That we are not leaves this approach vulnerable to conceptual attack and empirical criticism.

From the start, the concept has faced strong criticism from two general directions. One includes pedagogical critics who charge that this approach will not produce improved learning outcomes. Instead, they say, it will undermine good education and not induce high quality where schooling is now poor. The second includes those who argue that this approach is a diversion from addressing the real problems by blaming schools for not overcoming the consequences of racism and poverty. If rich learning is the desired goal, students must have adequate nutrition, housing, and health care as well as stable and caring families, communities, and schools. Racial segregation must be attacked anew. Schools themselves cannot do their job well without increased resources.[1]

My organization, FairTest, has concurred with the second critique while focusing primarily on aspects of the first. While schools can do better, and some do well in difficult circumstances, the current framework for school reform will not improve education. Since public schools are so important in the lives of our children and communities, the nation must pursue better ways to improve schools and to ensure all children receive the kinds of support they need so that, in the words of the Children's Defense Fund, we truly "leave no child behind."

As an approach to improving teaching and learning, the tests-and-consequences scheme has always been shaky. Standardized tests, even if based on decent standards, cannot be the primary goal or the measure of school improvement. The theory of action underlying this approach will not lead to high-quality changes.

Standards are not necessarily a bad idea. FairTest applauded the standards initially advanced by the National Council of Teachers of Mathematics (NCTM), seeing them as a vehicle to improve teaching and learning as well as assessment. However, questions soon arose as the professional standards became codified and mandated in state laws and regulations. Many of these standards are simply absurd and irrational, as authors such as Deborah Meier, Alfie Kohn, and Susan Ohanian have pointed out.[2] The volume of standards grew to gargantuan dimensions. It soon became clear that no living human, never mind a student, could actually meet all of them. As a result, any test based on them would have to be very selective and would inevitably not be comprehensive. On top of all this, standards-setting became the terrain of political battles as various groups, particularly conservatives, used state power to dictate their ideas of educational correctness.

The standards rubber hits the road with the tests. Study after study has found that state tests are not well aligned with their own standards. The tests focus on what is easy to measure, not what is important, relying primarily on multiple-choice questions. In New York, teams of scholars examined the Regents high school exams. Published authors of fiction evaluated the language arts exams, and historians considered the history tests. College admissions officers looked at several tests, including language arts, history, and environmental sciences. In all cases, the exams were excoriated as being largely irrelevant to what students needed to know and be able to do in college.[3]

More recently, Achieve, an entity set up by state governors to promote test-based accountability, surveyed professors who taught college freshmen. As is usually the case, the professors were unhappy with student preparation, but what they say is lacking is instructive: students do not have the ability to read complex materials with understanding, the ability to write extended papers, and oral proficiency. The tests do not measure or promote these important skills.

The tests, then, do not align with the standards. However flawed the standards may be, the tests are worse. Some may feature a solid open-ended question. Some of the declarative knowledge covered by the multiple-choice questions is valuable. But there are too few meaningful questions and far too much trivia. For example, the *only* question about the Civil War, its causes and consequences, on the Grade 10 Massachusetts MCAS U.S. history exam one year asked: Who was the commanding U.S. general at the Battle of Gettysburg?

With high stakes attached, the curriculum becomes mastery of often-disconnected facts and rote applications. Memorization is prized, thinking given short shrift. Because low-income and minority-group students are more likely to score low, they are most likely to find their schools turned into test-prep programs. Students from upper-income families may at least partly escape this consequence because the culturally skewed tests do not present the same kind of threat to them and because their parents have some idea what the children need to learn if they are to succeed in college.

In short, test-based sanctions backfire, if the goal is improving education rather than centralizing control over education or producing low-level thinking, compliant workers-to-be. Of course, education means different things to different people. To some, it does mean rising scores on narrow tests. For most people, however, it means a lot more, from academics that include critical thinking to preparing students for a complex range of adult activities. But that is not what school reform today seems to mean to most policymakers.

Thus, test-based accountability will fail our children by narrowing and dumbing-down education, to say nothing of denying diplomas to tens of thousands of students, mostly poor and of color, who will then have virtually no chance of economic security.[4]

State exams cannot be used to provide trustworthy evidence of educational improvement. Years of research find that teaching to the test produces score inflation: the scores go up but real knowledge, even as measured by other standardized tests, does not. No test assesses the range of academic knowledge our students need, never mind additional attributes the public desires, such as civic responsibility, creative thinking, and the ability to use knowledge. But the United States employs few indicators other than test scores as the main forms of evidence of school success. Two available indicators that are useful to look at are the National Assessment of Educational Progress (NAEP) and graduation rates.

On NAEP, high school scores have remained flat for decades: intensifying the stakes attached to state exams has not produced improvement either on NAEP or college admissions tests.[5] While NAEP results provide useful information, its exams are quite limited. Individual students take twenty- to thirty-minute slices of the whole exam, too little time to probe for conceptual understanding or the ability to do extended work. Worse, narrowing the curriculum to the tested subjects of reading and math is very common, likely producing the overall score gains seen across the nation on the Grade 4 NAEP. Through intense drill, scores increase modestly in the tested subjects, but at the expense of greater understanding in those disciplines and the reduction, if not elimination, of other subjects. The nation may be getting less real education while fooling itself that things are improving.

Turning schools into test-prep programs has been accompanied by an apparent drop in graduation rates, according to several studies. The Southern states, pioneers in high-stakes testing, have averaged a five-point decline.[6]

FairTest does not believe that all U.S. schools are a disaster because of test-based accountability. Many schools serve their students well. Teachers work effectively and caringly. Even in some schools with low scores and low college-attendance rates, educators may be doing great things under enormously difficult circumstances. Overall, however, test-based accountability is undermining, not enhancing, schools, especially for our most disadvantaged students.

Critiques of test-based accountability do not by themselves advocate an alternative approach: What if the nation went about school improvement differently? Could another path put useful attention on schools, avoid the clear harmful consequences, and actually improve schools? Is there any empirical evidence to support that direction and guide action?

FairTest has long promoted authentic performance and formative assessments in our own work and in collaboration with others.[7] Classroom-based assessment must be the foundation of all assessment work, which means skilled teachers employing a wide array of methods to discern students' strengths and weaknesses, how students learn, how best to help them, and how to ensure that students also learn to self-assess. Through this process, students and teachers can find and develop what Patricia Carini has described as the standards that emerge from each child's own work and growth,[8] as well as help students meet the formal standards of the school, district, or state. There is some evidence, from the United States and elsewhere, that qualified teachers using these kinds of assessments do lead to improved outcomes.[9] The work students do can be compiled in portfolios, which become the basis for shared understanding of how well students meet educational goals. Collaboratively reviewing portfolios and using them to enrich instruction is one key way for educators to improve schools.

FairTest has also helped develop ideas for improved accountability, using a richer array of measures (classroom- and school-based assessments, school inspections, and exams) and a different theory of action. These have included working with the Massachusetts Coalition for Authentic Reform in Education and with a national network that is "rethinking accountability."[10]

In addition to classroom-based evidence and limited use of external tests, school inspections as conducted in England, in Rhode Island, and with charter and pilot schools in Massachusetts can be a valuable tool for school self-reflection. Finally, educators need to report to the public on both academic measures and indicators of the overall climate and health of the school, and construct methods for public review and feedback.

This requires a different theory of action: that educators together with students, parents, and the community should be the core of improvement efforts, conducted not through threats or directed toward boosting test scores but cooperatively, with accountability looking at processes as well as a range of evidence on results.

Accountability, however, cannot be a one-way street. Policymakers have exempted themselves from the damaging consequences of test-based accountability and have too often abrogated their responsibility to ensure that schools have the resources to do their jobs well. They have conceptualized accountability as tests and punishments, not as obtaining rich evidence to be used for improvement.

FairTest has also built national coalitions of education, civil rights, and other organizations to point the way toward an overhaul of the NCLB law and the many state policies that head down the same dangerous road.[11] Complex questions remain as to how best to ensure that the federal government can help schools improve their capacity to serve all children well without micromanaging either through testing or through bureaucratic directives. We will be working on these questions in the months leading up to the 2007 reauthorization of NCLB.

We therefore welcome this powerful, illuminating, highly valuable book. It addresses the purposes and uses of accountability—to improve schools, to ensure they serve each and every child well, and to foster democracy. To attain the goal of a high-quality education for every child, we need to know how accountability processes can help, rather than undermine, progress toward the goal. This volume contributes greatly toward answering that "How?" and I commend it strongly to you.

NOTES

1. R. Rothstein, *Class and schools* (Washington, D.C.: Economic Policy Institute, 2004); D. Berliner, *Our impoverished view of educational reform*, Presidential Invited Speech to the American Educational Research Association meeting, Montreal, Canada, May 2005, available at http://www.tcrecord.org/search.asp?kw=Berliner&x=14&y=17; J. Kozol, *The shame of the nation: The restoration of apartheid schooling in America* (New York: Crown, 2005).
2. D. Meier, *In schools we trust* (Boston: Beacon, 2002); A. Kohn, *The schools our children deserve* (Boston: Houghton-Mifflin, 1999); S. Ohanian,

What happened to recess and why are our children struggling in kindergarten? (New York: McGraw-Hill, 2002).

3. See www.performanceassessment.org/consequences/ccritiques.html for details of the reviews.

4. The arguments on the consequences of high-stakes testing are summed up in M. Neill and L. Guisbond, *Failing our children* (Cambridge, Mass.: FairTest, 2004).

5. S. Nichols, G. Glass, and D. Berliner, *High-stakes testing and student achievement: Problems for the No Child Left Behind Act* (Tempe: Education Policy Studies Laboratory, Arizona State University, 2005), available at www.asu.edu/educ/epsl/EPRU/documents/EPSL-0509-105-EPRU.pdf; A. Amrein and D. Berliner, High-stakes testing, uncertainty, and student learning, Education Policy Analysis Archives (2002), available at http://epaa.asu.edu/epaa/v10n18/. S. Nichols et al. explain that only in grade 4 math is there some chance that greater test-based accountability pressure produced greater gain, greater exclusion of English-language learners and students with disabilities, among other things, probably explains the apparently greater gains.

6. P. Barton, *One-third of a nation: Rising dropout rates and declining opportunities* (Princeton, N.J.: Educational Testing Service, Policy Evaluation and Research Center, 2005); Southern Regional Education Board, *Getting serious about high school graduation* (Atlanta: Author, 2005), available at www.sreb.org/main/Goals/Publications/05E06-Graduation.pdf

7. M. Neill, et al. *Implementing Performance Assessments* (Cambridge, Mass.: FairTest, 1995); National Forum on Assessment, *Principles and indicators for student assessment systems* (Cambridge, Mass.: FairTest, 1995).

8. P. F. Carini, Dear Sister Bess: An essay on standards, judgment and writing, *Assessing Writing* 1, no. 1 (1994), 29–65.

9. P. Black and D. William, Inside the black box: Raising standards through classroom assessment, *Phi Delta Kappan* 80, no. 2 (1998), 139–48; see also various issues of FairTest *Examiner*, available at www.fairtest.org/examtoc.htm

10. Coalition for Authentic Reform in Education, *A call for an authentic state-wide assessment system*, available at www.fairtest.org/care/accountability.html; FairTest, Draft principles for authentic accountability, in M. Neill and L. Guisbond, *Failing our children* (Cambridge, Mass.: FairTest, 2004). Principles alone available at www.fairtest.org/nattest/Authentic%20Accountability/Draft%20Principles.html.

11. Joint Organizational Statement on No Child Left Behind (NCLB) Act, available at www.fairtest.org/joint%20statement%20civil%20rights%20grps%2010-21-04.html.

INTRODUCTION: RAISING SCHOOLS

What does it mean to be accountable? Ask this question in school circles these days and you will surely have a conversation about raising test scores. The chances are good that this conversation will be fraught with emotions—fear, frustration, a sense of injustice. As a teacher educator, I hear and feel these emotions on a regular basis, not just from educators but also from students and parents. Accountability has come to mean an unfair numbers game imposed from above rather than responsible behavior toward an agreed-upon goal. The word itself seems heavily weighted with top-down control and blame.

The fact is that the test-based system of school accountability that our policymakers have established for schools feels oppressive and doesn't make sense to the very people who are supposed to make it work. Not only is there a lack of belief in the fairness of the system but there is no confidence that it will lead to better schools and better learning for students. In fact, there is little evidence that it is doing so, even in terms of test scores, as Monty Neill points out in the foreword to this book. In a larger sense, we don't really know whether schools are improving because we haven't defined what a good school is in the first place. We have been busy raising test scores, not raising schools.

If we truly want to raise our schools to great heights, we will need to devote ourselves to a much deeper understanding of what schools are for and how they can best go about their business. By settling for the simplistic notion that school quality can be inferred by looking at the results of student testing, we have fashioned a form of accountability that looks at symptoms rather than causes and at a single measure instead of having a comprehensive look at a complex organization. Add to this the pressurized climate created by applying high stakes to these tests, and we have a system that yields very little reliable information about how well schools are functioning while alienating the people in them.

In order for an accountability system to serve the purpose of raising schools, it must do more than count. It must inquire into matters of context, process, and a host of organizational variables. And with respect to motivating people to do their best, it must do more than threaten them. It must inform them, support them, guide them, and develop their professionalism. Schools are about people and human development, not about manufacturing objects. An effective school accountability system must pay attention to what is good for people, not just to productivity and a set of measurable objectives.

This book is an attempt to redefine the meaning of school accountability in just such human terms. It stems from years of understanding the failures of the current test-based system and the need to envision a workable alternative. Many times we have heard the question, "If we don't hold schools accountable through testing, can we hold them accountable at all?" It is as if we cannot even imagine another way, a better way, of guiding schools toward excellence and equity. In this book, we ask the reader to imagine a better way.

My coauthors and I have come together to present a model for school accountability that is focused on high definition, not high stakes. In so doing, we paint pictures of what good teachers, schools, districts, states, and communities are doing, showing that there are realities now that can form an empirical basis for the vision. This model is not a quick-fix one, but rather one that will take time, commitment, and yes, money. We believe that this wealthy society can actually make good on its promise to leave no child behind, and that there is a way to do that through wisely investing in schools, teachers, and children and figuring out an honest and constructive accountability system that can serve as an effective guidance system.

Above all, we believe it is possible to do so in a democratic, not authoritarian, way. In fact, we believe it is crucial to do so. We want our children to grow up in a democratic society where equity is more than a rhetorical catch-phrase. This means that our schools must carry this torch, must operate democratically, must raise good citizens. The values that we hold for our children we also hold for our schools. It is not through control and command that we will help either of them grow into their full flower.

Growth is something we talk a lot about in our society, mostly in economic terms—sales, profits, market share, and so on. It appears that we have taken this same concept of growth into our thinking about schools, as we call for ever-increasing test scores. Our way of keeping account of schools is, in fact, very capitalistic. Growth as the indicator of the health of schools is the model. Yet it feels that the kind of growth we are imposing on schools is not at all healthy. It seems cancerous, destroying many good and promising things in our schools. Our obsession with the growth of test scores is creating negative side effects that are worse than the perceived ills the system was designed to address. And yet, we continue to hold to the test-based premise of the system, even as we look to make it "fairer," to soften its blows.

But growth need not be a bad thing. As one who has recently raised a garden, I can say that I have been most interested in growth. But here I mean not the kind of forced growth that comes from an agribusiness type of approach, but rather a homegrown caring that has to do with nurturing healthy organisms. I focus on husbandry of the soil, not fast-growth tonics that deplete the soil. I don't just observe things from a distant or technological vantage point, I get my hands into the mess of it all, digging, planting, weeding, mulching. I care about the growth of every one of my little seedlings. I think about relationships among different flowers and vegetables, about the changing contexts of sun and rain and bugs. I use my own judgment and the advice of knowledgeable friends to know how to make things better. I love a simple but good tool. I rejoice in my harvests and don't measure my success only by comparing my yield to last year's. Not a bad metaphor for schooling, I think.

I ask you as you read this book to allow this metaphor for organic growth to hold sway over the business growth model with which we are all so well acquainted. Even if you think such a metaphor implausible for schooling or possibly ineffective in achieving the hard goals of enabling our schools to provide equal opportunities for all, I ask that you give it a chance. Let the possibilities for defining school accountability take root in your thinking before you rush to judgment. As John Dewey might have said, this book is a thought experiment.

Each chapter in this book illuminates a different facet of possibility. After I outline the model in chapter 1, the authors of chapters 2 through 6 go into depth about specifics. Delwyn Harnisch and his Nebraskan teacher colleagues write about how a well-designed local assessment system can not only give a clearer picture of student learning than standardized testing but can also help teachers learn their craft in a powerful way. Jean Whitney expands the concept of opportunity-to-learn to include the necessity of engaging students, not just the provision of access. Barnett Berry zeroes in on the most crucial of all opportunities to learn, teacher quality, and demonstrates how it is teachers themselves who can foster and maintain the expertise of the profession and must be enabled to do so. Melody Shank uses two schools to illustrate how collaborative culture and structures are at the heart of developing a school's organizational capacity. Norm Fruchter and Kavitha Mediratta show how the power of a local community can be mobilized to guide and support schools.

Chapters 7 through 9 show some strategic possibilities for enacting the model. Katharine Pence speaks from her personal experience as a principal and as a school accreditation visitor to show how school visitations can provide data on school quality issues that cannot be measured through testing. George Entwistle, a businessman turned superintendent, gives a firsthand account of how his district has begun to enact a local school accountability model like the model proposed in this book. Patrick Phillips, the deputy commissioner of education in Maine, thinks about the proper role of the state in a system of reconfigured accountability.

In the last chapter, I attempt to synthesize some of the lines of thought developed in these chapters, articulate some underlying propositions, suggest some initial steps in the right direction, and conclude by dwelling on the obvious: kids.

I don't presume that this book is a well-defined answer to the complex problems of schooling in this country. It is meant as food for thought, an entry point for a new conversation about school accountability. So many of us can see that we need new direction and new leadership as we renew and improve public schools for the twenty-first century. We are parents and grandparents, sisters and brothers, neighbors and global citizens who are worried about the future of education and democracy in this country, as well as throughout the world. We are responsible and hardworking people who devote ourselves to raising children, raising schools, raising our society. It is in the spirit of this kind of accountability that my coauthors and I offer this work of hope.

Ken Jones
Westbrook, Maine
Spring 2006

1

A NEW MODEL FOR SCHOOL ACCOUNTABILITY

Ken Jones

So often when someone criticizes the current approach to school accountability, it is assumed that the person offering the critique is opposed to school accountability altogether. It is as if the current test-based approach is the only system possible, reasonable, or acceptable. I would like to get past that mind-set and explore ideas of school accountability that might indeed make more sense than what we now have in place.

First, I unequivocally agree with the premise that schools should be accountable to the public. So much is invested in our schools—and not just in money—that to have no accountability would be tantamount to planting seeds and not tending the garden. How can we trust that the hopes we have for our children, our communities, and our society in general will bear fruit unless we watch, understand, and act to promote the health of our schools?

The current concern about school accountability is important and well founded. Despite our best intentions and efforts over the years, we know that our schools are not functioning as well as we wish. We see continuing and unjust achievement gaps between our white middle-class students and our students from different racial and cultural backgrounds or less advantaged circumstances. We look at our changing world and realize that we need schools to not only cultivate basic literacy and numeracy but also to have more of an emphasis on complex thinking skills, collaborative dispositions, and an understanding of global issues. We see an increase in social ills and see that schools must provide more and more support to students in need. We see greater and greater cultural, linguistic, and ethnic diversity in this country and struggle with making our schools more adaptive and responsive. We deal with an increasing number of young people who are not motivated to succeed in schools as we have organized them and know that we must find ways to make school more engaging and relevant to their lives. The list can go on—there is much to do to improve and renew schooling in this country.

An essential part of accomplishing this improvement and renewal is to delegate responsibility for the work to education professionals and to check to see that they are doing their jobs well. This is the meaning of accountability: to ensure that those entrusted with the work are going about the business in a way that is visible, productive, and responsive to the agreed-upon goals of the enterprise.

But the school accountability system that we have recently developed is not working to address the critical issues just mentioned. In fact, our current accountability approach was created without much of a public discussion about how it would do this. Basic questions were not posed, such as: For what should schools be accountable? To whom should they be accountable? What means should we use to evaluate their accountability? Instead of working from such outcome-based types of questions, policymakers simply took the existing testing regimen as virtually the sole measurement for school accountability. This approach is proving to be not only very narrow but also quite counterproductive to our expressed purpose of leaving no child behind.

The problems with the existing approach are manifest. Based on the results of a single test, huge numbers of schools have been declared failures in a time when public surveys indicate very high public approval ratings for schools.[1] Struggling students are dropping out of school, are denied grade-level promotion, and are referred to special education programs in increasingly large numbers.[2] School curricula are inevitably narrowed to focus on test taking, with an emphasis on drill-and-practice pedagogy and a more authoritarian relationship between teachers and students.[3] Significantly, minority students experience these effects more frequently.[4] Teachers are becoming more and more demoralized and placed in the role of technician rather than professional decision maker.[5] They are leaving the profession in record numbers.[6]

In addition to these dire consequences, we can include the fact that this approach has created a classic case of goal displacement. Business guru W. E. Deming warned us years ago about this consequence of managing by objectives and quotas. What has happened in education is that attention has become fixated on the measurement objective (test score) and the quota (annual yearly progress) rather than the goal of greater excellence and equity. This fixation is largely due to the high stakes involved, which force teachers to do their best to win the game that has been set up. Test scores are the only currency in the realm of this accountability system. The means has become the end and the original goal has often been forgotten in the rush to improve test scores.

Another piece of advice given by Deming was that if there is a problem in the system, we should look to fix the system, not the people in it. This is very helpful advice in these times, when it seems that teachers are being blamed more and more for the problems encountered in schools. What we now have in place is an accountability mechanism that looks not at the whole system but only at end products. It's a model that looks to blame and punish people rather than to support and enable them.

Sometimes called outcome-based education or results-based accountability, the current model has come about in the last twenty years as part of a welcome shift in thinking from a strictly "input" model. Schools had been evaluated primarily on the basis of things like time-on-task, library resources, prescribed approaches to teaching, and so forth. What was not taken into account was student learning. Schools could be considered fine if they were doing the "right things," whether or not those things led to successful learning for students. And it didn't seem to matter if some kids did well and others did not. Schools were, and still are, clearly not the force of equity and equal opportunity we believe them to be. And so, the thinking went, let's go beyond talking about equal opportunity—let's insist on equal results. No "excuses" for less than that would be accepted.

Outcome-based accountability really took hold, however, not so much from equity concerns as from concerns about international competitiveness. The 1983 report *A Nation at Risk* painted the picture that our economic prosperity and way of life were in desperate jeopardy if we didn't fix our failing schools. The notion that school systems are responsible for the state of an economy has since been contradicted by the rise of the American economy and the fall of economies in Southeast Asia. The conclusion that our schools are failing because of performance on international testing has also been seriously questioned.[7]

At the time, however, the conviction that our schools were bad and needed to be fixed was widespread. As it still is today, in fact. From one camp came the concern about excellence compared to other countries. From another camp came the concern about equity for those who had been so ill served by our school systems. Excellence and equity—the same concerns then as now.

These forces led to the shift in thinking about accountability. Attention would now be paid to the outcomes of schools, not the inputs. It was a pendulum swing of sorts. Inputs would not even be considered. Outcomes would be defined and measured. Like profit and loss statements in business, these measures would provide the basis for deciding if a school was behaving accountably. What outcomes would matter? Student learning of academic subjects. How would we measure these? Through the time-honored American habit of standardized testing.

Interestingly, at that time, in the late 1980s and early 1990s, the outcome-based direction was portrayed as a form of deregulation. Schools were given new discretion in determining processes and means while states and districts would take on the new role of defining and measuring the outcomes. Schools would be free to decide upon their own curricula and pedagogy so long as the students met the outcomes as defined by the state. States would develop assessment systems to measure whether the outcomes were achieved and local decision making would be responsible for producing the achievement.

It all seems quite logical to first define outcomes, then develop a measurement system to see if they are met, and then plan toward those targets. After all, how could you begin a journey without a defined destination or a road map and have any hope of arriving where you hoped to go? In classroom practice, this kind of "backward" instructional planning can be very effective. At the school and district levels, such priority setting and consequent strategic planning can also work well to organize efforts and resources in a given direction.

The new outcome-based accountability movement took this planning strategy and made it a mechanism for large-scale change. At the same time, it coupled the idea with a historic shift in the locus of control of public schools. The new reform was focused on state-level initiatives. Governors and legislatures, often driven by court decisions, responded to the calls for school improvement by asserting their constitutional authority in state law to set new requirements for schools. Taking the outcome-based planning approach and applying it to a large-scale assessment system might have had some very good effects, depending on the quality of the assessment system, were it not for the large-scale change strategy it employed. The assumption was made that high-stakes consequences for performance on state assessments were needed in order to force school change, and that all planning should lead toward that outcome alone.

Other assumptions followed: that the outcomes should be about academic subject matter as presently organized, that an external testing system at the state level would be the best means for measuring student success, that schools should be rated according to the student results on such testing, that schoolwide test results should show an ever-increasing rise over time, and that a school's rating should have consequences in the form of rewards or sanctions to the schools. The biggest assumption of all, of course, was that this businesslike model would promote a new educational excellence and equity that would improve our public schools.

These assumptions must be questioned if we are to design a better school accountability model. Just as an improvement in student learning should begin with defining outcomes, an improvement in schooling should begin with defining the purposes and goals of schooling. From there, we can determine what schools should be accountable for. And to whom. Then, by what means. We have jumped to the end of the process by defining the means without examining basic premises first.

Simply put, we have approached school accountability in a way that is contradictory to the logical approach espoused for valid assessment. For assessment of student learning to be valid, it is understood that the starting place must be to explicitly establish the purpose of the assessment and the learning goals to be assessed. Yet we have not done the same with respect to school accountability systems—we have not had a public agreement about the purposes and goals of schools. One wonders how our school accountability systems could be deemed valid under such circumstances.

With the effects of the current approach becoming more and more problematic, it is time to have such a discussion. A beginning assumption for undertaking this process in a democratic society would be that the conversation should be public and should include students, parents, community members, and taxpayers. Presently, the discussion about educational priorities has been managed by business executives, elected officials, and policymakers. Unless we include the wider public, we are unlikely to change much in the existing system.

What is needed is a better means for evaluating schools, an alternative to the present system of using high-stakes testing for school accountability. I propose a new model for our collective thinking, based on a specific set of assumptions and understandings about school realities and approaches to power. It is based on the foundational belief that sustaining a modern democracy requires local schools that embody the values and practices underlying a government that is dedicated to government of the people, by the people, and for the people. All of its people.

DEMOCRATIC PURPOSES OF SCHOOLS

What shared values are important in a democracy? With public school serving as the primary means of enculturing citizens, what norms and practices should those schools embody? How should schools in a democracy be different than schools in a dictatorship?

These questions and others of their ilk are not new to educators. Questions about the proper role of public schools in a democracy have been debated for many years. Nearly a century ago, John Dewey explored what having a democratic purpose for schools meant regarding what should get taught and how it should be taught.[8] More recently, educators such as Carl Glickman, John Goodlad, and Deborah Meier have spoken insightfully and forcefully about the importance of developing schools as the engines of democracy.

The issue is a practical one, but at its base it is also about our most deeply held beliefs in the United States. This country was founded on a set of principles that became well established in documents such as the

Declaration of Independence and the Bill of Rights and that continue to be called upon in our political rhetoric and expressions of allegiance. As a people, we believe that our democracy should safeguard the life, liberty, and pursuit of happiness of all citizens, that all people are created equal, and that we have certain individual and collective rights that must be protected. We believe that this is the land of the free and that there is opportunity for all. We also believe that education should be the means to a better life for all.

Perhaps the most basic notion of democracy is the idea of participatory decision making in an open society. And perhaps the most basic ideals associated with democracy are that the government should promote freedom, justice, and equity for all of its citizens. We hold these ideals high as a nation, despite the cruel realities that exist for many of our citizens.

As Jefferson and many others have articulated, maintaining and enacting this noble view of democracy depends strongly on how well educated the people are. In order for the will of the people to work for the common good and to hold government officials accountable, the people must be literate, well-informed, and able to think critically about the issues of the day. In this light, schools can be said to have a moral mission to develop the citizenry needed to sustain the democracy. Goodlad stresses the moral dimensions of schooling:

Schools are not often thought of or spoken of as institutions having moral imperatives, but the skills, dispositions, and habits of intellect for democratic citizenship have to be developed somewhere. People are not born with them. This places a considerable burden on the shoulders of teachers, who are responsible to the children they teach as well as to their parents and to society as a whole. The moral dimensions of teaching are inescapable. When a teacher begins to teach, a whole array of moral choices and decisions inescapably come into play. What is omitted from a curriculum can be just as consequential as what is included. How information is presented can have a tremendous effect on how it is received. Teaching cannot help but be informed by values and guided by normative principles.[9]

With these democratic aims in mind, what do we want schools to provide for our own children, to enable them to be active and productive contributors toward such a society? Some qualities come easily to mind, such as strong literacy and numeracy programs and safe, respectful climates. But shouldn't schools also develop the ability of our students to make informed choices and act on them? What about collaborating with others for the good of the whole? What about instilling the desire for and experience with freedom, justice, and equity? Surely we want our schools to enact these values for our children in a way that goes beyond simply studying them. Our schools should provide living democratic experiences in order to prepare students to become the kinds of adults who can understand and promote these values in our government and society.

Having this democratic purpose for schools means that academic achievement, while important, cannot be the only indicator for school success. There are also matters of relationship and process that are important. There must be a concern for not just what is learned but also for how it is learned, and for giving all students a fair chance to learn and to have a say in what they learn. Schools must empower students to be active citizens, not just good workers, consumers, or captive audiences. Carl Glickman describes the need for a democratic learning environment in the following way:

> Democratic learning aims for freedom of expression, pursuit of the truth in the marketplace of ideas, individual and group choices, student activity and participation, associative learning, and the application, demonstration, and contribution of learning to immediate and larger communities. Such efforts are made in the context of justice and equality for all, a consideration of individual liberty and group freedom, and respect for the authority and responsibility of teachers in setting conditions for developmental learning.[10]

Clearly, if we want schools to be models for democracy in such a way, we must get beyond defining accountability as strictly a matter of outcome measures. There are important process variables to ensure as well.

At the heart of cultivating schools as democratic organizations is the issue of power. Who decides what gets learned, how it gets learned, and so on? Deborah Meier points out the vital necessity for maintaining local control. She argues that the more we take decisions away from the local teachers and administrators, the less they are able to behave as leaders in a democratic school environment. The less students see adults making important decisions in a collaborative way, the less they are inclined or able to do so themselves.[11] When the federal and state governments take over the decision making about curriculum, assessment, and instruction, as they are more and more with the current form of accountability, what we get in schools is regimentation, resistance, and other dysfunctional trappings of disempowered people.

On the other hand, we also know that many schools need guidance and assistance if they are to provide their students with a fair measure of participatory decision making, openness, freedom, justice, and equity. A new model for school accountability must combine local decision making with state and federal oversight, in a way that models the democratic values that we hope to see in our schools.

FOR WHAT SHOULD SCHOOLS BE HELD ACCOUNTABLE?

Given the democratic purpose of schools, for what should we hold them accountable? I offer the following list as reasonable categories for which our schools should be accountable: the physical and emotional well-being of students, the learning of students and the assessment of that learning, teacher learning and evaluation, equity and access to learning for all, and the continuous improvement and renewal of the organization.

The Physical and Emotional Well-Being of Students

As parents, we expect that our children will be safe from injury and violence in schools and that their emotional needs will be met. We want them to be well known and cared for by their teachers, to be challenged but not intimidated, to have their strengths acknowledged and their weaknesses fortified. We want a certain degree of orderliness, but not to the extent of quashing our children's spirits, curiosity, or creativity. We'd like our children to see learning as interesting and important. These care-tending aspects of schooling are known to contribute to cognitive growth as well as comfort and engagement. They are not "soft" goals for schools, but are essential for learning. Schools should be accountable for maintaining such warm and inviting human environments.

Student Learning and Assessment

Student learning is complex and multifaceted, not something that can be well gauged with one simple standardized test. We need to approach the assessment of learning with the same care that a doctor might evaluate health or an engineer might determine safety. As any good psychometrician will tell us, there are many variables to consider when trying to establish a valid measure of learning. And, given the conditions of the now-emerging information society, there are many aspects of learning to assess, including disciplinary subject matter, thinking skills, and collaborative dispositions. If we want to really understand what students know and can do, we must assess in multiple dimensions using multiple means, including assessments developed and administered at local and classroom levels, where learning can be assessed in the specific context of learning. More and more, in this age of increasing standardization, we hear the caution that one size will not fit all. This admonition must be taken to heart in a system of school accountability where each student is a unique individual, with different styles of learning and expressive strengths. Our assessment systems must have the capability of customizing measurements to exceptional circumstances. Schools should be accountable not only for creating the conditions for excellent student learning but also for assessing it well.

Teacher Learning and Evaluation

Having a knowledgeable and skilled teacher is crucial. Most of us remember the good teachers we have had with fondness and gratitude for the manner in which they helped to shape our knowledge and understanding of the world. Research and common sense support the notion that good teaching supports and enables good learning. What may not be understood, however, is that good teaching must itself be supported and enabled. Teachers, like other professionals, must have opportunities throughout their careers to keep up with the latest developments in the field and to try new ways of teaching. Schools must be provided with sufficient time and funding, and held accountable, for guiding teachers to improve their own performance, according to professional teaching standards. Evaluation must be done in a way that honors democratic processes, supports the teaching profession, and upholds high standards of performance.

Equity and Access

Much-needed attention has been given lately to the achievement gap that exists between white middle-class students and minority and underserved student populations. Federal legislation now requires disaggregated test scores that will provide important data about the deep-set inequities in our educational systems. But acquiring data is only a part of the solution. Schools need to use such data, as well as other information, to place a renewed and special focus on improving equity and access, providing fair opportunities to learn for all students. This includes adapting curricula and instruction to address the cultural and experiential backgrounds of students. They should be held accountable for doing so.

Improving and Renewing

The world is changing rapidly and so schools must continuously improve and renew their work. We need schools to be dynamic learning organizations, continuously engaged in self-assessment and adjustment with respect to meeting the needs of their students. Structures and norms may need to be changed. Ends and means may need to be reconsidered. The capacity to do this work depends on many factors, most important of which may be a school culture where teachers, administrators, students, parents, and others are conscious of and concerned with the health of the whole organization, not just their own individual parts of it. Developing such a professional learning community is necessarily an ongoing effort. Schools should be accountable for making that effort, working always toward getting better.

TO WHOM SHOULD SCHOOLS BE HELD ACCOUNTABLE?

With the current system of school accountability, schools are held accountable for their student test scores to state and federal requirements. Often enough, the rationale heard for taking a certain action related to curriculum or instruction is that "the state says we have to do it" or "No Child Left Behind requires it." Teachers and administrators feel disempowered. In fact, school boards themselves, in this era of high-stakes testing, have lost power. The shift in control is upward and outward in the bureaucratic hierarchy. Those closest to the work are having less to say about what that work is and are subject to accountability determinations and evaluations based on the decisions of state departments, federal regulators, and, indeed, testing companies.

It is a serious question as to whether this shift in power serves the democratic purposes of schools or is even organizationally effective. What seems to be getting lost is the long-held tradition in this country of local control of schools—and with it, a loss of accountability to the local community.

In the face of this historic shift, I argue that a local accountability system should be maintained. Schools should be held accountable to their primary clients: students, parents, and the local community. It is this local client relationship that serves the student best. Within certain professional guidelines, schools should be free to make decisions about the ends of education, not just the means, for their own specific contexts. Rural communities have different needs than inner-city neighborhoods. A primarily Latino community has a different context for making learning relevant than a primarily suburban white one. Where a written assessment might work best in one situation, a verbal interview might work better in another. A standardized approach toward school accountability cannot work in a nation as diverse as ours. The new model must be one that honors the principle of local accountability while also ensuring that schools are held accountable to the categories mentioned above.

What can the state and federal levels of government do at this point to protect and sustain a local accountability system? In order to reverse the shift of power that is part of the current accountability movement, the state and federal governments should focus on (1) supporting the improvement and renewal of school practices, especially the development of high-quality assessments at the classroom and school levels—rather than continuing to invest in large-scale, high-stakes testing; (2) providing guidance and information for local planning, evaluation, and decision making—rather than classifying schools as successes or failures; and (3) working to ensure equity and access for all students, examining the opportunities to learn provided by local schools and districts—instead of leaving that to the black box of unmonitored local discretion. This should all be done with an eye on nurturing the democratic values discussed above.

By what means can we develop such a system of local accountability? I propose a model that is balanced between various polarities, looking at inputs as well as outcomes, locating control in the local community while also providing external checks and balances, prompting improvement and renewal without declaring our schools failures.

A BALANCED MODEL

There is a framework for accountability currently employed in the business world called the Balanced Scorecard that can provide a useful perspective for schools.[12] This framework describes a four-part measurement system designed to give a comprehensive view of the health of the organization. The premise is that both outcomes and operations must be measured in order to have a feedback system that serves to improve the organization, not just monitor it. The four perspectives that form the framework for measurement are (1) financial outcomes, (2) internal business processes, (3) customer satisfaction, and (4) organizational innovation and learning.

Applying and adapting this four-part approach to education, the following aspects of school performance can provide the components of a balanced school accountability model: (1) student learning outcomes, (2) processes that provide equitable opportunities to learn, (3) responsiveness to students, parents, and community, and (4) organizational capacity for improvement. Each of these aspects should be attended to and fostered by an accountability system that has a sufficiently high resolution to take into account the full complexity and scope of modern-day schools.

Student Learning Outcomes

Principles of high-quality assessment have been well articulated by various organizations and can provide guidelines for developing valid approaches that go far beyond standardized testing in providing evidence of what students know and can do.[13] In the interest of both excellence and equity, we need systems that (a) are primarily intended to improve student learning; (b) align with local curricula; (c) emphasize applied learning and thinking skills, not just declarative knowledge and basic skills; (d) embody the principle of multiple measures, including a variety of formats such as writing, open response questions, and performance-based tasks (not just multiple choice); and (e) are accessible by students with diverse learning styles, intelligence profiles, exceptionalities, and cultural backgrounds.

In the past few years, there have been interesting developments in cognitive science and brain research that relate to human learning. We now know that human intellectual abilities are malleable and that people learn through a social and cultural process of constructing knowledge and understandings in given contexts—and yet we continue to conduct schooling and assessment according to beliefs that intelligence is fixed, that knowledge exists apart from culture and context, and that learning is best induced through the behaviorist model of stimulus-response.[14]

There is another belief that underlies our current approach to assessment that deserves mention: that scientific measurement can truly "objectify" learning and rate it hierarchically. Indeed, the history of testing has been fraught with questionable assumptions about what intelligence is and what knowledge is valued.[15] Test scores alone do not tell the whole story about a student's learning. Who among us can honestly say that it has been our experience that our learning has been fairly represented by a test score? Why do we put such faith in such an approximate science? It would be better if we made decisions about the quality and depth of an individual's learning based on informed judgment, constrained by agreed-upon criteria and protocols for decision making. Although test scores and other assessment data are useful and necessary sources of information, a fair determination about a person's learning can only be made by other people, most preferably by those who best know the person in his or her own context. Rather than letting a formula "objectively" make decisions about student success, we might, for example, convene local panels of teachers, parents, and community members to review data about student performance and make decisions about promotion, graduation, placement, and so on. Of course, such approaches take time and human resources.

What is missing in most current accountability systems is not just a human adjudication system but also a local assessment component that addresses local curricula, contexts, and cultures. A large-scale external test is simply not sufficient to determine a student's achievement. District, school, and classroom assessments must also be developed as part of a comprehensive means of collecting data on student learning. The states of Maine and Nebraska have been developing just such local assessment systems.[16]

Most importantly, locally developed assessments depend upon the knowledge and "assessment literacy" of teachers. Most teachers have not been adequately trained in assessment and need substantial and ongoing professional development to develop valid and reliable tasks and effective classroom assessment repertoires. This means that an investment must be made in teacher learning related to assessment. The value of such an investment is not only in the promise of improved classroom instruction and measurement. Research also shows that improved classroom assessment results in improved student achievement on external tests.[17] That is, there is evidence that high-quality classroom assessment practices are in fact also high-quality instructional practices, contributing to improved achievement. This sort of investment in teachers pays dividends not seen in the investments we now make in testing contractors.

One note about a potential barrier to developing authentic local assessment efforts. There is a need for the state to determine the effectiveness of such local efforts as well as the health of the larger state school system. Depending on the approach taken to accomplish this, state requirements can either support or undermine local assessment efforts. If state or federal agencies require aggregated data from local to state levels, an undue emphasis will be placed on standardized methods and local decision making will be weakened. If, however, the state and federal agencies rely on methods other than aggregation of local scores, much may be gained. In New Zealand, for example, a system of educational monitoring is in place that entails using matrix sampling on tasks that include one-to-one videotaped interviews, team tasks, and independent tasks.[18] No stakes are entailed for schools or students. The data is profiled and shared with schools for the purpose of teacher professional development and as a means of developing model tasks for local assessments. Such a system supports rather than undermines local assessment efforts. At present, federal regulations require aggregated data at the state level. This is a problem.

Opportunity to Learn

How can students be expected to meet high standards if they are not given a fair opportunity to learn? This is *the* question that must be addressed if we are to develop a fair and equitable system for students. Not until we solve this problem can the standards-based movement be said to promote democratic values of justice and equity. To truly provide fair opportunities for all to meet our new high standards, we must have the political will and investment needed to remedy the inequities in the present system.

What could be done if our society really had the will and made the investment to leave no child behind? The most apparent problem that must be addressed is the inequitable funding of public schools, particularly the disparity between the schools of the haves and those of the have-nots. The schools of many urban and rural disadvantaged students often suffer debilitating conditions that would not be tolerated in suburban settings. Over the past decade, there have been lawsuits in various states attempting to redress this imbalance, which is largely a factor of dependence on property taxes for school funding. Small progress has been made. In a recent lawsuit, *Williams v. State of California*, the plaintiff school districts argued that all schools and school systems in the state should receive adequate resources from the state to provide qualified teachers, adequate instructional materials, and sound facilities. The state settled out of court, agreeing to provide for those prerequisites.

What is needed is more than the settlement of an individual case like this. A definition of financial adequacy in school funding must be legally established and enforced by the courts. In the literature about school accountability, there is a concept referred to as reciprocal accountability, wherein state and federal agencies are as accountable to provide resources for schools as schools are accountable to demonstrate performance. Two-way accountability. That would be another good requirement to establish.

But there is more to this issue than just funding. Jeannie Oakes describes a framework that includes opportunity-to-learn indicators for access to knowledge, professional teaching conditions, and "press for achievement."[19] Linda Darling-Hammond stresses the "fair and humane treatment" of students in a set of standards for professional practice.[20]

As such standards for opportunity to learn are articulated, the question arises as to how to monitor and report on them. Clearly this cannot be done through the proxy of testing. What is needed is a means of observation in schools and classrooms in order to determine the degree of adherence to these standards. Two aspects of this must be considered: the quality of individual teachers and the quality of the school as a whole.

Teacher evaluation has received a great deal of criticism for being ineffective. The hit-and-run observations so often done by principals do little to determine whether teachers are meeting established professional teaching standards. Unions have been described as more interested in protecting their membership than ensuring high-quality teaching. One promising development that has potential for breaking through this impasse is the peer review processes now conducted by a number of teacher unions. Dal Lawrence, who created the union-led Toledo model for teacher evaluation over twenty years ago, has this to say about the value of such systems:

> Highly complex work is normally performed by workers who are valued. Teaching is complex work, yet nearly half of all new teachers leave the occupation within five years. If one looks even casually, one can see that the school workplace needs a makeover. If we continue to run schools like American automobile plants in the 1950s, is it any wonder that many frustrated policymakers suggest that competition will produce better students, or schools?
>
> If ever there was a practice based on the assumption that a boss unquestionably has to be in charge, it is the way we bring novice teachers into the profession and measure their work and growth thereafter. The notion that principals are the only ones who should evaluate, hire and fire,

> or reassign teaching positions unilaterally, isn't far removed from where the auto industry was five decades ago. Yet, the great man, or woman, theory of school reform still gets prominent mention by reformers.
>
> It is my contention that until we challenge the way schools operate by rearranging roles and responsibilities of teachers and managers, most reform efforts will continue to be marginal at best. I know many will disagree, but I suggest that those who do are the ones most comfortable, or familiar, with existing adult relationships in schools.
>
> Twenty-four years ago we put in place an initiative that changed teacher and principal roles and produced more effective student results. The Toledo Plan is aimed at the very heart of teacher effectiveness. It gets results.[21]

In order to evaluate the performance of a school as a whole, a school review process will be needed. Variations of inspectorates and school quality reviews have been developed in New York, Rhode Island, Maine, and other states, as well as in Britain, New Zealand, Australia, and other countries.[22] School accreditation agencies are more and more focused on standards related to opportunity to learn. In order for such reviews to serve the purpose of school improvement, it is essential that the data collection be done in a "critical friend" manner through a combination of school self-assessments and collegial visitations. Findings from such a process should not be stated or used in a bureaucratic and judgmental way, but rather should be given as descriptions to local boards and councils charged with evaluating school accountability. As with all aspects of any school renewal initiative, the quality and effectiveness of a review system will depend upon the time, resources, and institutional support given to it.

Who will ensure that adequate opportunities to learn are present in schools? As described below, a system of reciprocal accountability must be set up so that both local accountability councils and the state itself serve to "mind the store" for all students. Equitable funding must be resolved through courts or legislatures.

Responsiveness to Students, Parents, and Community

We must look to empower students, parents, and communities as the primary clients of schools. How can we do this in a way that ensures that they will hold in trust the need for schools to serve the greater good of society, not just a local parochial interest, and not just the interests of one faction or another? This is the challenge—to entrust to local decision making the schooling of their own young while at the same time focusing schools on directions needed to sustain our democracy, our economy, and our national well-being.

One might say that this has been the role for school boards and that the current accountability movement actually goes around the role of the school board. Even if the testing approach were a given, it could have been that the tests were submitted to local boards for their consideration about what to do. Instead, the decision about what is expected on those tests and what to do has been preempted by the state and federal governments. To some extent, school-board decision making has been superceded by the current accountability approach.

Some argue that school boards, especially in urban areas, have not worked to the benefit of minorities and others who are not in the mainstream and that it is not a bad thing that they have been superceded. Certainly, the achievement gap and a host of inequitable practices in the schools confirm this analysis, but is it in the interest of equity to move accountability to a more remote agency, far from those who are closest to the children and teachers in the local context? To the extent that the local context is biased against certain students, this may have appeal—to look to an outside, higher, more objective system for holding schools accountable for fairness and equitable opportunities.

But what are the trade-offs for the underserved? Will their students do better in a state-controlled system of accountability? This must be the hope, but judging from current evidence, one must think it unlikely. With the state defining standards and tests, the consequences for those who have previously been left behind look no better. The litany of ill effects has been cited elsewhere.[23] Here let us just note again that the increase in dropout rates, retentions, referrals to special education, regimented instruction, and underqualified teachers has fallen most heavily on minority groups.

If we attempt to reverse this shift in power away from localities by calling for schools to be more accountable to their own students, parents, and community—for the elements just described above—what mechanisms could serve to guide and constrain school-board decision making?

Local school-based councils have been created in Chicago, Kentucky, and elsewhere that have been given authority to make decisions about curriculum, instruction, staffing, and other matters. They have received mixed reviews about their effectiveness in improving schooling. But what if local councils were organized more deliberately to serve an accountability function? These councils could review accountability information from state and local assessments as well as from school quality review processes and make recommendations to school boards about school policies and priorities. They could publicly hold school boards accountable for the development and implementation of school improvement plans. Phil Schlechty discusses how such councils might work:

> Community leaders who are concerned about the futures of their communities and their schools should join together to create a non-profit corporation intended to support efforts of school leaders to focus on the future and to ensure that lasting values as well as immediate interests are included in the education decision-making process. It would also be the function of this group to establish a small sub-group of the community's most trusted leaders who would annually evaluate the performance of the school board as stewards of the common good and would make these evaluations known to the community. . . .
>
> In a sense, the relationship between the school district and the monitoring function of the new corporation should be something akin to the relationship between the quality assurance division of a corporation and the operating units in the corporation. . . .
>
> When the data indicate that goals are not being met, the president of the corporation, working with the superintendent and the board of education, would seek to discover why this was the case, and would seek as well to create new approaches that might enhance the prospect of achieving the stated goals and the intended ends. It is not intended that the new corporation simply identify problems and weaknesses, it is intended that the leaders of this organization also participate in the creation of solutions and participate in creating support for solutions once they have been identified or created.[24]

Questions about how to comprise and sustain such councils and ensure that they do not pursue narrow agendas would need to be determined. How councils are composed in urban settings would likely vary and be different from those in rural or suburban settings. Standards and acceptable variations for councils would be important topics for public discussion.

Another intriguing possibility for resituating the locus of accountability control at the local level to ensure the responsiveness of schools to their primary clients lies in the advent of powerful community organizations that have served as advocates for school improvement.[25] From the Bronx to Texas to Oakland, citizen groups have come together to pressure schools to respond to important student needs. How could these types of organizations serve a role in a localized accountability system? What if they were given a seat at the table, included in discussions and decision making of school boards or local accountability councils? Treated and acknowledged as legitimate voices of the community? Surely, the kind of accountability that they now exert on schools could have an even more beneficial effect?

Whatever structures are invented to ensure responsiveness to the primary clients, one thing is certain: Such structures must go beyond current notions of parent involvement. Efforts from schools and districts, through PTA-like outreaches, are usually focused on gaining parental support for existing school practices, not in changing or improving such practices. New structures must also go beyond existing efforts at gathering survey information about satisfaction. Real accountability to the primary clients for schools entails shifting power relationships. These clients must be given a real decision-making role in the schools.

What sort of visible manifestations might be seen by a visiting school quality review system that would indicate some degree of responsiveness to students, parents, and community? Here are a few possible indicators:

- there are multiple opportunities provided for these clients to be heard and taken seriously;
- engagement from client representatives is assured for any major decision making;
- regular communications come from the school to the clients, both to invite and inform, sent in the primary language spoken; and
- curricula are adapted to the local contexts, needs, and interests of the clients.

Current educational reform efforts give a great deal of lip service to involving local families and community members. An accountability system ought to ensure authentic responsiveness.

Organizational Capacity

If schools are going to be held accountable to high levels of performance, they need to have the internal capacity to rise to those levels. To what degree, we must ask, are the resources of schools "organized into a collective enterprise, with shared commitment and collaboration among staff to achieve a clear purpose for student learning?"[26] In many cases, the present answer to this is "not very much." Teaching is known for its isolating circumstances, where teachers each work alone in their separate rooms, often not knowing what is going on in the next room over. From a client point of view, this is clearly not desirable. What schools should provide is a more coherent, continuous experience where teachers worked together to shape and deliver an agreed-upon curriculum with instruction and assessment practices that are jointly considered and studied in the light of what students demonstrate about their learning.

In the world of business, there is much talk about being a learning organization, developing the means to assess and respond to changing circumstances, considering the health of the whole as well as the parts of the organization, and making adjustments as needed. This way of operating is also needed in schools. But schools are largely not well designed to do so. Creating better organizational capacity will take some thoughtful redesign of schools. It will also take ongoing and job-embedded teacher professional development to support teachers as they undertake new collaborative roles, keep up with changes in their fields, and expand their classroom practices.

This issue—providing high-quality professional development and effective school environments for our teachers—will take greater investment than we have so far been willing to make, particularly as we expect higher and higher levels of performance from students. The logic is straightforward and simply common sense: better learning for students means better learning for teachers. Just as students need improved opportunities to learn, so do the adults who are expected to provide students with those opportunities.

A great deal of research has shed light on what kind of professional development is most effective in promoting school improvement.[27] Unfortunately, the in-services and workshops that are so common in schools and districts do not reflect this research. Often enough, these experiences stand alone in isolation or are shallow treatments of instructional strategies, with little follow-through or connection to the overall goals of the organization. Providing greater time and funding for professional development must be founded on the requirement that the learning experiences provided be high-quality ones, based on existing research and standards for teacher learning.

But we must be careful not to approach this with a top-down stance of doing something to or for teachers. It is crucial to honor and build on teacher knowledge and to safeguard their professional decision making. To do otherwise not only would be counterproductive to their learning (and so too the learning of their students) but would also undermine the democratic values we hold for schools, fostering followers rather than informed decision makers. The process of learning for teachers is much the same as the process for students. Both need to be engaged as active contributors, empowered to make choices and connections, and given opportunities to apply their learning in a supportive environment.

What we increasingly see, however, are professional development events where teachers are told what to do and how to do it. It seems to be part of the pressurized milieu resulting from high-stakes testing. This kind of teacher disempowerment leads to a decreasing sense of efficacy and professionalism and an increasing sense of job dissatisfaction. Teacher disempowerment has, in fact, become a key factor in the drain from the profession causing the growing teaching shortage.[28]

In order for schools to have the kind of capacity we are discussing, it is important for principals, curriculum directors, and superintendents to lead in a way that empowers teachers to be informed and responsible leaders themselves. This means that in many cases, administrators must also learn new ways of doing things. Some think that collaborative and effective leadership may be the most critical piece of the puzzle in school reform. It is certainly hard to imagine a school that has great capacity without a talented administrative leader or constructive central office support and guidance. It is such interdependency that speaks of the need for districtwide systems-thinking approaches.

Within a given school, capacity requires that there be a kind of internal accountability system. That is, the professional community in the school must take responsibility for developing goals and priorities based on the ongoing collection and analysis of data, monitor its performance, and report its findings and actions to its public. Many schools have not moved past the condition where individual teacher responsibility rather than collective responsibility is the norm. States and districts should cooperate with schools to nurture and insist upon the development of such collective internal norms. It may well be the case, as some researchers argue, that external accountability measures will have no effect on a school until there is just such an internal approach in place[29]—so much more the reason to focus on developing a new form of accountability that is centered locally rather than at the state level.

THE STATE ROLE

But this is not to say that we should disempower the state either. There is an important oversight role for the state to maintain. For a balanced and localized model of school accountability to succeed, there must be a system where states and districts are jointly responsible, along with schools and communities, for student learning. Reciprocal accountability is needed, where one level of the system is responsible to the others and all are responsible to the public.

This means that the present role of state and federal agencies with respect to school accountability is much in need of redefinition. Agencies at these levels should not be primarily in an enforcement role. Rather, their role should be to establish standards for local accountability systems, to provide resources and guidance, and to set in place processes for quality review of such systems. Certainly the state and federal levels should establish no high-stakes testing or prescribed growth in test scores, no rewards and sanctions, no mandatory curricula, and no manipulation through funding. All of this constitutes an undemocratic approach to schooling, with chilling trickle-down effects that go to the heart of learning in the classroom.

So what happens, we might ask, if schools are failing, even by the terms defined in this new accountability model? What should the state do then? Doesn't the state need to have some "teeth" to maintain local accountability? The answer is yes, but what to do depends on the specific circumstances. There is not an absolute or prescriptive answer to how a state should approach failing schools, except to say that it should be done in an open way that takes local context into account.

Where there are clear cases of faulty local accountability systems—a lack of appropriate local assessment systems, adequate opportunities to learn, responsiveness to students, parents, and community, or organizational capacity—supportive efforts should be initiated by the state.

Under what circumstances should the state intervene forcibly in a school or district? This question must be addressed in a way that acknowledges the multilevel nature of this school accountability model. One might envision at least three cases where the state would take on a more assertive role: (1) to investigate claims or appeals from students, parents, or the local community that the local accountability system is not meeting the standards set for such systems; (2) to require local schools and districts to respond to findings in the data that show significant student learning deficiencies, inequity in the opportunities to learn for all students, or lack of responsiveness to students, parents, or communities; or (3) to provide additional resources and guidance to improve the organizational capacity of the local school or district.

Is it conceivable that a state might actually take over a local school or district in this model? Yes, but only after the most comprehensive evaluation of the local accountability system has shown that there is no alternative and then only on a temporary basis.

A NEW MODEL IS NEEDED

It is of great importance to the health of our public schools that we begin as soon as possible to define a new model for school accountability, one that is balanced, comprehensive, and localized in nature. Schools can and should be held accountable to their primary clients for much more than test scores, in a way that supports improvement rather than punishes deficiencies. The current model of using high-stakes testing is a recipe for public school failure, putting our democratic nation at risk.

Schools have many purposes in our society. In the current national discussion about accountability, the only one that is given much currency is the economic purpose of preparing our students for the workplace. Lest we create a system for our children that is imbued only with the values and concerns of corporate interests, it is vital to understand the role our schools play in maintaining our democracy. It is this role that is ignored in the current model of school accountability. Reconnecting democratic purposes to our schools must be the starting place and touchstone for establishing a new generation of accountability that serves the interest of the people, is managed by the people, and works for the people.

NOTES

1. L. C. Rose and A. M. Gallup, The 35th annual *Phi Delta Kappa*/Gallup Poll of the public's attitudes toward the public schools, *Phi Delta Kappan* 85, no. 1 (September 2003), 41–56.

2. W. Haney, The myth of the Texas miracle in education. *Education Policy Analysis Archives* 8, no. 41 (August 2000), available at http://epaa.asu.edu/epaa/v8n41/.

3. L. McNeill, *Contradictions of school reform* (New York: Routledge, 2000).

4. G. Madaus and M. Clarke, The adverse impact of high-stakes testing on minority students: Evidence from one hundred years of test data, in G. Orfield and M. Kornhaber (Eds.), *Raising standards or raising barriers? Inequality and high stakes testing in public education* (New York: Century Foundation, 2001).

5. B. L. Whitford and K. Jones, *Accountability, assessment and teacher commitment: Lessons from Kentucky's reform efforts* (New York: SUNY Press, 2000).

6. National Commission on Teaching and America's Future, *No dream denied: A pledge to America's children* (Washington, D.C.: NCTAF, 2000).

7. D. C. Berliner, B. J. Biddle, and J. Bell, *The manufactured crisis: Myths, fraud, and the attack on America's public schools* (Cambridge, Mass.: Perseus, 1995); G. Bracey, *Setting the record straight*, (Alexandria, Va.: Association for Supervision and Curriculum Developers, 1997).

8. J. Dewey, *Democracy and education: An introduction to the philosophy of education* (Old Tappan, N.J.: Macmillan, 1916).

9. J. Goodlad, C. Mantle-Bromley, and S. J. Goodlad, *Education for everyone: Agenda for education in a democracy* (San Francisco: Jossey-Bass, 2004), 28.

10. C. Glickman, *Revolutionizing America's schools* (San Francisco: Jossey-Bass, 1998), 29.

11. D. Meier, *The power of their ideas: Lessons for America from a small school in Harlem* (Boston: Beacon Press, 2002).

12. R. S. Kaplan and D. P. Norton, The balanced scorecard: Measures that drive performance, *Harvard Business Review* (January–February 1992), 71–79.

13. National Forum on Assessment, *Principles and indicators for student assessment systems* (Boston: FairTest, 1993), available at www.fairtest.org/k-12.htm.

14. L. A. Shepard, The role of assessment in a learning culture. *Educational Researcher* 29, no. 7 (October 2000), 4–14.

15. S. J. Gould, *The mismeasure of man* (New York: W. W. Norton, 1996).

16. Maine's Local Assessment System, available at www.maine.gov/education/lsalt/LAS/; Nebraska's School-based, Teacher-led Assessment Reporting System (STARS), available at www.nde.state.ne.us/stars/index.html.

17. P. Black, C. Harrison, C. Lee, B. Marshall, and D. Wiliam, *Working inside the black box: Assessment for learning in the classroom* (London: Department of Education and Professional Studies, King's College, 2002).

18. T. J. Crooks, *Design and implementation of a national assessment programme: New Zealand's National Education Monitoring Project (NEMP).* Paper presented at the annual conference of the Canadian Society for the Study of Education (CSSE), May 2002.

19. J. Oakes, What educational indicators? The case for assessing the school context. *Educational Evaluation and Policy Analysis* 11, no. 2 (summer 1989), 181–99.

20. L. Darling-Hammond, *Standards of practice for learning centered schools* (New York: National Center for Restructuring Education, Schools, and Teaching, 1992).

21. D. Lawrence (2005, February 22–27). Top-down to team-work: Unraveling the resistance to reform. *The challenge of education reform: Standards, accountability, resources, and policy*, 12th conference, 20(2), 1–2. Washington, D.C.: Aspen Institute.

22. J. Ancess, *Outside/inside, inside/outside: Developing and implementing the school quality review* (New York: National Center for Restructuring Education, Schools, and Teaching, 1996); New Zealand Education Review Office, *Frameworks for reviews in schools*, available at www.ero.govt.nz/EdRevInfo/Schedrevs/SchoolFramework.htm; D. R. Smith and D. J. Ruff, Building a culture of inquiry: The school quality review initiative, in D. Allen (Ed.), *Assessing student learning: From grading to understanding* (New York: Teachers College Press, 1998).

23. K. Jones and B. L. Whitford, Let them eat tests: High-stakes testing and educational equity. *Journal of Thought* 37, no. 4 (winter 2002), 35–49.

24. P. Schlechty, unpublished manuscript (2005).

25. K. Mediratta, N. Fruchter, and A. C. Lewis, *Organizing for school reform: How communities are finding their voice and reclaiming their public schools* (New York: Institute for Education and Social Policy, Steinhardt School of Education, New York University, October 2002).

26. F. M. Newmann, M. B. King, and M. Rigdon, Accountability and school performance: Implications from restructuring schools, *Harvard Educational Review* 67, no. 1 (spring 1997), 47.

27. J. W. Little, Teachers' professional development in a climate of educational reform, *Educational Evaluation and Policy Analysis* 15, no. 2 (1993); M. W. McLaughlin and J. Talbert, *Professional communities and the work of high school teaching* (Chicago: University of Chicago Press, 2001).

28. R. M. Ingersoll, *Who controls teachers' work? Power and accountability in America's schools* (Cambridge, Mass.: Harvard University Press, 2003).

29. C. Abelman, R. Elmore, J. Even, S. Kenyon, and J. Marshall, *When accountability knocks, will anyone answer?* CPRE Research Report Series RR-42 (University Park: Consortium for Policy Research in Education, University of Pennsylvania, 1999).

2

CONNECTING HIGH-QUALITY LOCAL ASSESSMENT TO TEACHER LEADERSHIP

Delwyn L. Harnisch, Ronald Shope, Mitzi Hoback, Michael Fryda, and Darin Kelberlau

Who best to design high-quality assessments that measure student learning than classroom teachers? Good assessment practice involves designing assessment instruments that are not only based on the state curriculum standards but are also rooted in the curriculum that is taught by the classroom teacher. Local classroom teachers can and should play a key role in developing assessments because they understand the learners as well as the state and national standards.

ASSESSMENT AS ACTION RESEARCH

High-quality assessment can be viewed as a form of action research. The outcome that is being measured is student learning. The teacher identifies appropriate measures, collects data to determine the level of student learning, analyzes the results, and takes appropriate action. This process is illustrated in figure 2.1.

Three important conclusions can be drawn from this model. First, the model illustrates that assessment methods are directly related to the learning targets and to instruction. Second, assessment data is often collected multiple times and with different methods to determine student

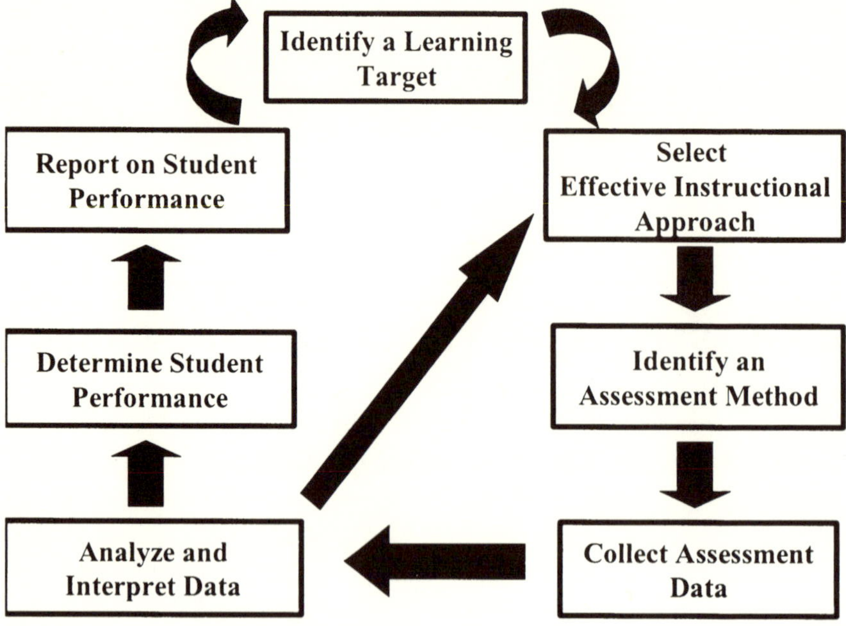

Figure 2.1. The Assessment Cycle.

performance. Finally, assessment does not end at the student report, but is used to identify further learning targets. High-quality assessment, therefore, is an ongoing process that has a direct impact on student learning. This means that in addition to providing information for school accountability, assessment also must focus on student learning. Stiggins refers to this idea as assessment *for* learning, making the point that high-quality assessments do more than the assessment *of* learning.[1]

THE CASE FOR A BALANCED APPROACH

This model illustrates the need for an approach to assessment that is broader in scope than simply using standardized tests alone. Such tests, commonly used to compare school districts using national or state norms, or to determine the extent to which students have mastered particular areas of learning, may be needed, but they are not sufficient.

There are two reasons that standardized tests alone do not provide an adequate basis for assessment. First, standardized tests do not provide the data teachers need to make decisions regarding instruction and curriculum. In many cases, standardized tests are given only once each year and may not measure all of the learning targets specified by state standards. Teachers need more immediate, frequent, and comprehensive feedback to guide their teaching. For example, if a standardized test indicates that students are performing poorly in an area of mathematics, it will in most cases be too late to design further instruction to address the issues during that year.

Second, standardized tests provide only one source of data about student learning. Some students tend to perform poorly on standardized tests even though they can demonstrate learning in other ways. The resulting inaccurate or incomplete measure of achievement does not meet the intention of No Child Left Behind. High-stakes tests without supportive classroom assessment environments can harm struggling students.[2] If standardized tests are the primary means of assessment, low-performing students could be left with the feeling that they can't learn and this could eventually lead these students to just give up.[3] To succeed, these students must view themselves as successful learners. The key to doing this is through helping them to achieve, as noted by Chappuis and Stiggins,

> First comes achievement and then comes confidence. With increased confidence comes the belief that learning is possible. Success must be framed in terms of academic attainments that represent a significant personal stretch. Focused effort with an expectation of success is essential. Students must come honestly to believe that what counts here—indeed the only thing that counts here—is learning that results from effort expended.[4]

Finally, standardized tests alone, even when the tests are aligned to state standards, are not an adequate means to measure all of the learning targets in the curriculum. Chappuis points out,

> Some state tests assess only standards that are easily measured, with important content standards eliminated from the test. Narrowing the curriculum to teach only those items covered on the test undermines a balanced curriculum, as valuable learning goes untaught simply because it is untested at the state level.[5]

What is needed is a balanced approach to assessment that incorporates standardized testing into an overall assessment plan that includes locally developed assessment measures that are linked to learning targets based on state standards. Rather than relying on measures that are developed by outside developers, such an approach is learner-centered because it incorporates locally developed measures that are tied to the learning process. It becomes part of the learning process because it stresses continual improvement. As Stiggins and Chappuis note, "Wise teachers who use the classroom assessment process as an instructional intervention to teach the lesson know that small amounts of progress are normal. Success is defined as continual improvement over the long haul."[6]

Learner-centered assessment is an important part of the instructional process for two reasons. First, through the assessment process the teacher communicates what the learner needs to do to be successful. Second, the teacher designs an assessment that allows the learner to make progress. Thus, the assessment not only serves to measure progress toward standards but also helps the learner and teacher to see what must be done to help the learner be successful.

THE NEBRASKA MODEL

The state of Nebraska has adopted an assessment system known as School-based, Teacher-led, Assessment and Reporting System, or STARS. STARS is a standards-based accountability system using assessment that is balanced with the use of instruments developed by local teachers. What is unique about the STARS system is that individual school districts can decide which assessment they want to use. There is no one single standardized instrument that is chosen by the state. Districts are free to determine what assessment instruments provide the best alignment between state standards and their curricula. School district assessment plans usually consist of both standardized tests and locally developed assessments.

The state has developed a writing assessment that relies largely upon the involvement of the state's classroom teachers. Panels of teachers participate in the development and field-testing of writing prompts, set anchors or exemplar papers used for scoring and training, develop rubrics, and score the assessments each year. Teachers are also involved in setting the cut scores, or proficiency levels, for the assessment.[7] Scoring of the writing essays takes place at a central location and involves teams of teachers who teach in the grade levels covered by the assessment. Teachers view this as a personal development activity as well as an opportunity to participate in assessment because the teachers have the opportunity to interact with other teachers about writing and many times take these ideas back to their own classrooms.[8]

There are two important initiatives that provide the framework for this process. The first is training in assessment literacy for teachers and administrators. Teachers and administrators must learn how to develop high-quality assessments that have reliability and validity and are aligned with state standards. In addition, administrators must also learn how to provide leadership and support for assessment. As Roschewski, Gallagher, and Isernhagen note,

> Administrators must have the opportunity to grow and to develop their capacity for instructional leadership. The administrative role must be to advocate on behalf of balanced assessment and its development. Administrators must understand how to recognize assessments of high quality and know how to use them effectively in order for schools to improve.[9]

One criticism of assessment developed by local teachers is the concern that teachers may not be capable of developing high-quality instruments that have validity and reliability. While this is a very valid criticism, it is being addressed in Nebraska by giving teachers the skills that they need. There can be no question that if we want high-quality assessment, we must also provide high-quality professional development for our teachers. Teachers also need to have the support of leaders who can provide the support and resources they need to develop good quality assessment instruments and practices.

TRAINING ASSESSMENT LEADERS IN NEBRASKA

In Nebraska, we are developing leaders in assessment by training teachers and administrators in assessment practices and leadership. Teachers receive training in assessment through the Nebraska Assessment Cohort

(NAC) while administrative leaders receive training in assessment leadership and practice through the Nebraska Leadership for Learning (NLL) cohort. The teachers and administrators are selected for NAC and NLL from applicants all over the state. These are educators who have demonstrated leadership in their schools or districts and have an initial understanding of assessment and a desire for further training. In both of these programs, the participants return to their schools and districts to become leaders of assessment practice and to train others.

The hope is that these teachers and administrators will form the core leadership of Professional Learning Communities (PLCs) that focus on assessment in their schools and form the basis for a culture of assessment within the school. PLCs provide a means for teachers and administrators to collaborate to develop a shared vision for assessment for learning, emphasizing relationships and shared ideas. Collaboration allows teachers to test ideas about teaching and expand their expertise. It also reduces the fear of risk taking because a PLC provides encouragement and moral support. Most importantly, collaboration results in higher quality decisions because there is an emphasis on collective inquiry in which the teams focus on continuous improvement by developing goals and strategies for improvement and criteria to evaluate the progress toward improvement. The result of this collaborative effort is a clear vision that motivates and energizes people, gives direction, establishes standards for excellence, and creates a clear agenda for action that is shared by both teachers and administrators.[10]

A Practical Hands-on Curriculum

Both the NAC and NLL programs consist of eighteen hours of courses that are organized into two six-hour blocks offered in consecutive summers and six hours of practicum during the intervening school year. During the practicum, students work on research projects using data they collect from their school.

The goals for NAC are to increase the assessment literacy of classroom teachers, to improve classroom assessment practices, and to prepare teachers for leadership roles at either the building or district level. The curriculum is structured around six main assessment skills. These are: (1) Identify and develop classroom assessments designed to meet the informational needs of specific users, uses, and targets; (2) Develop assessments that reflect the specific achievement targets students must master; (3) Use a variety of assessment methods to gather data within a particular context; (4) Sample student achievement to draw confident conclusions about instruction and student learning (knowing how much you need to assess); (5) Control for relevant sources of bias; and (6) Use student involvement to motivate students (know how to involve students in the assessment process).[11]

The first goal for the NLL is the same as the NAC, the second and third goals focus on building leadership. These are: to improve educational leadership with an understanding of the principle of the PLC, and to prepare educational leaders to understand the process of building collaborative cultures that focus on results. In addition to assessment skills, the Nebraska Leadership for Learning cohort targets key leadership skills that administrators must have to lead and support assessment in schools. These are understanding the need for clear academic targets; planning professional activities that help teachers plan and produce quality assessments; evaluating the teachers' competencies in assessment; and devising appropriate plans for reporting the results to the school, parents, students, and community.[12]

One of the foundational issues addressed in both of the cohorts is that good assessment must be data driven. Cohort participants receive instruction on how to design appropriate quantitative and qualitative measures for given learning targets. They also learn how to analyze the data that come from these assessments and draw conclusions regarding student learning. Finally, they learn how to communicate the results to various target audiences such as students, parents, administrators, and the community.

Black and his colleagues in the Assessment Reform Network emphasize that assessment training must provide teachers with practical ideas on how to implement assessment in their classrooms through what they call a "variety of living examples of implementation."[13] Not only do cohort participants receive classroom instruction, but the collaborative format used for the instruction allows participants to work together and learn from each other about how assessment works in the classroom. In addition, during the year between each of the summer sessions, teachers and administrators are engaged in action research in their own schools. They write research proposals, engage in data collection and analysis, and then report on their projects to the other members of their cohorts as well as to their schools. By being provided with practicum opportunities as part of the program, participants have the chance to try their skills in an atmosphere where feedback and dialogue are possible.

Throughout the program, participants have an opportunity to use technology tools that will help them in their data analysis and in communicating their results. In addition to MS Office products such as Word and PowerPoint, they are introduced to ActivStats, a statistical software program that is built around Excel. This product is relatively inexpensive and can be used easily by a single user in a school. In addition, participants are introduced to qualitative software packages and are given the opportunity to code qualitative data. Application is made to the analysis of assessment data that is in the form of written or visual texts.

What Have We Learned?

Data from the evaluations of the cohorts reveal that both teachers and administrators are developing the skills to create quality assessments and to support the development of assessment in their schools and school districts.

There are three themes that describe what cohort participants feel are essential to leading in high-quality assessment. These are: a collaborative community, development of vision and skills, and empowerment.

A Collaborative Community A collaborative community is essential to developing a culture of assessment that is focused on student learning. This community must involve not only teachers but also administrators and the community. As one participant noted,

> I see the classrooms of tomorrow being labs of learning for students. I see teachers who are assessment literate and take advantage of classroom and standardized assessment data to develop strategies to improve student learning in collaborative teams. I see the district and building leadership along with the community providing resources and time to support classroom instruction of and for learning. The challenges include: The process takes time and requires hard work from all stakeholders; resources from

the community are needed to support our schools; resources that we have should support student learning.

This can be accomplished by developing PLCs at schools and within districts. PLCs provide teachers, administrators, and outside stakeholders with the ability to interact about matters regarding student learning in a professional way. PLCs provide the collaborative framework for school improvement. One participant commented,

> Professional learning communities can drive school improvement! As staff work in professional collaborating groups, relying on current research and best practices and sharing responsibility for learning to take place, we will see improved student learning, which is the basis of school improvement.

Developing Vision and Skills PLCs provide the structure in a school or school district to help administrators and teachers formulate the vision and build the resources and skills necessary to develop and support balanced assessment that focuses on student learning. As one participant wrote, "Leadership creates the vision, provides the resources and helps keep a district on the course. Modeling, communication, collaboration and the climate that is created and sustained by an administrator is essential."

In addition to helping leaders of assessment to create vision, the NAC data from 2003–2005 indicate the extent to which teachers have grown in their assessment skills. There are three areas that were measured: assessment competence, assessment confidence, and technology competency. Evaluation instruments in these areas were administered to the participants at the beginning and end of each of the summers that NAC met. There were three major areas that were measured by the evaluation. First, there were ten areas of assessment competence targeted, dealing with large-scale assessment, including competencies needed to develop local assessments.[14] Second, there were four areas of assessment confidence that asked the participants to rate their confidence in four areas of assessment design.[15] The final area for evaluation was in technology competency. Technology skills are important because technology tools are needed to analyze and communicate assessment data. The instrument used to evaluate technology skills was based on competencies drawn from the International Society for Technology in Education (ISTE).[16]

Changes that occur between the pre- and post-administrations of evaluation instruments are summarized as effect sizes. The effect size represents the magnitude of the discrepancy in the participant behavior represented by the item. When the effect size is large, or a pattern of moderate effect sizes exists, it is likely that the quality of the participant experience is appreciably different and, therefore, may be of practical as well as statistical significance (.20 is a small effect, .50 is a medium effect, and .80 is a large effect). Table 2.1 indicates that there were large effects for each of the areas of assessment competency measured after the first summer of classes for those in the 2003–2005 NAC groups.

After the first summer, the area of assessment confidence that increased the most was in the area of assessing student achievement, which had an effect size of 1.0. In the area of technology competency, the area that increased the most was using technology to facilitate effective assessment and evaluation strategies (.81). Results from the second summer were similar in the area of assessment competency. One notable change was in the area of design and development of classroom-based assessments; it went from .91 after the first summer to 1.0 after the second. The largest change in assessment confidence was in communicating effectively and accurately about student achievement, which went from .94 after the first summer to 1.08 after the second.

Empowerment The final theme that describes the impact that assessment training had on cohort participants was empowerment. Lead-

Table 2.1. Assessment Knowledge after First Summer Session NAC 2003–2005

Assessment Knowledge Area (N = 59)	*Effect Size*
Nebraska assessment system	2.0
Large-scale assessment practices	1.6
Assessment methods	1.6
Achievement targets	1.5
Standards movement from national perspective	1.4
Standards needed for high-quality assessments	1.3
Technical Issues: Reliability, validity, and bias	1.2
Grading and report cards	1.2
Conferencing	1.2
Design and development of classroom-based assessments	0.9

ership is essential to empowering teachers and administrators to develop a culture of assessment. As a cohort participant noted, "Leadership is crucial to changing the culture of a school. That trust must be built by the leader so staff feel empowered to take risks. Leaders are found throughout the school, not just principals and superintendents."

Empowerment results from the collective vision for student learning and the resources to accomplish that vision. A cohort participant stated that empowerment could be achieved in this way: "By keeping the mission and purpose for assessment, increased student learning, in the spotlight at all times, and by providing the environment for collaboration, support and resources to empower teachers to use classroom assessment to achieve the mission."

TEACHER EXPERIENCES

Three short case studies below illustrate the ways in which teachers and administrators were empowered as a result of their participation in the program. The first case study is written by Mitzi Hoback, who is a staff developer with one of the Educational Service Units (ESU) in Nebraska. These units provide training and support services for Nebraska schools. Mitzi has not only facilitated seminars in assessment for K–12 teachers in Nebraska but has also been one of the facilitators for assessment workshops for teacher education faculty from colleges and universities in Nebraska. The second is written by Michael Fryda, a science teacher at Millard South High School, a large urban high school in central Omaha, Nebraska. The final case study is written by Darin Kelberlau, who, when he was in the program, was a secondary math teacher from Fremont, Nebraska.

Mitzi: A Whole New World

We often say that teachers went to sleep one night and when they awoke the world had changed—the educational world, that is. In Nebraska, this change was from a traditional educational system to one based on standards and assessment. No longer are teachers teaching what their textbooks dictate or their favorite unit on dinosaurs or the

Civil War. The curriculum is now based on the standards adopted by the state of Nebraska in the core content areas: language arts, mathematics, science, and social studies. No longer are the tests at the end of the chapter and norm-referenced tests the mainstays of assessment. Teachers are writing and using assessments aligned to the Nebraska state standards. These changes are *huge* and have happened over the last five years as Nebraska has implemented STARS.

As a staff developer at ESU 4 for the last five years, I have been involved in this change process from the beginning. As a graduate of the University of Nebraska Lincoln Assessment Cohort Program, I have been able to utilize the training I received to help in the facilitation of this process with the school districts I serve in the five counties of southeastern Nebraska.

The key to the process has been *teachers* and the assessment literacy they have developed as they have embarked on this assessment journey. In the summer of 2000, ESU 4 hosted a workshop in collaboration with ESU 5 (Beatrice) for language arts teachers in the benchmark grades of four, eight, and eleven. The task was to develop the assessments needed for reporting progress on meeting the standards, required for the first time in June 2001. The assessments developed at that workshop little resemble the assessments the same teachers are using today, as they have rewritten, revised, and refined them. The language arts teachers have met frequently over the last five years to complete this process. We have subsequently convened groups of mathematics, science, and social studies teachers as well. The process described below has been undertaken by all four of these content area groups and is in various stages of completion.

Teachers from multiple school districts attend ESU 4 summer workshops that last from one to three days. Special education teachers are also included in the training because special education students are included in the STARS reporting process. The special education director at ESU 4 is a part of the Staff Development Assessment Team and encourages and even insists that special education teachers participate in all workshops.

At the beginning of the workshop, teachers are divided into teams of three to four districts and assigned several state standards. The first step of the process is to "unpack" the standard. As teams they answer the question, "What knowledge and skills must a student have in order to master this particular standard?" Once the group agrees on this, they write proficiency level descriptions, detailing exactly what a student would know and be able to do at each of the four reporting levels of beginning, progressing, proficient, and advanced. We say that the ensuing discussions result in "million-dollar conversations." Often for the first time, teachers talk about student learning and what the standards mean in those terms.

Once the proficiency-level descriptions are written, the teacher groups receive training that will help them write criterion-referenced assessments that match their assigned standards. Assessment literacy is woven throughout the workshops. Teachers are given a primer on different types of assessments and how to write good assessment items. They also discuss the concept of matching appropriate methods of assessment to instructional targets, and what is necessary for sufficiency of coverage. Research is shared in terms of best practice regarding breadth and depth of coverage.

Next, we introduce the assessment topic of avoiding bias in assessment. We show teachers what constitutes bias, by giving them examples of bias and then give them guided and independent practice in identifying bias issues. Finally, before we have them write assessments, we cover readability and grade-level appropriateness.

After assessments are written, teams of teachers trade assessments and review them. This peer review requires teachers to check for alignment with the standard, sufficiency of coverage, bias issues, readability, and grade-level appropriateness. The reviewing teams recommend changes and return the assessments to the development teams for appropriate changes. Teams also use the Modified Angoff method to determine appropriate mastery levels.[17]

Then the assessments are ready to be piloted. After the assessments have been given, teachers reconvene to repeat the process described above. Now teachers have data that they can use to help them in the revision and refinement of the assessments. This results in rich conversations as teachers analyze their students' performance and make changes in the assessments based upon that data.

Teachers also receive training in determining reliability of assessments. They learn about methods of internal consistency (KR20, KR21, and Coefficient Alpha) and when each might be appropriate to use.[18] Teacher rescoring and decision consistency are also presented as methods that may be used for teachers to report reliability.

When teachers began writing and administering these criterion-referenced assessments, most of them had received little or no training in assessment literacy. As a facilitator of the process, I have had to stay one step ahead of the teachers in all of these issues. Training through the NAC, as well as that received through the Nebraska Department of Education and Buros Institute for Assessment and Consultation and Outreach have been invaluable.

The teachers have grown increasingly sophisticated in their understanding and use of sound assessment practices. At the beginning of the process they were mostly concerned with getting assessments written and being "finished" with reporting. Over the five years, however, they have seen that good assessments are all about student learning and that they inform the process of instruction. Teachers who once complained and hoped assessment would "just go away" are now leaders in the process and help others who are just beginning to understand the hows and whys of good assessment.

To assist teachers in the analysis of assessment data, ESU 4 schools are invited to participate in annual workshops that allow them an opportunity to analyze the wealth of data they collect. This is integral to the assessment process. As schools become more sophisticated at assessing their students, they must also become adept at interpreting the data that result from these assessments. The data analysis workshops involve teams of teachers from each district in a process of collaborative reflection. Teams leave the workshop with a plan for involving the rest of their faculty in understanding and interpreting their school's data and using it to continue their school improvement plan.

We have found that schools that have principals who understand assessment and buy into Nebraska's assessment process generally have been successful, while those who are less involved have experienced less success. We have invited our principals to serve as coaches during our summer assessment workshops. As coaches, they receive all of the training the teachers receive, as well as some additional training. They are then able to assist our Staff Development Assessment Team in leading teachers in developing and revising assessments. As we observe the principals who have participated and monitored their student performance in STARS, we have seen huge growth in understanding and support of assessment and standards-based education.

Assessment is an important part of every school's improvement process. As districts become more proficient at assessing their students, they have more relevant data to measure the improvement of their students. School improvement is now focused on student learning, so as the assessment literacy of teachers' increases, it is hoped that student learning will also increase. Teachers and administrators increasingly see that assessment and school improvement all fit together.

I have found that this has been a rewarding experience to lead our teachers and administrators in the STARS process. I believe that ESU have been instrumental in making it work at the local level. As educators, every effort we make should be directed at student learning. Assessment plays a key role in informing instruction.

Michael: A Way to Serve

I am a science teacher at a public high school in central Omaha, Nebraska. This is the end of my second year as a teacher. Like many teachers in science, I started with a degree in hard science before switching to education. Frustrated by a lack of emphasis in service to people, I entered an excellent accelerated eighteen-month master's program in science education. This program did not require courses in assessment to fulfill the needed credits. I knew that my limited knowledge of summative multiple choice assessment alone would not make me an effective teacher.

Before entering an education program, I was a teaching assistant in biology at a local university. The assessments we were given to test our students were cognitively thorough, emphasizing almost every level of Bloom's taxonomy. Unfortunately, I found this to be a completely impersonal and unfair process. Students had one chance to succeed. They never had the opportunity to review the concepts in the same form again. We were actually instructed to "give no mercy" on helping students relearn ideas because such deviation would tamper with the Bell curve. Although I wasn't an educator at this point, this grade-centered assessment strategy was very unsettling to me. All that seemed to matter was the grade, not whether the student had mastered the concepts. I never questioned it because people had been using this form of grading for years. So I thought that it must be right!

It wasn't until I started assessing my own students in my first year as a teacher that I became truly frustrated. I noted that some of the same assessment methods used in college were being used at the secondary level. I observed that many teachers used these assessment methods simply because their professors had used them. I kept asking myself, "Where does student learning factor into all of this?" I needed a way to justify questioning these traditions through educational research.

Through my participation in the NAC, I began to find the answer to this question. My certification program had gotten me excited about bringing learning-based change to education. The NAC has now given me a research base for and the practical tools I need to construct assessments that are centered on that kind of change. I feel fortunate that I have been able to receive this guidance so early in my career when it can be put to practice early. By starting early, I am starting to establish myself as someone willing to actually effect change, not just talk about it.

I have had the unique opportunity to effect change in how assessment is used in my classroom and my department early on in my career. After two NAC summer courses, I began to use my new knowledge immediately in a very practical way. One of my tasks was to develop a program to use sound assessment practice to improve my classroom over the course of the next school year.

The one area that I had struggled with my first year that I wanted to improve was in communicating expectations to students. I knew that part of the reason my students might not have been learning as much as they could is that they were not sure about either what I wanted them to do or the high quality of work I expected them to aspire to.

I also looked at past educational research and found evidence that what teachers expect of students can have a significant impact on them. Rosenthal and Jocobsen showed whether students improved or regressed was dependent in part on their teacher's expectations.[19] Teachers who showed that they expected a student to do well and communicated this to the student found a performance increase. Conversely, teachers who showed negative expectations found that students did poorly, regardless of past performance. This finding has been echoed in a more recent study of expectations that found that elementary teachers who were more skilled at communicating expectations during the first days of school were more effective in helping students learn than teachers who did not.[20]

I was convinced by my new knowledge of targets and expectations that this was an area of teacher performance that I could work on to help improve student learning. I made a goal to start and finish the school year with clear expectations for my students. I selected specific areas of improvement that I personally struggled with in my first year. The first idea that I had was to post a broad list of academic expectations that were geared to learning skills, not behaviors. My list emphasized my expectations for thinking, questioning, and specificity rather than more common lists I had seen emphasizing complete sentences and turning work in on time. These things are important and I still emphasize them, but it is far more important for me to encourage my students to think, question, and be specific from the first day. This posted list also aided me in reminding my students of my expectations frequently. My students can read my expectations at all times and I can be sure to communicate them effectively if I have a momentary lapse in concentration and forget to mention one of them.

I supplemented this posted list with what I called "Big Idea" lists throughout each concept area of study. My experience with the NAC helped me to realize that I often got so caught up in meeting knowledge-level content standards that I was forgetting to emphasize ideas and process. I knew there were concepts that my students were hearing about through association, but I had never explicitly stated them or written them down. I want my students to be able to connect the content knowledge they gain to the broad ideas associated with them. I hope that this will further emphasize for them that my expectations extend to critical thinking and questioning, not just knowledge.

The final phase of my project to increase my student's understanding of my expectations involved showing them models of quality work. I constructed examples of quality work on labs and assignments that they could use as models on future assignments of that type. I decided that there was no better way to show them what I consider quality work than to actually show them examples of quality work. By showing examples of hitting the learning targets, I am encouraging my students to believe that they can all achieve those targets too.

To make sure that I could accurately assess whether my students understood these expectations, I involved them in my action research by gathering feedback from them throughout the second semester. I asked them whether certain methods of increasing expectations actually helped them to understand what I expect. These data were collected both before and after a new method of communicating expectations was implemented to see if there was a change in my students' understandings of expectations. This data will help me to better serve my students by helping to improve student learning.

In addition to improving communication about classroom expectations, I have begun to incorporate the technology of classroom multiple-choice response systems into my assessment practices to further increase student participation in the process. This system uses a device similar to a television remote that allows students to click in their feedback without fear of uncomfortable peer or teacher evaluation. Students in a class are shown a question that asks them how they feel about something. They are then given response options that correspond with the buttons on their keypad. They then respond by pressing the appropriate button on their keypad. The results are immediately tabulated and shown to the whole class.

I also plan to collaborate with my colleagues to develop grading systems that are more based upon student achievement. NAC introduced me to the research-based practical grading methods of Ken O'Connor.[21] O'Connor's suggestions focus on grading that reflects achievement only, not effort, behavior, or other nonacademic variables. It will be a difficult task to convince many of my colleagues that a student's grade can or should reflect achievement only.

My experience with the assessment cohort has already helped me in collaborating with my colleagues on a separate project. Part of my experience with the cohort has been learning best practice in large-scale assessment. My district has given science teachers that opportunity to write our high school science assessments for No Child Left Behind. My experiences with the NAC have given me the skills to choose which assessments would be best for the standards we are trying to gauge, as well as the ability to write quality assessments. I have also had the good fortune of taking a leadership position in writing assessments in all science content areas. These positions probably would not have been possible without the knowledge and confidence I gained from the program. With the endorsement in assessment that I will receive for my work with the program this summer, I may even be able to participate in assessment at the district level.

All of my experience with the cohort has been stimulating and makes me proud to be an educator. I think that my experience will be unfulfilling if I can't help to spread good assessment practices to my colleagues. I have learned that my knowledge alone will not be enough to convince many of my colleagues that they can improve learning by changing what they may have been doing for years. Communicating that knowledge in a respectful way is probably one of the greatest challenges facing students of sound assessment practice.

All educators have the best interests of children in mind. At the same time I think that educators, because they are human, fear changing professional practices that have been taught consistently to them over time. There is a lot to risk when changing the way in which students are assessed and learn. Some view it as a risk of job security and some see a risk of lost time for learning. As my colleagues see more and more of the research support behind sound assessment, I think these fears will gradually slip away. I have found, though, that the risks are worth it because I now have the tools to better serve my students.

Darin: A Teacher's Toolkit

Before entering NAC, I didn't realize how little I knew regarding basic assessment principles. NAC helped develop a new vision for assessment and provided me with the tools to develop assessment that are built around student learning.

The ways I assessed my students were very similar to the ways that my teachers assessed us. Assessments were administered after learning had taken place. I viewed assessment like many teachers in terms of the assessment *of* learning. What I learned in NAC was that the purpose of assessment should also be assessment *for* learning. That was the key idea that changed the way I viewed assessment in my classroom.

I decided to implement this idea in my classroom by involving students in assessment that focuses on their learning. This changed my classroom! While at the beginning of the school year I often heard students say, "I'm going to fail" or "You can't study for a math test," I found that when I involved the students in identifying the learning objectives of the day, tracking their achievement, and assisting in creating the assessments, they were more eager to participate in the learning process. The students took pride in their work and many wanted to know how they were doing compared to others in the class. Those prior comments have been replaced with comments like "I have the third-highest grade in class" and "I need another worksheet so I can practice for the quiz."

I also began to use different methods to assess the students based on the different learning objectives. Even though the mathematics department standards-based tests were selected response, I started to use more performance-based assessments. I restructured my questions and asked students to "think aloud" or "tell us what you are thinking as you solve the problem." The student had to explain the process to the class. Increasing the use of these types of open-ended questions showed me immediately the level of student understanding and showed the student how important the process is—not just the answer. What I found was that when the assessment and objective were correctly aligned, assessment enhanced learning.

In addition to aligning assessments with my objectives, I was concerned that I was developing assessments that were reliable and valid. NAC gave me tools that helped me to know how to do this. We studied the four types of reliability: inter-rater, test-retest, parallel forms, and internal. Inter-rater reliability is the degree to which the different raters are in agreement. This is used for our statewide writing assessment. We also learned how to run a Kuder-Richardson 20 to test for internal consistency. We use the KR20 when we report our statistics to the Nebraska Department of Education.

We also studied three types of validity: content, criterion, and construct-related validity. Content validity refers to the sample of items being representative of the skills, content, or behaviors of interest. Not only did we learn the methods for establishing validity, but we were also given practical examples of how to do this in our school. For example, to establish content validity I could have a group of teachers, who are the content experts in a particular area, make a judgment on the appropriateness of each item in the assessment to the overall coverage of the domain.

I also learned how to construct high-quality assessments and analyze and use assessment data. I learned to ask two key questions: "What are the results telling me?" and "What is the appropriate course of action?" As a result, I began to look at each item's *p* value and discrimination index to determine which items were too difficult or too simple.[22] I also began to look at distracters in multiple-choice items. Distracter analysis would tell me what distracters were attractive to those answering the item incorrectly. Performing a distracter analysis was most helpful on pretests. I could use class time much more efficiently. I was able to more time on the objectives for which my students did not score well and less time on the objectives for which they did. It allowed me to identify common mistakes the class made and correct specific errors. All of these statistics aided me in identifying assessment items that needed revising. Revision of items could be based on poor wording, diagrams not clearly marked, bias to gender or ethnic group, or ambiguity. When analyzing the results I could see *proof* of student learning. I didn't have to just *think* I was doing a good job.

I learned to summarize these results using a graphical tool called the Student-Problem (S-P) Chart (figure 2.2).

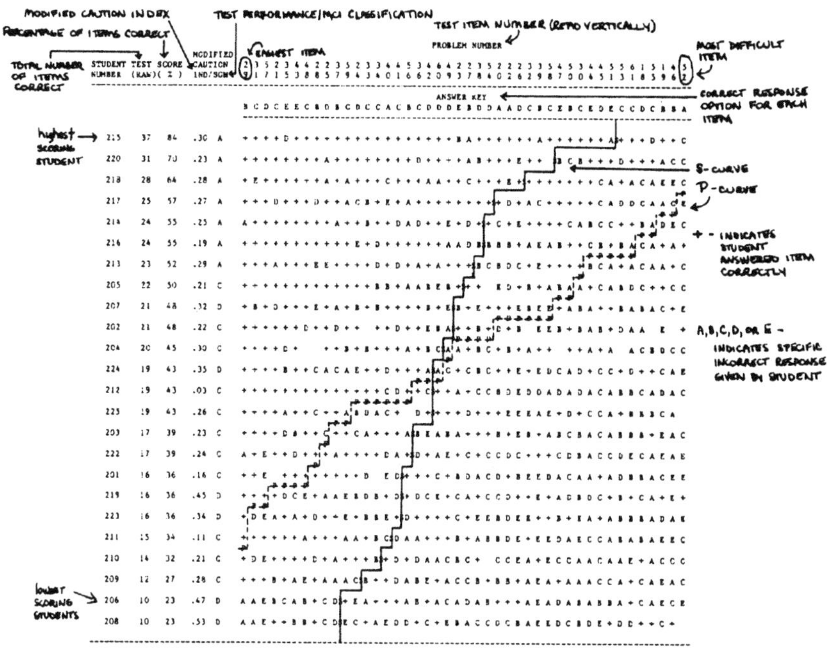

Example of a Student-Problem (S-P) Chart for a classroom of 24 students on 44 problems.

Figure 2.2. Sample Student Problem (S-P) Chart.

This chart organizes students vertically from low-achieving to high-achieving students. The matrix also sorts the items horizontally from least challenging to most challenging. The graph shows a student curve and a problem curve. To the right of the student curve are the items that each corresponding student should have missed and to the left are the items that the student should answer correctly.[23] One can quickly see if a student is answering items incorrectly that he or she should answer correctly or vice versa. This curve helps identify irregular response patterns. Such a response pattern could be due to being absent from school, not mastering a particular objective, or academic dishonesty. To quantify this irregular response a pattern, a Modified Caution Index (MCI) is computed.[24] A MCI that is above 0.3 is recognized as being unusually high. This means that we should be cautious of this learner's response pattern. Above the problem curve are the students who should have answered the item correctly and below are the students who should have answered the item incorrectly. From the problem curve, one can detect distracters that are attractive to the high-ability learners and compare it to the distracters that are attractive to the low-ability learners.

Right away, the training I received had practical benefits to my school. The mathematics department at my high school created a criterion-referenced test for each quarter of each course. This assessment is now used to document how well our students meet local graduation requirements, along with state standards. During the assessment cohort, I reviewed one of the tests we created. I found a few items that needed revision and discovered that our curriculum needed to be slightly realigned. Upon completion of the review, I analyzed five other assessments. Using a reliability coefficient (KR20) I could determine if we met the state's requirement of 0.7. The correlation coefficient was calculated to determine the relationship between the even items to the odd items. I was very pleased to find that the KR20s and correlations were satisfactory. After examining the distracters I believe that if we revise some items we could increase our reliability index even higher.

I also was given the opportunity in the assessment cohort to learn software packages that could help me in data analysis. For example, in the second summer sessions, we learned how to use the *Statistical Package for the Social Sciences* (SPSS) software package to perform many statistical tests. KR20s, correlations, point-biserials, and many other statistics were computed in time-saving fashion. The portion of the output that I found to be most helpful was "Alpha if item is deleted." This allowed me to see results of the internal reliability if we were to omit a particular item. The other statistics would alert me to possible problematic items while this portion of the output would tell me any possible increase in the alpha statistic. We also worked with Excel. Many of the participants said this was not as intimidating as SPSS. Creating charts became very quick and simple with Excel and teachers and administrators could use them in their schools.

Through this experience I realized the power that there was in collaboration. I found that each individual within the cohort had his or her own specific strengths. E-mailing each other became common practice. Knowing that there were other professionals in the same boat as I gave me access to resources when I needed assistance in the future.

I hope that I can build the level of collaboration in the team at my school that we built during the assessment cohort. Next year, I have been granted a team leader position in my course and have the opportunity to emphasize grading for learning. This will be a great challenge, as many of my colleagues have been successful with traditional practices for many years. I have noticed so far that the difficulties involved in communicating sound assessment practices to teachers pales in comparison to the positive changes that I have already seen in my classroom. I want to facilitate collaboration among my colleagues to combine the best of past and current research to improve learning in our classrooms. By working together we can construct a vision for assessment that is centered on student learning in the core academic areas and incorporates the STARS standards.

REFLECTIVE VIEWS OF NEBRASKA ASSESSMENT APPROACH

As we have seen, teachers can and should play the key role in developing assessment. The NAC and NLL cohorts are helping teachers and administrators develop a new vision for assessment as well as providing them with the tools for developing a balanced approach to assessment that is rooted in the STARS standards of the state of Nebraska. Through this program, a core group of leaders of assessment are emerging who are returning to their schools and school districts to establish communities of practice in assessment that share the common goal of assessment *for* learning. This vision is also being taken to the teacher education institutions across the state and is being incorporated into the teacher education curriculum.

This task is not easy, yet it is the best way to help schools to be accountable. More importantly, it is the best way to focus on student learning to ensure that no child is left behind.

NOTES

1. R. J. Stiggins, *Student involved classroom assessment for learning*, 4th ed. (Upper Saddle River, N.J.: Prentice Hall, 2005).
2. Stiggins, *Student involved classroom assessment for learning*, 24.
3. P. Black, C. Harrison, C. Lee, B. Marshall, and D. William, Working inside the black box: Assessment for learning in the classroom, *Phi Delta Kappan* 1, no. 86 (2004), 8–21.
4. R. J. Stiggins and J. Chappuis, Using student-involved classroom assessment to close achievement gaps, *Theory into Practice* (winter 2005), 13.
5. S. Chappuis, Leading assessment for learning: Using classroom assessment in school improvement. *Texas Association of School Administrators Professional Journal—INSIGHT* (winter 2004), 21.
6. Stiggins and Chappuis, Using student-involved classroom assessment, 14
7. B. Plake, J. Impara, and C. Buckendahl, Cut scores for district performance classifications for the State of the Schools report based on the percentage of students meeting the reading, writing, speaking, and listening standards, unpublished manuscript (Lincoln: Buros Institute for Assessment Consultation and Outreach, University of Nebraska-Lincoln, 2001.
8. S. Anderson, *Statewide writing assessment scoring: Effective professional development for the classroom teacher*, unpublished manuscript (Lincoln: University of Nebraska, Lincoln, 2004).
9. P. Roschewski, C. Gallagher, and J. Isernhagen, Nebraskans reach for the STARS. *Phi Delta Kappan* 8, no. 82 (2001), 611–15.
10. R. Dufour and R. Eaker, *Professional learning communities at work: Best practices for enhancing student achievement* (Bloomington, Ind.: National Education Service, 1998).

11. Based on Stiggins, *Student involved classroom assessment for learning.*
12. Chappuis, Leading assessment for learning, 19
13. Black et al., Working inside the black box.
14. Derived from R. J. Stiggins, *Student-involved classroom assessment*, 3rd ed. (Upper Saddle River, N.J.: Prentice Hall, 2001). See also Stiggins, *Student involved classroom assessment for learning.*
15. Stiggins, *Student-involved classroom assessment*; Stiggins, *Student involved classroom assessment for learning.*
16. D. L. Harnisch, M. L. Connell, and R. J. Shope, Are teachers "TechReady?" Evaluating the technology competencies of preservice teachers. Proceedings of the Society for Information Technology in Teacher Education 13th International Conference, USA Chesapeake, Va.: Association for the Advancement of Computers in Education, (2002), 1085–88.
17. The Modified Angoff method uses expert judgments to determine how difficult a test is. The easier the test, the higher the pass point; the more difficult a test, the lower the pass point.
18. KR20, KR21, and Alpha Coefficient are methods for estimating the reliability of assessment scores by measuring internal consistency to determine if the test content is consistent. The KR20 formula is used to measure dichotomously scored items (e.g., true/false or right/wrong) by calculating the proportion of correct responses and the standard deviation. The KR21 is similar to the KR20 but assumes the items have equal difficulty. Alpha Coefficient is used when tests of nondichotomous responses, such as scale items.
19. R. Rosenthal and L. Jocobsen, *Pygmalion in the classroom: Teacher expectation and pupils' intellectual development* (New York: Holt, Rinehart, & Winston, 1968).
20. C. M. Bohn, A. D. Roehrig, and M. Pressley, The first days of school in the classrooms of two more effective and four less effective primary-grade teachers. *Elementary School Journal 104*, no. 4 (2004), 269–87.
21. K. O'Connor, *How to grade for learning: Linking grades to standards*, 2nd ed. (Glenview, Ill.: Skylight/Pearson, 2002).
22. *P* value refers to the proportion of the learners answering the item correctly. The Item Discrimination Index is the difference between the proportion of high and low scorers who answer a dichotomous item correctly.
23. See D. L. Harnisch, Item response patterns: Applications for educational practice. *Journal of Educational Measurement* 2, no. 20 (1983), 191–206.
24. Modified Caution Index (MCI) is used to detect abnormal response patterns on tests to determine if a student was being careless, was confused, or needs special help. Normal response patterns occur when students answer easy items correctly and miss difficult items. Abnormal response patterns are those in which students may miss easy items and get a more difficult one correct.

3

OPPORTUNITIES TO LEARN: BEYOND ACCESS TO ENGAGEMENT

Jean Whitney

I work with high school students, primarily those with identified disabilities, in urban and rural schools with students from diverse racial, ethnic, and socioeconomic backgrounds. I talk to students, observe them in school, give them cameras, and ask them to describe for me, in pictures and word, both written and spoken: who they are in school, what they do in school, who they imagine they will become, and who is helping them along the way. I use my emerging understandings to help teachers better understand and engage students in their own education, link students' visions for the future with the standards that guide curricula, and identify services and supports that enhance the probability for students' success in the future. I have learned that while educators might think about opportunities to learn as access to resources and institutional structures, students describe not only the physical environment of schools, the text books and materials they use, and the creativity and expertise of their teachers but also opportunities for self-discovery and connections with others. Students see schools as places where they can build relationships with peers and teacher, share ownership of the classroom, and participate in a community of learners.

In this chapter, I share insights gained from the students I work with to explore the notion of opportunities to learn (OTL). I have come to understand that while educators and scholars have described the multidimensional nature of OTL, students take a holistic approach to their education. They focus on relationships in which they engage at school (with teachers, peers, etc.) and they understand that they are learning skills, learning about themselves, and learning about the way the world works. I have structured this chapter in a way that moves back and forth between the voices of educators and students. I start with a description of what educators have described as OTL. I use vignettes to describe opportunities fulfilled and denied. From the students' experiences, I build the argument that our consideration of OTL should move from merely access to engagement. I describe how the principles of Universal Design provide a framework and tools to accomplish this. Finally, I close the chapter with considerations for a new model for school accountability.

WHAT ARE OPPORTUNITIES TO LEARN?

Literature on OTL began to proliferate in the 1980s as school reform efforts responded to national reports such as *A Nation at Risk*.[1] In 1989, Jeannie Oakes set forth the proposition that in order to have equitable OTL, schools must provide access to knowledge, enact a press for achievement, and maintain professional teaching conditions. In addition, Oakes pointed out that the organizational considerations for these commitments, such as time, emphasis given to particular subject areas, organization of the curriculum (e.g., grouping practices), availability of extra support, and extent and type of parent support, are inherently alterable. The public educational system enhances or deters OTL through resource allocations and policy decisions.[2]

The construct of OTL developed through the late 1980s and 1990s with the school reform movement and Goals 2000. In the 1990s, documented inequities for many specific groups of students caused lawmakers to more clearly articulate common commitments across laws that mandate educational services. A prime example of this can be seen in the 1997 reauthorization of the Individuals with Disabilities Education Act (IDEA), which clearly emphasized the participation of students with disabilities in the general curriculum and state and local assessment systems. Opportunities to learn are, to some extent, being discussed again as No Child Left Behind (NCLB) and its strict accountability mandates are implemented. In fact, opportunities or lack thereof are being brought to the attention of the courts through cases about the equitable financing, adequate physical spaces, and material resources in states such as California, Texas, and New York.[3] The questions being asked in the current context are similar to those asked twenty years ago: If students do not have access to opportunities to learn that for which they will be held accountable, how can high-stakes assessments on this curriculum be justified?

Dimensions of OTL also include the physical spaces in which students learn, the curriculum and instruction they receive, the materials and tools they use for learning, and the quality of their teachers.[4] Since the passage of NCLB and the standards/high-stakes accountability nexus, OTL increasingly means opportunities for students to interact with curricula that have been aligned with standards and the presence of "highly qualified" teachers in each classroom. There is, nevertheless, a paradox emerging in this environment. Even as we come to understand the complexity of opportunities to learn (e.g., rich curricula, teachers with expertise in their content as well as pedagogy, instruction that is based on varied modes of presentation, and active engagement by students in a variety of ways), educational practice is actually exhibiting decreased opportunities. While the majority of states report rising scores, there are questions about the depth of students' learning.[5] Educators express concerns that students are learning to respond to the tests and not to understand the content. While it is not always clear what the academic outcomes of the accountability mandates are, there is no doubt that practice in schools is changing, with a greater emphasis on test prep and correspondingly narrower curricula.[6]

These changes in our schools have a direct impact on OTL for many students, particularly those most likely to struggle in class and on state assessments. While students' learning styles, preferred performance media, and expressions of knowledge are as diverse as the students themselves, instruction and professional development are becoming increasingly focused on standardized testing format and response options. As a result students are often not given opportunities to learn in ways that fully engage them. Similarly, students are being asked to demonstrate what they have learned through mechanisms that fail to capture the complexity of their knowledge and academic needs. While some might interpret increased numbers of referrals to special education or delivery of remedial, test-prep courses as provision of services necessary for students to pass the state test, these programs often deliver a parallel curriculum that bears little relationship to what is assessed at the state or local level, or is presented in the same way that has proven to be unsuccessful for these students in the past.

WHAT OPPORTUNITIES DO STUDENTS SEE IN SCHOOL?

More and more, student voices are joining conversations about schooling.[7] Students often reinforce what common sense might tell us: that their experiences are influenced by classroom culture, organization, and physical arrangements and that they have expectations for instruction and the roles that teachers should play in their lives.

When I work with students to document their education with photography, almost every student has many pictures in his or her collection of a teacher or paraprofessional who helped in times of struggle. These students indicate that good teachers, to them, create and manage learning environments to enhance the full participation of *all* students. This indicates to me that students are not only interested in what their own educational experiences feel like, they are also concerned for their fellow classmates. They have a deeply rooted sense of what is fair not only for themselves but, by extension, for all students. They feel that the best teachers are those who demonstrate to every student a warm, caring personality and a professionalism, both in terms of instructional expertise and classroom management. Students also tell me stories of their schooling with frequent references to others who have been influential: an older sibling, a teacher, a parent, an employer, or friends. These dimensions of their lives define what school means to them, how they make their way through their educational experiences, and whether educational opportunities are fulfilled or lacking for them.

When asked to talk about school, students invariably weave themselves into the narrative. Most notably, they talk about their strengths and challenges as learners, describe their families, and look to the future. Students' challenges often come through as they list classes they struggle with. They use phrases to describe themselves, such as "Not much of a reader," "I have trouble spelling," or admit to not remembering what was read. Their struggles often extend outside of school and come from the financial worries of their families, their responsibilities for younger siblings or their own children, or inconsistencies across their education as a result of moving from state to state, immigrating to this country, or even just changing schools.

My work has also allowed me to hear students' dreams for the future. Many students know school is instrumental to achieving their goals. For these individuals, school provides them the place to learn things they will need later. For others, school is a hoop to jump through before getting on with the business of life on the other side.

Taken as a whole, students I have worked with describe the following facets of their education, which can be understood as opportunities to learn and factors that influence their learning:

- the physical spaces in which they spend their time;
- strategies that teachers use to help them learn;
- the tasks and expectations of the classroom;
- ways that teachers establish personal relationships with them; and
- their individual struggles to stay engaged when they are not succeeding academically.

The following vignette tells the story of Helen, a student who agreed to work with me on a project in which she took pictures of her education. She wrote short descriptions of her pictures, talked with me about school, and let me observe her in classes. This story is drawn from these observations, interviews, and her own pictures. It is a glimpse into how Helen moves through her school day experiencing both fulfilling opportunities to learn and times when opportunities are denied.

Helen's Story: Opportunities Denied, Opportunities Fulfilled

This is Helen's junior year. She splits her time between her town's high school and a regional vocational center. She has invited me to visit her English class, the resource room, and the vocational center where she participates in a medical occupations class. She loves her medical occupations class more than anything because it is a way of making her dream to become a nurse a reality. Helen told me, "My grandmother is a nurse and I love working with patients, taking care of them, and helping people. It is something I am good at. I won awards last summer at the national competition and am secretary of our Health Occupations Club at school."

On the first day of my classroom visits, Helen and I meet outside her English class. She greets me with a wrinkled brow and heavy sigh. "I am stressed today," she says. "I think I will be all right, but I have to tell my teacher about how I am feeling." She leaves me to go to her English teacher, who asks how she is and if she needs to take a break. "No," Helen says, "I'll be all right." She takes her seat. She and I do not have any other opportunity to talk before class begins. I watch and take notes as Helen sits in silence, follows the teacher with her eyes, writes notes in her notebook, and moves her finger along the text as the class reads together.

After English, I meet Helen in the resource room, where she receives extra academic help due to a learning disability. She comes in with her books and sits next to me at one of the large tables in the room. She begins to explain what she was stressed about earlier. "My medical occupations teacher called my mother yesterday and told her that I shouldn't try to become a nurse. She said that I really couldn't do it and it was wrong to get my hopes up. My teacher wants my mother to get me to think about another job." We talk about how this makes Helen feel and what she is doing about it. "I think I just really need to study and concentrate on my work. I think that will help get my mind off things." Helen turns to her books and spends the rest of her time in the resource room studying for a test later in the day.

The next morning, I arrive at the classroom in the regional vocational center and introduce myself to the teacher, who knows I am coming. She invites me to sit at a table at the back of the academic area of the room. The students are sitting at tables in front of a white board, in pairs and alone. Some are talking to each other. Some are sitting quietly. Helen sits by herself on the right side of the classroom, her textbook open in front of her, studying as she had in the resource room. There is going to be a quiz later in class today and Helen is preparing. One boy is sleeping with his head on his backpack.

The other end of the room is set up like a medical area with beds, some of which have mannequins lying in them, an area with easy chairs, and a sofa. There is a desk on one side of the room with a computer, and magazines and journals on a rack on the wall above it; this area is labeled the "Health Information Center." Across the room, there is an area filled with medical equipment such as wheelchairs, toileting supplies, and IV poles. Shelves and hanging files separate the room into two areas. Hanging on the walls are Health Occupations Student Association banners, bulletin boards with information about medical technician licensure, a CPR state championship banner, student-created posters, scholarship information, schedules, behavior guides, and the like.

As class starts, the teacher and students have a conversation about the test they are going to have today. "Isn't it a quiz?" says one girl with a note of anxiety in her voice. "You said it was a quiz yesterday."

"What difference does it make?" asks the teacher.

"A test is worth more than a quiz," answers another girl.

Another girl asks with a plaintive voice, "Do you expect us to know *all* the words?"

The teacher shakes her head in a way that shows discouragement and responds, "These are words you are going to have to know in the medical field. I gave you time to study in the class." Most of the students in the room groan or complain and try to negotiate with the teacher for fewer words or for the quiz to be worth fewer points. Helen is quiet during this conversation. Her book is still open and she bends her head to review one or two last words.

Before the quiz, the class has a guest speaker. In preparation for his visit, the teacher and the students rearrange the tables so they can sit in a circle, listen, and discuss. The boy whose head is down on his desk in the back of the room still appears to be sleeping. The teacher asks if he can rouse himself and "fake it" for the speaker. He silently moves over to the table and joins the group.

Their speaker is the director of medical and disability services at a local insurance company. He introduces himself and says that he is going to be talking about insurance, counseling, and various job opportunities in "the medical-related arena." He starts by asking the students, "Who's thinking about going to college?" Most raise their hands quietly. "Are you all juniors and seniors?" he asks. The students nod and murmur quiet affirmations.

The speaker then asks the students what each of them wants to do as a health career, starting with the young man sitting next to Helen. He says he wants to be a professional firefighter/paramedic. He is currently on the volunteer list in his home community, as are other members of his family.

Helen is next to offer her vision of the future and she immediately says, "Nurse." As soon as she says this, three or four of the nine other students exchange looks with each other. One of the girls hides her mouth in her sweatshirt, suppressing laughter, and two boys glance down, hiding their eyes and avoiding the looks of the others who are trying not to laugh. This happens relatively quietly, but nonetheless obviously, while Helen and the speaker talk. The teacher keeps her eyes on the speaker and does not remark on what the other students are doing.

The speaker moves on to the next student and proceeds in this way around the table. A number of girls say they want to be nurses. Other students say paramedic, vet assistant, respiratory therapist, and child-care worker. One young man says that he is interested in the electrical field and there is brief conversation about scheduling complications that brought him into this class instead of a class more relevant to his goals. When they complete the circle around the table, the speaker returns to the idea of nursing and says what a need for nurses there is. Helen nods and adds, "Always will be, that's what I hear." The other students around the table again exchange looks and barely suppress silent laughter.

After the speaker leaves, the class prepares for its test (or quiz). Some students study together in groups of two and three. They ask each other vocabulary questions or skim their books together. Even the young man who was asleep on his backpack earlier has joined a small group of girls. Some students have markers out. Other students' books are closed next to them. Among the students who are reviewing together there is a buzz of soft voices, although it is hard to tell how much of the conversation is focused on the quiz material. While this is going on, Helen's head is down as she focuses on her book and notes. The teacher hands out the test questions and Helen starts looking around the room. Other students are reading the test questions, but not Helen. This strikes me as unusual, since she was so focused earlier. The teacher then hands out a bubble sheet for test responses and Helen gets up and asks if she can go to the student services office to take the test with "Mr. D."

I leave the room with Helen and she tells me that it was hard to study while the kids were talking earlier in the class. In the student services office, Helen sits at a round table in the middle of the suite of offices and begins reading the test aloud to herself. I sit at a computer terminal on the edge of the room and hear her talking through the items saying, "I don't know. . . . I don't know. . . . Skip it."

When Mr. D. gets off the phone, I go into his office and introduce myself, explaining my presence. With a warm smile and a firm handshake, he says, "Great, well, let's see what she needs." He goes out and sits next to Helen, greets her and begins to help her through the test. He reads the items, emphasizes key words, and walks her through the multiple-choice options, as she talks them through.

Occasionally, she says, "I don't know."

To which Mr. D. responds, "Okay, then do what you do best."

"Guess!" she says eagerly.

"Narrow it down," he coaxes. As Helen vocalizes her thought process, Mr. D. praises her by saying, "I love the way you talk through that."

Mr. D. has a joking, friendly manner. He stays focused on Helen and her work and seems to be thinking about things that might influence her performance and concentration. When there is noise from a speaker in the hall, for example, he gets up and quietly closes the door.

When Helen is finished, they go back over her work together. Helen keeps the answers about which she is confident and talks through the ones that still confuse her. When they are done, Mr. D. says, "Okay, the vast majority you got right." Mr. D. estimates the score to be a 90. "That was outstanding. I think you did a fine job on this. I was glad to see you work through this. Good job."

Helen remarks that she and one of her other teachers "talked yesterday about how it's okay to reword and rephrase the questions on tests—because it's on my IEP [Individualized Education Program]."

Mr. D. says to me, "I tell some of the kids they should carry around a copy of their IEP—know your mods [modifications]." They have a brief conversation about what career ideas she is exploring. She says that she is thinking about radiology and practical nursing.

Mr. D. nods and says, "The good news is that you are going to be with us at the vocational school again next year, so you can really do some exploring." I suspect that he has framed his response to be realistic and encouraging at the same time.

This is spring and Helen's annual IEP review is scheduled for later in the week. This will be a time to talk about what classes she takes, what goals she and her team want to set, and what accommodations she needs.

Helen asks Mr. D., "You'll be at my meeting?"

"Is there food?" he asks, with a twinkle in his eye.

"Yeah."

"Ok, I'll be there." Then he pauses and says with feeling, "I wouldn't miss it."

What Helen's Experiences Tell Us

We can see in Helen's story examples of how educational opportunities are fulfilled and denied across settings in just one day. We can see opportunities fulfilled and denied in the places of learning, instructional methods and activities, expectations, personal connections between the teachers and students, and characteristics or aspects of the students themselves.

Helen moves across multiple learning environments during her school day. She usually begins at the regional vocational center, which is a bright, new, and comfortable building. The classroom spaces I saw were well equipped to provide learning experiences for students in specific fields. It is important to note, however, that environments are characterized by more than just the physical space and furnishings. Many students describe the tone that the teacher sets in a classroom as fundamental to establishing opportunities to learn.

In Helen's classrooms, her teachers established different tones, with varying results. Helen's English teacher is a trusted adult to whom Helen can turn and express her feelings of stress. Helen feels comfortable enough in her English class that being there and focusing on her work provides a measure of reassurance. Helen's student services counselor, who works one-on-one with her in testing situations, plays the roles of advisor, learning strategist, and cheerleader. Helen clearly feels comfortable in his office, where she comes into her own, as evidenced by her hard-earned test score. The tone in Helen's medical occupations classroom, however, makes it a place where it is not safe for her to express herself. The teacher seems to have abdicated responsibility for making the space one in which all students feel respected and eager to work. Instead, the students disengage by sitting silently or sleeping. Some students shut others down by complaining and making fun of others.

In this vignette, we can see a variety of ways that students engage or disengage, depending on the instructional methods or activities that are provided. Generally, Helen was very engaged in the learning activities I observed. In conversations with her teachers, these glimpses were representative of what they see from Helen on a daily basis. They have come to know her as "very hardworking." Although I didn't have the chance to observe this, Helen says that she enjoys her medical occupations class the most when they are practicing the nursing skills with equipment in the room and when they are working with actual patients at a nearby nursing facility. She also appreciates the clear rubrics, or task descriptions, that her teacher provides the students for each skill. She reported enjoying working together with other students in groups, being active, and doing things that were directly related to what she understood nurses to do in the "real world."

Other students I have worked with report that they disengage from school when there is too much learning "from the book," when they spend most of their time working individually, or when they are expected to passively take in information that the teacher presents. Glimpses of this can be seen in Helen's medical occupations class as students complained about the quiz or slept. Even the most disengaged students in the class, however, perked up when they were given the opportunity to study together for the quiz.

One of the most alarming elements of Helen's story is the explicit expression of a teacher's low expectations for her. Many students I have worked with have told me that clear, supported tasks and high expectations help them engage in opportunities to learn and result in greater achievement. In Helen's case, she too appreciates clear directions, as seen in the support that she gets in the student services office and through her IEP. She is, however, severely challenged by her medical occupations teacher's low expectations for her, which have been communicated not only to Helen and her mother but, clearly, to the other students in the class. To Helen's great credit, she continues to persevere.

She and her mother are actively looking into colleges with prenursing programs and supportive disability services.

In a prior study that I conducted with teachers in an urban Massachusetts school, close to three hundred high school students said that one of the most important elements of good teaching was drawing students into positive interpersonal relationships by exhibiting care and respect, making help and support accessible, and reaching out to all students.[8] Helen is fortunate to have this type of relationship with her English teacher and with the student services counselor. In my work with student photography, the majority of students took pictures of teachers, educational technicians, or other school personnel with whom they were close or by whom they felt well served. On the other hand, many students in our large-scale Massachusetts study reported that teachers who are demeaning, sarcastic, unavailable, or who focus on only a few students in the room epitomize those who provide inadequate opportunities for them to learn.

Finally, it is important to connect OTL to individual students. Explicit links between OTL and students' goals and learning styles can mean the difference between engagement and disengagement. Helen's struggle with her medical occupations teacher is mitigated by her deep commitment to becoming a nurse and the genuine happiness she finds in working with patients. Helen sees school as a priority in her life and her classes as a means to a future goal. She enjoys the friends she has at school, and the time she spends there is important to her. Many other students do not find themselves in the same situation as Helen. The young man in the medical occupations class whose goal is to become an electrician has missed opportunities to learn skills that would be relevant to his vision for the future due to school policies and/or practices that worked against him. Others were clearly bored or had given up, as evidenced by their sleeping, joking, and inattention.

Providing access to learning is merely the first step toward providing adequate opportunities to learn. What is also needed are ways for students to *engage*. Teachers, administrators, and educators at all levels of the educational systems can create physical spaces, furnish them with tools, and lay out a curriculum for students to learn. This, however, is often not enough to engage students in learning. This is especially true when students struggle with the curriculum, are not guided through the use of tools meant to facilitate learning, or are not scheduled into classrooms that are relevant or meaningful to them and their visions for the future. Opportunities to learn are not fulfilled until students fully engage in them.

FOSTERING ENGAGEMENT THROUGH UNIVERSAL DESIGN

Universal Design (UD) is a concept that is well established in architecture and urban planning and is becoming more and more widely used in education as well.[9] Buildings and public spaces that are universally designed have been built with a diverse array of users in mind from the conception to the construction. Elements that provide access so that a variety of people can engage in their community in a variety of ways can be seen in simple and flexible features that are integrated into the design. One common example is the use of curb cuts at intersections. Originally designed for individuals in wheelchairs, curb cuts are used by workers with dollies, parents with strollers, as well as kids on skateboards, allowing for greater freedom of movement for all.

Thinking about how a diverse set of users might access and engage with an environment in flexible ways has been brought into the realm of education by organizations such as the Center for Applied Specialized Technology (CAST), in Massachusetts, and Alltech, in Maine. The educational consultants in these organizations began with the notion that technology can now provide tools for access in education that have not previously existed. Many technological tools offer access to print for individuals who may not be able to see printed pages or for whom the motor demands of writing are too much. UD goes beyond the use of technology that is developed and implemented with an individual in mind and considers how tools and technology can be used to meet the needs of as wide a range of learners as possible.

Once the basic hurdles of access have been accomplished, the principles of UD invite educators to consider how students will participate or engage with the media in a sustained way so that learning occurs. Access is, therefore, the first step, sustained engagement is the second, and demonstration of knowledge is the third. These ideas have changed the notions of access and inclusion in the minds of many special educators today. Inclusionary practice began with the goal of establishing a physical presence for students with disabilities in spaces where diverse groups of children learn, including those with and without disabilities. Now, however, we understand inclusion to mean access, participation, and progress in shared opportunities to learn from a common curriculum. This complex definition speaks more fully to engagement and the outcomes that should result.

Alltech's approach to UD focuses on the physical, social, and learning environments of schools and classrooms.[10] The need for access to and engagement in the *physical environment* is fairly self-evident in that all students need to be in classrooms where learning is taking place (including science, media, and computer labs, field trips, etc.). They need to physically be in the arrangements that the teacher has organized (groups, circles, teams, etc.), and they need physical access to the tools and materials that are being used as part of the curriculum (textbooks, math manipulatives, tools for writing, science equipment, etc.). Access and engagement are denied when students are tracked into programs that teach different curricula. Access and engagement may also be denied when classrooms are not organized in ways that encourage or support the presence and participation of all. Finally, access and engagement are likely to be denied when instruction relies too heavily on traditional tools such as written texts and oral presentations.

Access to and engagement in the *social environments* of classrooms and schools is premised on the notion that learning occurs in a social context. Students learn together through discussions, projects, and reflections on shared activities. Teachers and students engage in social interactions and relationships as they work together on learning goals. In order for students to be able to fully participate in the social environments of schools, classrooms need to be structured so that there are ways to communicate, arrangements are made to enhance and encourage social interactions, and tools available that facilitate the social processes of learning. Unfortunately, universal access and engagement are denied when learning opportunities and assessment are predominantly individualistic and even, in some cases, competitive.

Finally, access to and engagement in the *learning environment* can be thought of as the students' access to and participation with the curriculum. The curriculum that all students have access to and engage in should be aligned to content and performance standards. The delivery of watered-down or unrelated parallel curricula denies educational opportunities to students.

CAST's theoretical foundation for UD is built on emerging brain research and our growing understanding of how different networks within the brain engage in different ways.[11] The most basic finding in this research is that the brain needs new information to be presented in multiple and flexible ways, the learner needs to be able to engage with this information in multiple and flexible ways, and learning outcomes can be expressed in multiple and flexible ways. Universally designed classrooms use tools that promote such multiplicity and flexibility. They effectively engage the recognition network (that which perceives new information and relates it to prior knowledge), the strategic network (that which works with new information to establish novel understandings or solutions), and the affective network (that which relates to the emotional or motivational elements of information). For example, Helen is better able to engage in learning opportunities when she recognizes relationships between new information and prior knowledge, when she uses thinking skills successfully to make sense of new information, and when she feels comfortable and supported in her learning.

We can see how the opportunities to learn that are the most meaningful to students are related to this brain research. First, when the places that students learn are comfortable and well equipped, the teacher imparts a caring and positive tone, and the classroom feels safe, students' affective networks are engaged. Just as students say, this classroom environment is an essential ingredient in providing a fair opportunity to learn. In contrast, opportunities to learn are denied when spaces feel like jails, equipment is lacking or goes unused, and the general tone is negative or demeaning. In these places, students are not encouraged or even safe to engage.

Second, the instruction, activities, and academic expectations in the classroom determine how well students recognize the learning outcomes and incorporate them into what they already know. Students' recognition networks can be stimulated by clear, yet challenging, expectations and scaffolds that build on their prior knowledge. Students' strategic networks are more likely to be engaged when teachers organize activities that are hands-on, active, and built on cooperation and collaboration among students. When a variety of tools and equipment are made available, the choices and flexibility expand and students are encouraged to engage in learning opportunities in new ways. When instructional strategies and activities are primarily passive, rely too heavily on one media (e.g., printed text), or are not connected to what students understand as "the real world," their strategic networks are not challenged and they are less likely to engage due to frustration or boredom.

Finally, students themselves bring qualities, characteristics, and expectations to the classroom that enhance or impede their readiness to engage in opportunities to learn. When a student can connect learning to his or her future goals, when he or she has felt previous success with a subject or task, or when he or she shows a predisposition toward hard work and perseverance, the likelihood for engagement is, of course, enhanced. From the perspective of UD, the student's affective networks are stimulated by an inherent excitement or motivation to learn. He or she is more readily able to recognize the relationships between new information and prior learning. Prior learning and present scaffolds allow the student to use strategies that have worked in the past and can be applied in the current physical, social, and learning environments.

Clearly, the student who comes to school eager to learn, makes his or her own connections between content and life goals, and can successfully match prior learning to present challenges is a student for whom engagement in opportunities to learn is not a problem—provided that the opportunities are there in the first place. Challenges exist for students, parents, and educators when standards and content seem hopelessly irrelevant, when a student's goals are not clearly articulated or do not even exist, and when struggle and denial of opportunities has been the status quo to such an extent that the student's affective networks have been preconditioned for boredom, frustration, and anger. For this student, his or her recognition networks process new information as unrelated to prior knowledge. Strategic networks have not become accustomed to working in systemic ways and, more often than not, employ a strategy of giving up.

We may not completely understand the concepts of access, engagement, and Universal Design until we see all of them in action and related explicitly to what students say about the best opportunities to learn. In the following vignette, I describe a project implemented in an urban Maine high school over the course of one grading period in winter 2004. The teacher in this classroom used the principles of UD to design a highly engaging instructional unit that was based on the state standards and provided students with new and fulfilling opportunities to learn.

STUDENTS USE PICTURES TO DESCRIBE THEMSELVES AND THEIR VISIONS

Looming in the high school chorus room is a large movie screen, set up against one wall. Mrs. K. sets up chairs in front of the screen for a small audience of teachers, parents, students, and other invited guests. Ashley, Sarah, Kayla, and Melissa, juniors and seniors in Mrs. K.'s life-skills class, arrange coffee, tea, donuts, and muffins on a table covered with a green cloth. The girls mingle nervously near the food and stay close to Mrs. K., who sets up a computer for a PowerPoint presentation. Kayla is quietly feeding and rocking her eight-month-old daughter until she falls asleep. The audience filters in, sits in chairs arranged for them, and waits expectantly. This gathering is the culminating experience of their winter term project in their "Daily Living Skills" class in which the students used cameras and short narratives to define who they are as learners and where they want to go in life after high school. Mrs. K. designed this project to explicitly address literacy, technology, and career development standards that are part of the state curriculum.

One by one, each young woman stands near the screen and reads text that she has prepared to accompany her pictures in the slide presentation. The pictures illustrate each girl's likes and dislikes, her learning style, people in school upon whom she relied for help, and what worked or didn't work for her in school. The girls read carefully in each presentation. Their voices carry across the room. They smile as they present images that mean the most to them: their favorite teacher, activities, or accomplishments. Kayla's face lights up and her voice strengthens when she reads, "I'm proud to be a mother," accompanied by a picture of her two children. Each girl stumbles over a word here or there. Occasionally, the wording of a sentence seems awkward as it is read aloud.

Nevertheless, each girl moves steadily along, never expressing self-consciousness or concern for her performance.

In the last slide, the girls and Mrs. K. smile and stand together with arms around each other, the words on the screen reading simply, "Thank you!" The girls sit back, breathe audible sighs of relief, and the audience erupts in clapping. Afterward, over coffee and donuts, the girls talk animatedly about their first successful public performances. "I kept messing up!" "I was so nervous!" they agree. Everyone present acknowledges that this had been a powerful presentation and that the girls have clearly expressed themselves as individuals and learners. Ashley, Sarah, Kayla, and Melissa accomplished all this in spite of the fact that each of them struggles with reading, writing, and academic performance due to identified disabilities.

The third-quarter project began with one-to-one interviews with me, as I served as project consultant. In these interviews, the girls answered questions about themselves, their day-to-day school life, their academic strengths and weaknesses, and their visions for the future. Mrs. K. guided the students through vocational and learning style inventories that helped the girls understand themselves from a new perspective. Each girl was given a disposable camera to practice taking pictures and then supported in making a list of images that would represent herself, her school experience, and her vision for the future. Mrs. K. or I took each girl on a "photomission" to capture the images on her list with digital cameras. When the pictures were developed or printed, class time was used to write about the images to answer questions such as "Why is this picture important to you?" "What does this picture show an audience?" and "What would you like an audience to think about?" The girls also spent time integrating their pictures with information gathered from their career and learning inventories in order to present themselves as learners with dreams for the future and look for themes that were common across the group.

This project was based on the *Photovoice* process, developed by Carolyn Wang and Mary Ann Burris in the field of public health.[12] *Photovoice* is often used for needs assessment and program evaluation and puts cameras into the hands of people who are considered or feel disenfranchised from decision-making processes that affect their lives. According to Wang and Burris, *Photovoice* builds on the power of the visual image, the tradition of documentary photography, and literacy building techniques to give participants opportunities to engage in "*v*oicing *o*ur *i*ndividual and *c*ollective *e*xperience [notice the acronym VOICE]." *Photovoice* processes have been carried out by women in rural China, African American women, and students with disabilities.[13]

Using Universal Design to Enhance Engagement in the Photovoice Project

This vignette about the girls' project and presentation illustrates ways that a universally designed project can be embedded into the curriculum and used to help foster engagement in opportunities to learn. I will discuss elements from this vignette as they relate to places for learning, instructional strategies and activities, expectations, personal connection to the teacher, and the students themselves.

The project was orchestrated in Mrs. K.'s special education resource room. Her classroom is a haven for the girls and other students. They come there daily for academic support and targeted instruction in various curricular areas. Knowing that students are not able to focus on work when they are hungry, Mrs. K. has handy supplies of food including cereal, fruit, granola bars, milk, juice, and water. There is technology available to the students, including, for example, iMAC computers, alphasmarts,[14] and large-display and talking calculators. The tone of the classroom is positive and warm. Students know they can talk about their concerns, and they encourage each other in their work.

Outside the special education setting, Mrs. K. takes steps to support engagement in all the spaces her students frequent around the school. She and other special education staff members assist in general education classrooms. Mrs. K. communicates frequently with general education teachers and team-teaches a math class. She works with the students and their teachers to put accommodations and modifications in place on an as-needed basis or as specified in a student's IEP.

The strategies that Mrs. K. used in the photography project with the girls were hands-on in that the girls took their own pictures and wrote the accompanying narratives themselves. The project kept the girls active in that it took them out of the classroom, around the school, and into their communities and homes. In addition to becoming familiar with some of the aspects of photography, they worked with Mrs. K. to develop their PowerPoint slide show and presented it themselves to an audience of their choice.

Throughout the project, Mrs. K.'s expectations were clear to the students. Rubrics for the final products were developed and shared. The girls understood how this project fit into their curriculum and contributed to their quarterly grade. The girls also knew that supports were readily available to ensure their success. For those who didn't feel comfortable taking pictures around the school, an adult accompanied them on "photomissions" and took pictures that the students pointed out or orchestrated. The narratives that the students wrote to accompany their pictures were composed and revised as part of their academic day with the support of staff and tools in the classroom. With clear rubrics, adequate and appropriate supports, and the excitement of an innovative project, each girl exceeded expectations.

One of the most important elements in Mrs. K.'s classroom is her personal connection to the students. She is their advocate, acts as a counselor, sets clear and firm limits on behavior, and is ultimately their greatest cheerleader. Mrs. K.'s commitment to the students influenced the girls' commitment to the project. Although there were times that one or two of them didn't want to participate, they came back to their project with guidance from Mrs. K. The outcomes of the project included more than a grade for the quarter and demonstration of academic standards on the state curriculum. They also included meaningful outcomes related to preparing these students for lifelong learning. The girls learned about themselves as learners, illustrated for others what they wanted to try for work experience, realized they could complete a complex project, and found that this helped make school a priority in their lives.

ENGAGEMENT IN OPPORTUNITIES TO LEARN IN A NEW MODEL OF ACCOUNTABILITY

How are these stories from students' experiences related to a new model of accountability? As Ken Jones points out in chapter 1 of this book, our entire public educational system, from the federal to the local level, should be held accountable for the physical and emotional well-being of students, student learning, equity, and access. As the vignettes above make clear, physical and emotional well-being are the starting places for access and engagement. Jones also suggests that the public educational system should be accountable to students, parents, and the local communities. Incorporating students' firsthand accounts of their school experiences is a step in this direction. I would add that in order for us to be accountable to students, parents, and local communities for equitable, accessible, and engaging opportunities to learn, we need to consider processes and the need for rich descriptions of practice.

Accountability for Processes

In a new accountability system, we need to emphasize processes as well as the products. That is, the way that students get to their learning outcomes is itself a critical school responsibility. In today's standard-based world, why do we not use opportunity-to-learn standards as well as content and performance standards? In other words, why not set an expectation not only for how students perform on state and local tests but also for how schools provide opportunities for students to meet academic standards?

Here a word of caution is in order. Angela Valenzuela reminds us that using OTL standards in the same way that we now use student performance standards (as high-stake scores) is a recipe for failure.[15] Opportunities to learn cannot be easily measured, nor should their complexity be condensed into a score and used against struggling schools. Establishing accountability for educational processes should involve careful consideration of how environments, curriculum, instruction, and individuals are likely to influence students' engagement in opportunities to learn. These considerations should be documented continuously from the design stages through implementation. Using the principles of UD can help in this process. It is important that this documentation be used for the purposes of improvement rather than punishment.

Rich Description

In a system of accountability that relies solely on quantitative measurement to assess performance, indicators of OTL are unlikely to be validly measured. Part of the complexity of OTL is the fact that such indicators are contextual—these opportunities exist in schools, each with its own unique culture. Our understanding of a specific school's approach to OTL cannot be separated from its place and people. In order to explore, understand, and document opportunities that exist, equitable access, and substantive engagement, we need to expand our evaluation repertoire. We need to hear the voices of students and teachers, see what is happening in schools and classrooms, and share what we learn with others in accessible formats. *Photovoice* is one example of a process for accomplishing this. Other tools include in-depth interviews with students, classroom observations, focus group discussions, and examination of teaching and learning artifacts (such as student work samples, lesson plans, texts and software used, etc.).

MIND AND HEART

I close this chapter with the perspectives of two teachers. The first is Mrs. K., who designed and implemented the *Photovoice* project with her high school students. When I asked her to reflect on the impact of this unit on the learning and lives of the young women involved, she said that they gained greater understanding of their personal strengths and weaknesses. She saw growth in their ability to demonstrate their knowledge and skills through pictures and written and oral language. She felt confident that each student knew ways to seek out the help in the future. One of the most important outcomes of the project for the young women, however, was their increased commitment to each other and to school. This project led to greater engagement socially as well as academically.

Mrs. G., another teacher who works with secondary students with disabilities, has said that "You can't overestimate the importance of making the classroom a place for relationships." The relationships in her classroom are founded on her deep and long-term commitment to her students' learning. "They need to know that you are into doing it [working on challenging material or skills] for as long as it takes; that you won't throw your hands up and give up with them." Students who struggle have experienced enough giving up. In the face of rigorous standards and high-stakes testing, their first reaction is likely to be surrender. To prevent this and increase the likelihood of success for all students, we need to provide opportunities to learn by engaging the whole child—mind and heart.

I thank Kelli Doody and Mary Guhl, who have shared with me their classrooms, time, and thoughts on teaching students. They have contributed not only to this chapter but also to the lives of many students.

NOTES

1. The National Commission on Excellence in Education published *A Nation at Risk: The Imperative for Education Reform* in 1983, available at www.ed.gov/pubs/NatAtRish/title.html.
2. J. Oakes, What educational indicators? The case for assessing the school context, *Educational Evaluation and Policy Analysis* 11 (1989), 181–99.
3. Legal cases include *Williams v. California*, Superior Court of the State of California for the County of San Francisco (2001), available at http://justschools.gseis.ucla.edu/news/williams/; the protracted battle between the Mexican American Legal Defense and Education Fund (MALDEF) in the Texas Court of Appeals for fair educational funding, available at www.maldef.org/publications/pdf/2002-2003_Annual_Report.pdf; and the Campaign for Fiscal Equity case in New York, available at www.cfequity.org/.
4. S. Denbo, C. Grant, and S. Jackson, *Educate America: A call for equity in school reform* (Chevy Chase, Md.: National Coalition of Educational Equity Advocates, Mid-Atlantic Equity Consortium, 1994); J. L. Herman, D. C. D. Klein, and J. Abedi, Assessing students' opportunity to learn: Teacher and students' perspectives, *Educational Measurement: Issues and Practice* 19, no. 4 (2000), 16–24; W. Schwartz, Opportunity to learn standards: Their impact on urban students (1994), ERIC Clearing House on Urban Education, Reproduction No. ED389816.
5. Center on Educational Policy, *From the capital to the classroom: Year two of the No Child Left Behind Act* (Washington, D.C.: Author, 2004).
6. See J. Jacobs, *School culture and assessment data: A review of the literature*, unpublished paper (April 2005); M. G. Jones, B. D. Jones, B. Hardin, L. Chapman, T. Yarbrough, and M. Davis, The impact of high-stakes testing on teachers and students in North Carolina, *Phi Delta Kappan* 81 (1999), 199–203; B. M. Stecher and S. Barron, Unintended consequences of test-based accountability when testing in "milepost" grades, *Educational Assessment* 7 (2001), 259–81.

7. See A. Cook-Sather, Authorizing students' perspectives: Toward trust, dialogue, and change in education, *Educational Researcher* 31, no. 4 (2002), 3–14; D. Corbett and B. Wilson, What urban students say about good teaching, *Educational Leadership* 60, no. 1 (2002), 18–22; J. Schultz and A. Cook-Sather (Eds.), *In our own words: Students' perspectives on school* (Lanham, Md.: Rowman & Littlefield, 2001); and B. L. Wilson and H. D. Corbett, *Listening to urban kids: School reform and the teachers they want* (Albany: SUNY Press, 2001).

8. J. Whitney, M. Leonard, W. Leonard, M. Camelio, and V. Camelio, Seek balance, connect with others, and reach all students: High school students describe a moral imperative for teachers, *The High School Journal* 89, no. 2 (Dec. 2005–Jan. 2006), 29–39.

9. Websites with useful information and resources related to universal design include www.cast.org; www.alltech-tsi.org/; www.design.ncsu.edu/cud/; and www.udeducation.org/.

10. C. Curry, Universal design: Accessibility for all learners, *Educational Leadership* 61, no. 2 (2003), 55–60.

11. Center for Applied Specialized Technologies (CAST) information and full text of Educating All Students in the Digital Age (Rose and Meyer, 2002) is available at www.cast.org.

12. C. Wang and M. A. Burris, *Photovoice*: Concept, methodology, and use for participatory needs assessment, *Health Education and Behavior* 24 (1997), 367–87.

13. See T. T. Dyches, E. Cichella, S. F. Olsen, and B. Mandlesco, Snapshots of life: Perspectives of school-aged individuals with developmental disabilities, *Research and Practice for Persons with Severe Disabilities* 29 (2004), 172–82; C. M. Killion and C. C. Wang, Linking African-American mothers across life stages and station through *Photovoice*, *Journal of Health Care for the Poor and Underserved* 11 (2000), 310–25; C. C. Wang, *Photovoice*: A participatory action research strategy applied to women's health, *Journal of Women's Health* 8 (1999), 185–92.

14. Alphasmart is the brand name of a portable keyboard with word processing tools and widely used in schools. For more information, go to www2.alphasmart.com/.

15. A. Valenzuela, The accountability debate in Texas: Continuing the conversation, in *Leaving children behind: How "Texas-style" accountability fails Latino youth*, edited by A. Valenzuela (Albany: SUNY Press, 2005), 1–32.

4

TEACHER QUALITY AND THE TEACHING PROFESSION: NEW MESSAGES, NEW MESSENGERS

Barnett Berry

The history of teaching in America is stormy and convoluted—and often framed by the struggle to determine who teaches what and how, as well as under what conditions they do so. Teaching's history can be traced back to colonial times when community leaders turned to those with good moral character who would ensure that our nation's youth could read "the good book." More than two hundred years ago, America's teachers were hired to transmit values, and then to some extent the basic skills of the day. One could argue that midway through the first decade of the twenty-first century some things have changed, while others have not. Teachers have seen their salaries and working conditions improve. They are better educated than ever before. And schools and districts are beginning to pay attention to novice induction and professional development programs that have been common in the other professions (and in teaching in other nations).

However, teachers often face a barrage of demands imposed upon them by policymakers and administrators who are quite distant from the practice of teaching. At an average salary of about $45,000, teachers are not paid well relative to other similarly prepared professionals. Inside the school organization, today's teachers are treated more like a twentieth-century factory worker than a twenty-first-century knowledge worker.

Unlike other practitioners in fields, such as law, medicine, and architecture, the vast majority of America's 3.3 million teachers struggle to become members of a *true profession.*

In fact, teaching has long been noted as a semiprofession due to its truncated training and unenforced standards, an ill-defined body of knowledge, and less autonomy afforded to its practitioners.[1] For many in American society, teaching is not a prestigious profession, and the occupation still has many of the markings it did some fifty or more years ago. Even today the popular press often characterizes teaching as rather simple work that does not require much more than subject matter that needs to be taught in a rather straightforward way to children and adolescents. To be sure, teaching is developing a body of knowledge, in part due to the work of cognitive scientists and research on how humans learn, the emerging methodologies in diagnosing and remedying literacy difficulties in children and adults, and by the creation (but slow spread) of the National Board for Professional Teaching Standards (NBPTS). However, a host of political and cultural factors stunt dissemination of effective teaching practices and codification of professional knowledge among teachers in America's 100,000 schools and 13,000 school districts. One teacher does not often emulate the effective practices of another, even if the two teach down the hall from each other.

To make matters more challenging, teaching has not been a self-regulating occupation, and teachers have little control over who enters classrooms with common forms of preparation. The most accomplished teachers have little say-so when it comes to what content is taught, what teaching methods are used, and how students are assessed, as well as how teachers are educated, licensed, developed, paid, and held accountable. The lack of teacher control over and voice in the day-to-day matters of the teaching profession has been heightened considerably with the advent of the No Child Left Behind Act (NCLB).

NCLB hinges on standardized tests with high stakes for schools, students, and teachers by mandating annual testing at every grade level as well as disaggregating test scores by racial and socioeconomic backgrounds. With a single definition of "adequate yearly progress," schools must increase test scores for all subgroups of students in order not to be sanctioned and thereby lose federal funding. Characterized as a powerful accountability tool to address the student achievement gap, NCLB also places a premium on "highly qualified" teachers, defined primarily by their knowledge of content,[2] and the equal distribution of them.

The teaching profession's response to NCLB has been framed primarily by the National Education Association—with its lawsuit against the federal government because of inadequate NCLB funding[3] as well as its successful effort to ensure that veteran teachers did not have to take a subject matter test in order to be identified as "highly qualified." Most states, with few exceptions, are "either exempting veteran teachers from any course work or asking them to complete activities that have little connection to the subjects they teach."[4]

Teachers have been portrayed as resisting both accountability and a willingness to demonstrate that they are willing to be judged by what they know.[5] To be sure, many teacher union leaders still are apt to resist paying different teachers differently and policing their own, for fear of losing solidarity among the rank and file. Without a strong voice from teachers (emphatically insisting that all teachers must meet high standards), in times of shortages policymakers typically lower standards to ensure a "teacher" is in every classroom. In doing so, policymakers—who are the ones in control of the teaching profession—end up *not* having to make the deeper investments in both teacher education and in competitive salaries necessary to ensure highly qualified teachers for all students.

Despite these tensions, over the last decade or so, some progress has been made in efforts to professionalize teaching. More states are testing teachers before they enter teaching; education schools have instituted more rigorous clinical preparation; new teacher induction programs have begun to crop up; and now almost 48,000 teachers from across the nation have become National Board Certified Teachers (NBCTs)—passing a performance assessment that is similar to those doctors pass to become board certified in their respective fields.

However, the truth is that teaching is still very much a semiprofession marked by an influx of underqualified teachers entering classrooms who are far more likely to be teaching in our nation's urban and rural schools serving primarily poor children. And the same policymakers who lower standards in order to fill classrooms with unskilled teachers are now, with high-stakes accountability systems, initiating even tighter curriculum and testing controls over all of America's schools.

In public education many tensions exist: between costs and quality; between public regulation and professional self-governance; between controls that ensure competence among practitioners and those that create self-interested monopolies; and between those who envision a public education system that offers opportunities for all students to achieve at the highest levels and those who envision a more limited mission and reach. These tensions often play out in rancorous debates among researchers, policy wonks, and politicians, where teachers and teaching quality solutions are viewed in terms of a zero-sum game. Teacher union officials, administrators, and school boards, Democrats and Republicans, and right-wing and left-wing think tanks often "duke it out" over the definition of good teachers, how they are prepared (or not), and how they should be judged and compensated. As Lorraine McDonnell claimed over fifteen years ago, "The greatest obstacle to states in their struggle to balance popular control and professionalism may well be the inability to resolve the questions of who should evaluate teachers and how they should be evaluated."[6]

Unfortunately, much as in other political spheres, the teacher-quality tensions most often play out in rather dichotomous ways. Advocates for infusing market principles in teaching and using external, high-stakes accountability to control teachers square off against advocates for professionalizing teaching and using internal, low-stakes accountability to empower teachers. The rhetoric from the opposing teams are intense, with both sides fueling the debates with dueling data, often from reputable researchers and scholars like Eric Hanushek and Linda Darling-Hammond.[7] The result is that the struggle over the future of teaching in America gets played out in a very rough "red states" and "blue states" game.

Market advocates often hinge their views on conservative policies—built from a belief that government maintains order, promotes self-interest, and limits social programs (which only spoils people by giving them things they haven't earned and keeping them dependent). Public education is important, but many market advocates see it as a private, rather than a public, good. Professionalism advocates often hinge their views on progressive policies—built from a belief that government offers safety nets and opportunities, such as universal public education designed for the common good. Each camp has "differing notions of evidence, fairness, results, progress, public benefit, the American way, and other key ideas," and their respective ideologies are driven by "ideas, ideals, values, and assumptions about the purposes of schooling, the social and economic future of the nation, and the role of public education in a democratic society."[8]

What often gets lost in the squabble is that both sides can make compelling cases. On the one hand, the market advocates decry longstanding teacher union rules over single-salary schedules and seniority transfer rights. Although these compensation policies have been designed to overcome gross inequities of the past, they do not reward good teaching and do not take into account the need to offer incentives for good teachers to teach in the subjects and schools where they are needed most. Market advocates rightfully claim that many traditionally certified (and National Board Certified) teachers are not willing to teach in hard-to-staff schools, but that young, bright Teach for America teachers, who enter without preparation, are more than willing to do so.

On the other hand, the professionalism advocates belittle short-cut alternative certification programs that make it easier for individuals with only content knowledge to enter teaching. Although these alternative entry programs have been created to overcome cumbersome certifying and hiring procedures, they often pave the way for lesser-prepared teachers to teach the most challenging students. The easier it is for someone to enter teaching and be called a teacher, then the less policymakers have to make deeper investments in teacher preparation and salaries and improved working conditions.

Most often, university professors and researchers, policy wonks, administrators, teacher union officials, and elected politicians are the voices in the teaching-quality debate. These players can provide much needed evidence, nuanced analyses, management perspectives, and representation of the will of the electorate. Lost in the war over teacher quality is the knowledge and wisdom of highly accomplished teachers.

In the 2001 report *Redefining the Teacher as Leader*, a task force organized by the Institute for Educational Leadership (IEL) urged education decision makers to "exploit a potentially splendid resource for leadership and reform that is now being squandered: the experience, ideas, and capacity to lead of the nation's schoolteachers . . . the unique voice of teachers is too seldom heard or their views even solicited."

Teachers possess vital knowledge about students—and because of this knowledge they can provide much needed leadership for the changes needed to improve public education. There is a history of teachers serving in formal leadership roles as department heads and union leaders, where teachers take on administrative tasks. More recently, a small percentage of lead teachers are beginning to spread their instructional expertise as staff developers, curriculum specialists, and mentors for new and underperforming teachers. What I am finding is that this is not enough. Our public schools need more teachers who are change agents for their schools and communities and have the knowledge and skill to lead the teaching-quality debates. They are teaching in our schools; however, they have not been able to define their profession. The IEL panel said it best: It is time for our best teachers to "get in the game."

In this chapter, I bring the voices of the Teacher Leaders Network—a vibrant virtual learning community of some of the nation's best teachers—into the teacher-quality debate. These teacher leaders can add a new, clearer, and more compelling voice to the debate between those who argue for market or professionalism reforms in teaching. It is time for our nation's policymakers to hear, understand, and embrace the wisdom of expert teachers as they consider new strategies for improving the teaching profession. The bottom line is that what these accomplished teachers want in terms of quality for their profession is very similar to what the public wants. Both the public and these teachers seek a *true profession*, one where all members are well prepared and supported and have fair opportunities to hold themselves accountable. The tools of the market advocates are not totally discarded, but must be used in ways that are respectful of the challenges teachers face every day in our nation's diverse classrooms. I begin by unpacking the teacher-quality debates and the impasse that needs to be broken.

THE TEACHER-QUALITY DEBATES

First of all, there is no debate among policymakers, researchers, and practitioners over the fact that teachers and how they teach—not class size, curricula, or facilities—make the *most important* difference in whether or not students will achieve. Unfortunately, there is a huge debate over how to identify quality teachers and recruit, prepare, develop, and pay them. Little, if any, consensus exists on what should be done to promote teacher quality and how best to evaluate teachers. Second, there is no debate that standards-based reforms and accompanying accountability systems are critical to defining emphatically what all students should know and be able to do. (By this I mean that most educators and the public believe that standards, accountability, and testing are means to an end, but should not be the end itself.) However, there is a huge debate over the purpose of the accountability systems in terms of what kind of information is collected and how it is used. Some reformers want the information to identify weaknesses in the system and marshal more support and dollars for underperforming schools. Others want the information to identify good and bad districts, schools, and teachers and then use "carrots and sticks" to make them do better. Similarly, some see that teachers, with the right resources and opportunities, will do what is needed to ensure the success of all students. Others believe that teachers need rewards and punishments in order to teach effectively.

As previously noted, these debates often evoke a larger set of contentious issues clearly defined by two opposing ideological camps—those who seek to enhance teacher quality by using the tools of the market versus those who seek to do so using the tools of professionalism. There are at least two major areas where market and professionalism advocates depart from each other, with major implications for the future of teaching—the definition of good teachers and how they are prepared, and how teachers are evaluated.

Defining and Preparing Good Teachers

Market advocates tend to define good teachers by high verbal skills and content knowledge as well as by the student achievement scores of their students. They point to research that teachers tend to score lower on measures of academic ability (e.g., the SAT) and graduate from less competitive colleges than those who enter other professions, and claim that these measures are more likely to affect student achievement. Because teaching does not rest on a stable body of knowledge like medicine, a good teacher is one who has "a solid general education, who possesses deep subject area knowledge, and who has no record of misbehavior."[9]

In defining the good teacher, market advocates also discount the importance of extensive, pedagogical training on two counts—limited research evidence and the fact that assessment of teaching skills may discourage potentially good teachers from entering teaching. Consequently, they downplay teacher education—and in some cases call for its abandonment. In his 2002 teacher-quality report to Congress, then-Secretary of Education Rod Paige called for the dismantling of teacher education systems and the recasting of what it means to be a "highly qualified" teacher to include little, if any, preparation for teaching. Like other market advocates, Paige claimed that current teacher certification systems are "broken," and teacher education course work is "burdensome":[10] Most university programs are too theoretical and prepare teachers for schools that do not exist. What needs to be learned about teaching can be learned on the job where schools have a curriculum that needs to be taught. As Finn has noted,

> We should welcome good teachers of every size and shape and should welcome them no matter what path they follow to the schoolhouse door. We shouldn't just welcome them. We should recruit them. We should reward them. . . . What we should not do is go crazy about their inputs, their formal credentials.[11]

On the other hand, professionalism advocates tend to define good teachers much differently. These advocates also call for teachers to have high verbal skills and stronger subject matter knowledge—but a lot more as well. Citing a synthesis of recent research on human learning and teacher education, the National Academy of Education, has found that good teachers

> use many different tools to assess how their students learn as well as what the students know. They use this information to help all students advance from where they are to where they need to be. They carefully organize activities, materials, and instruction based on students' prior knowledge and level of development so that all students can be successful. They know what conceptions students bring with them about the subject and what misconceptions are likely to cause them confusion—and they design their lessons to overcome these misinterpretations. They adapt the curriculum to different students' needs; for example, making content more accessible

> for students who are still learning English and for those who have special educational needs.[12]

For professionalism advocates, these skills cannot be measured by content tests and, in stark contrast to market advocates, call for more extensive preparation, licensing, and certification. They call for more professional accountability in the form of tougher inputs as well as new structures like professional development schools (the equivalent of teaching hospitals where teachers are both prepared more extensively while serving students and families).

Evaluating Teachers

Market advocates call for evaluating teachers by looking at results—either on paper-and-pencil tests or in the kind of student achievement results they produce. With little faith in typical teacher evaluation systems (that rarely discriminate among teachers who are highly effective and those who are not), they tend to promote the idea that principals need to have more authority to hire and fire teachers, and that current tenure rules are an impediment to quality control. Market advocates promote the use of content-focused, multiple-choice teacher tests that are aligned with the kinds of basic skills-oriented standardized tests that students take. With substantial backing from the U.S. Department of Education (USDOE), the market advocates are supporting the American Board for Certification of Teacher Excellence (ABCTE)—a relatively inexpensive way to "certify" teachers without any training or performance measures before they begin teaching. The computer-based exam, which costs $500, is viewed as an important antidote to currently ill-designed and misguided preparation and licensing that do not prepare teachers for the reality of schools and present too many bureaucratic hurdles to clear.

The market advocates also turn to outcomes as the way to define a good teacher. As Finn has claimed,

> A good teacher is quite simply one whose students acquire plenty of skills and knowledge, one who adds academic value to her pupils. She may do lots of other worthwhile things as well, but if she doesn't add academic

> value, then she is not a good teacher, and if she does add academic value, then she is a good teacher. That is the only definition of being a good teacher that truly matters in the real world. If she is a good teacher, I don't much care where she came from or how she got to be that way.[13]

For market advocates, student test scores have become the sine qua non for evaluating teachers. Indeed, the idea of using test scores to judge teachers has taken on a new saliency, due to the rise in popularity of value-added methodologies (VAM). Popularized by Bill Sanders, a statistician, who developed the model at the University of Tennessee, VAM draws on several years' worth of student test scores to provide a longitudinal picture of individual student progress. By using both teachers and students as statistical controls for themselves, results can be used to gauge an individual teacher's effect on student learning. In Sanders's model, "good teachers" are not penalized for having ineffective colleagues because the past effects of these teachers are considered in calculating current value-added scores. Far more equitable than using a cohort model (i.e., when one school's third grade is compared to the next year's third grade—that is, the test stays in third grade, measuring different cohorts of students as they matriculate through the elementary school), many reformers, and especially the market advocates, are calling for VAM to be the sole measure of whether teachers are hired, paid more, or fired.

Valued-added methodologies are seductive, and with good reason. Researchers have found have "above average" or "more effective" teachers for three or more years can "substantially offset or even eliminate the disadvantage of low socioeconomic background" on student achievement.[14] As Katie Haycock, who directs the Education Trust, has asserted, "By looking at scores on year-end standardized tests, one can have a pretty good idea who's cutting it and who isn't."[15] While Haycock (and other market advocates) admits that standardized tests may have limitations, she also claims that these "are not so great that they compromise the tremendous utility of value-added information."[16] She and others often criticize teachers who resist being judged by student test scores, claiming that they are the only objective way of measuring academic progress across schools and districts. They often articulate the point that standardized tests are the best tools to see which students are getting high-quality teachers and which are not, putting a spotlight on the current inequities in the system.

Professionalism advocates focus on inequities as well, but depart substantially from market advocates relative to their views on how teachers should be evaluated. First of all, they do not discount the need to examine student results. For them, some value-added measure of student performance on standardized assessments, properly used, could provide an important data source. However, for them, identifying and rewarding teachers solely on the basis of standardized test scores would be like rewarding doctors solely on the basis of their mortality rates, no matter whether they are a pediatrician or an oncologist. This does not mean that mortality rates should not be used as useful information in evaluating doctors or test scores in evaluating teachers.

The professionalism advocates often point out that the models now in place can be fraught with technical problems—some of which are identified by market advocates themselves. For example, Dale Ballou, in examining VAM used in Tennessee, found that student gain scores in reading were far more unreliable than those in math. He also noted that value-added assessments might not adequately control for factors like poverty and limited English proficiency that may affect a student's rate of progress, as well as his or her absolute performance.[17] RAND researchers recently concluded that despite the significant advancement in statistical methods for explaining student achievement and teaching effectiveness, the research base is "currently insufficient" for VAM to be used in teacher evaluation decisions.[18] For professionalism advocates, VAM may be a case where a bright idea has so dazzled its proponents that they have failed to ask themselves whether the mechanisms are in place to make it work for high-stakes decisions.

Even if the statistics become more reliable as technologies improve, many other problems exist. For example, VAM requires at least three years of data to get reliable estimates of teacher effects. However, as the market advocates propose, if no other teacher-quality control means are used, then students may have a teacher for three years who is totally unprepared and ineffective, and where there is no evidence collected on whether that teacher can teach reading, work with second-language learners, and more. For professionalism advocates, this danger of letting anyone begin to teach and then figuring out later if they know how to teach effectively could have very bad consequences for students.

Professionalism advocates turn to more complex and expensive measurement tools, such as NBPTS and its relatively expensive performance-based exams.[19] The National Board certification includes both a portfolio and a standardized teaching exam. Almost antithetical to the ABCTE testing process, the portfolio assessment takes about six months to complete. Teachers submit four portfolio entries, including videotapes that document the candidate's teaching practice, and provide examples of student work. The portfolio process requires teachers to demonstrate how they analyze student performance and adjust instruction. The portfolio also demonstrates how teachers work with students' families and the larger community and how they collaborate with professional colleagues. Near the end of the certification cycle, NBCT candidates participate in a rigorous daylong, timed essay exam where their knowledge of subject matter is tested.

Professionalism advocates often criticize traditional teacher evaluations, usually based on principal observations. In this process, 95 percent or more of observed teachers are typically deemed above average. The process is relatively easy to administer, and does not require content-specific expertise on the part of the evaluator. Often these evaluations are "an activity that is done to teachers"[20] and a perfunctory procedure that they must endure. Several new models of teacher evaluation, such as the one developed by Charlotte Danielson, have emerged over the last several years that require teachers to analyze student work and produce a video demonstrating their teaching expertise (not dissimilar from the NBPTS process).[21]

Professionalism advocates, in promoting the idea that teachers need to be accountable to themselves, also have turned to peer review, a practice that has been around for over twenty years and is found in a handful of districts. Not widely practiced, and often going against the grain in typical union-management relations, peer review provides for content-specific consulting teachers to conduct formal evaluations, offer ways for new and veteran teachers to improve their knowledge and skills, and then recommend whether the participating teacher should be retained or let go. Although some teacher unions have dropped their long-standing opposition to peer review, most have not. The program is expensive, and it does break ranks with the traditional union conception of worker solidarity. Although some modest evidence suggests peer review is more rigorous than the traditional administrator-driven evaluations,[22] continued union resistance to the idea fuels the criticism of the market advocates and furthers the perception that teachers do not want professional accountability.

A STRUGGLING PROFESSION AND FUTURE PROSPECTS

Professionalism advocates have not gotten their way. First of all, only twenty-four states assess the subject-specific pedagogical skills of new teachers and only thirteen assess teaching performance—either through a portfolio, classroom observations, or videotaped lessons—prior to licensure.[23] Second, although there are almost 48,000 NBCTs nationwide these accomplished teachers are less likely to be found in high-poverty, high-minority schools—and few districts, if any, have figured out how to systematically utilize them for improving schools and closing achievement gaps.[24] Third, fewer than 1 percent of novice teachers have access to high-quality induction programs.[25] Fourth, most professional development is still best characterized by one- or two-shot workshops that rarely support long-term changes in teaching practices.[26] Fifth, with the lack of investment in clinical training and tight connections with K–12 schools, most teacher education programs still do not adequately prepare new teachers for challenging urban and rural schools.[27] Finally, teachers are still not paid well, compared to other similarly trained and college-educated professionals. With just a few exceptions, most teacher unions and administrators still get bogged down when it comes to finding new ways to pay teachers more and differently.[28]

The tough financial and political decisions don't get made. Low-performing schools, especially in urban areas, continue to be beset by declining rates of certified teachers, high turnover among new teachers, and inequities in the assignment of qualified teachers to schools.[29] If the data appear more promising of late, it is because states and districts have easily identified their underprepared teachers (who tend to be enrolled in alternative certification programs) as "highly qualified" under the

NCLB guidelines. Efforts to improve teaching have been stymied by an impasse pitting progressives against conservatives and the education establishment against reformers. However, one effort to address teacher compensation problems may have promise in resolving some aspects of the teacher quality debates, possibly offering a way to fuse the best of the market and professionalism models.

In 1999, the Denver Classroom Teachers Association and the Denver Public Schools agreed to a potentially cutting-edge approach to professional compensation that focuses on student learning, knowledge and skills, professional evaluation, and market incentives. Led by union activist Brad Jupp, the professional compensation plan was thoroughly vetted with teachers and the community for over a year, and then piloted in sixteen schools. Jupp's extraordinary leadership has led to a plan that is "something else altogether"—not only rewarding individual teachers, which has been anathema, but it has been "designed, tested and sold to a majority of the city's teachers by the union itself."[30]

In terms of student learning, Denver teachers will set two performance objectives around growth in student achievement and receive bonuses based on achieving those objectives. Further, teachers serving in schools designated as distinguished (based on thirty to forty indicators) will receive additional compensation. The plan will not use a value-added model, because of the limitations of the methodology and the need for teachers to understand clearly how student gains will be attributed to them. In addition, under the new plan new teachers will only receive salary advancement for education and demonstrated skill directly related to district goals. A teacher- and administrator-led committee will approve all professional development choices, and ensure that they are aligned with student learning priorities and are known to improve practice—for example, the National Board certification process or special training in specific literacy strategies.

Also, teachers will receive additional pay for working in high-poverty schools or teaching subjects like math and science, where qualified instructors are in short supply. The amount of money that teachers can earn for the different components still is being considered, but the plan will raise the maximum pay for most teachers to $100,000, from $60,000.

Finally, the union and district administrators are creating a new evaluation process that goes beyond using principals in observing teachers and "checking off" teaching behaviors on a list. Increases in compensation will be granted only for satisfactory performance on what promises to be a more rigorous evaluation that will focus on expanded areas of focus, definitive criteria for meeting standards, and use of student work samples (artifacts of teaching). Teachers will receive a 3 percent increase every three years for satisfactory evaluations and 6 percent for distinguished evaluations.

The Denver model, in a sense, offers a more "pragmatic value-added model" that is more transparent to teachers themselves. The Denver model represents a blending of professional and market models, and in doing so, fits more with the expectations the public has for the future of teaching. The plan was funded in November 2005 with a $25-million referendum.

WHAT THE PUBLIC WANTS IN TEACHING AND FOR TEACHERS

Recent polling data suggest that the public actually has far more respect for teachers than most people (including teachers) believe, and would seemingly invest in professional compensation programs such as the one unfolding in Denver. A 2005 poll released by the Teaching Commission revealed that the majority of Americans want to improve teaching quality by investing heavily in teachers, even if these investments result in higher taxes.[31] Democrats, Republicans, and Independents all want to pay teachers more and pay them even more if they produce results. Granted, Democrats are more likely to support salary increases without more accountability. But 60 percent of the Republicans polled would pay more in taxes to pay teachers more—and 77 percent would do so if salary increases were tied to some form of accountability. For the public, professionalism is not a partisan matter (see table 4.1).

These polling data indicate that Americans do expect teachers (and other educators) to be held accountable. The Teaching Commission, a high-profile panel primarily composed of business leaders, policymakers, and a few educators,[32] revealed that more than 93 percent "favor" (strongly or somewhat) the idea that teachers need to be tested on knowledge of subject(s) and how to teach them. The majority of the

Table 4.1. Public Support for Teacher Pay Raises and Accountability (By Political Affiliation)

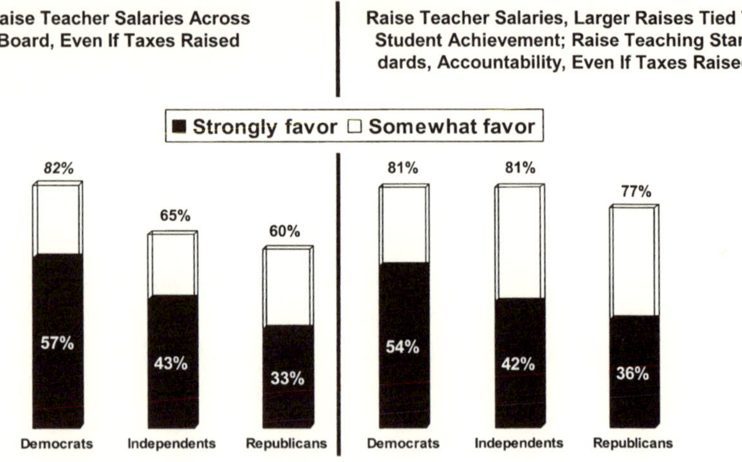

The Teaching Commission (2005). America's Commitment to Quality Teaching in Public Schools. Findings from a National Survey Conducted by Hart-Harris.

public also believes that teachers should be compensated based on some measure of performance. Two-thirds (67 percent) of the public believes that teachers should be paid extra for "gains in student achievement as measured by test results—and *other indicators*." On the other hand, only one-third (32 percent) of the teachers polled nationwide felt the same (see table 4.2). The disconnected views of the public and teachers may have something to do with the measure, and not accountability.

In fact, the Teaching Commission poll also revealed that both the public and teachers have little confidence in the accuracy of standardized tests. Only 35 percent of the general public (and even less, 25 percent of teachers) believe that current standardized student achievement tests are fair measures of what students learn and how well teachers teach (see table 4.3). Even the Teaching Commission, a group dedicated to using standardized tests to measure teacher performance, claimed, "Until people have more confidence in the accuracy of standardized tests, they will be reluctant to tie teacher compensation to the results and will be particularly uncomfortable with any system that uses test results as the sole measure of teacher performance."[33]

Table 4.2. Should Student Achievement Determine Extra Teacher Pay

Should "gains in student academic achievement as measured by test results and other indicators" determine whether a teacher receives extra pay?

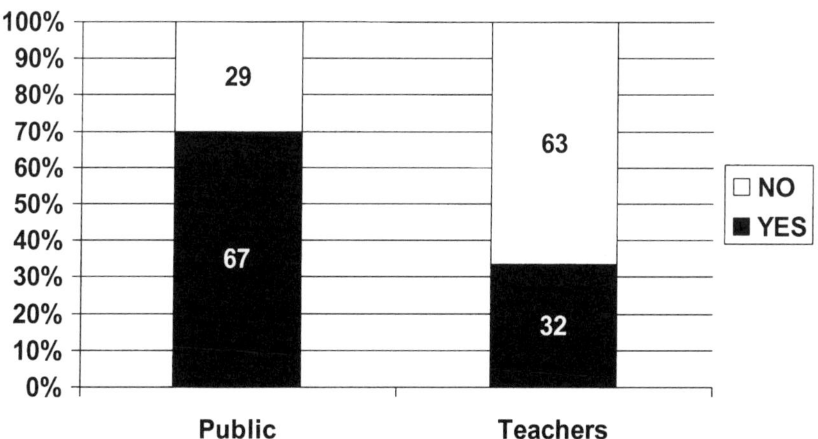

The Teaching Commission (2005). America's Commitment to Quality Teaching in Public Schools. Findings from a National Survey Conducted by Hart-Harris.

Table 4.3. Little Confidence in Accuracy of Standardized Tests

In general, do the standardized tests students currently take in your state accurately measure student achievement?

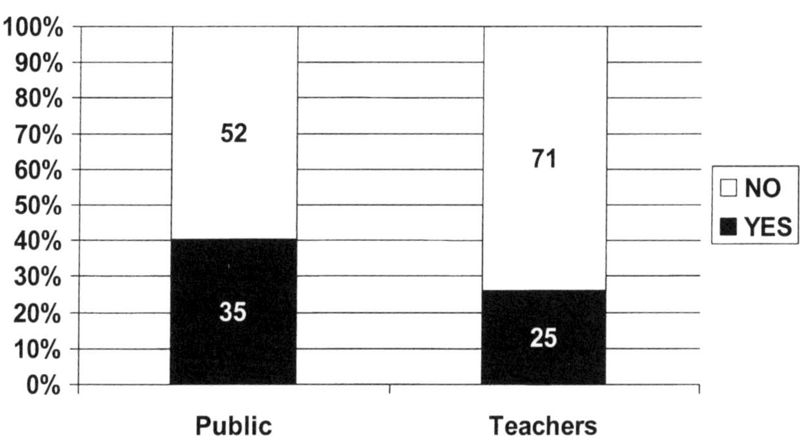

The Teaching Commission (2005). America's Commitment to Quality Teaching in Public Schools. Findings from a National Survey Conducted by Hart-Harris.

According to the Teaching Commission poll, the public believes that teachers, like other professionals, should be paid on a differentiated basis—for what they know, where they teach, and how well they perform. Over 76 percent of the public (and 77 percent of teachers) support teachers being paid more if they teach in high-poverty schools and 72 percent of the public (and 52 percent of teachers) support teachers being paid more if they teach hard-to-staff subjects. Almost two-thirds of the public (62 percent) believe that teacher education should be more rigorous and extensive and almost nine in ten adults call for "guarantees" that teachers have access to high-quality professional development. But as in other knowledge-based professions, performance cannot always be tied accurately to a single simple measure, like standardized test scores. When asked what was their "biggest" concern about teacher performance pay, almost one in five adults (18 percent) believed it is "inappropriate to base teachers' pay on student achievement," and another one in five (19 percent) believed there was no fair way to measure student achievement gains. However, the biggest concern, with 44 percent of the public weighing in, was that linking teacher pay to student achievement would be "unfair to teachers who have to teach the most difficult students" (table 4.4).

These polling data mean the public does want more teacher accountability and performance-based compensation. But whatever the approach, the public clearly wants it to be fair, and perhaps the Denver model may best represent their views—one that pushes teachers to be more responsible and accountable, without relying too heavily on unreliable and narrow standardized achievement scores. However, if such a hybrid, market/professionalism model is going to work, then many more conceptual, philosophical, and implementation issues need to surface and be addressed. How do teachers respond to such evaluation processes? Do they want the responsibility associated with professional models? What is actually known about standardized test scores and their use in evaluating and rewarding teachers? How would teachers accurately measure their impact on student achievement? What kinds of incentives are necessary for effective teachers to teach in hard-to-staff, low-performing schools? Our nation's best teachers—whose voices are rarely if ever heard in policy debates—have considerable insight into these teaching-quality matters, and will be presented next.

Table 4.4. Public Reservations about Linking Teacher Pay to Student Achievement

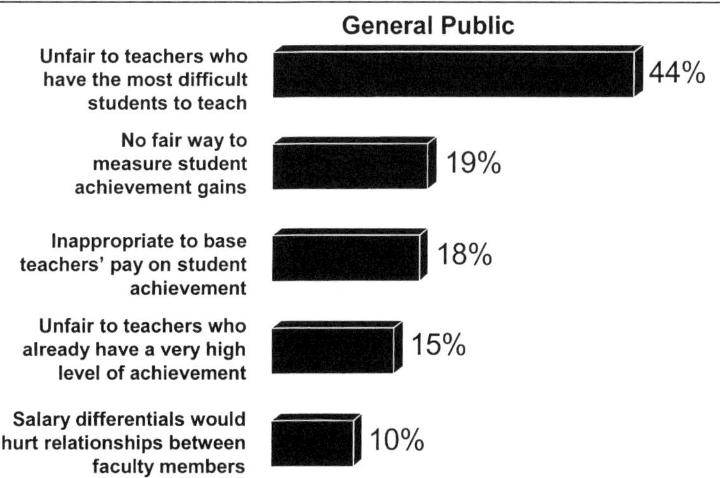

The Teaching Commission (2005). America's Commitment to Quality Teaching in Public Schools. Findings from a National Survey Conducted by Hart-Harris.

ACCOMPLISHED TEACHERS AND ACCOUNTABILITY IN THE TEACHING PROFESSION

Much of the teacher-quality debates often take place without the voices of accomplished teachers. Researchers, with different ideological bents, dispute the evidence on best ways to recruit, retain, and reward teachers. Policymakers continue to receive conflicting messages, and little gets done to transform teaching. Market advocates often portray teachers as unwilling to be held accountable for student results, and therefore needing high-stakes accountability. This may be the case for some, but not for the accomplished teachers of the Teacher Leaders Network. What follows are excerpts from a structured dialogue among 300 accomplished teachers (NBCT, Milken award winners, Teachers of the Year) who drew on a range of research studies and their own day-to-day classroom experiences, in describing the key issues regarding teacher quality, accountability, and their teaching profession.[34]

First of all, these accomplished teachers are focused intently on student learning. Jeanne, an exceptional needs teacher in Virginia, reflected that the ultimate measuring stick of a teacher's performance must be student achievement, as hard as that may be to define:

> I guess that I find that the best measure of how well I am teaching isn't really *about* how well I am teaching. It's about how well my students are learning. I can be the best teacher in the world, and use the best methodology in the world. I can have the best materials and the best lesson plans. I can use every wonderful teaching technique known to man; but, if my students aren't learning . . . then, in my opinion, I'm not teaching.

Elaine, an applied technologies teacher and NBCT, is willing to be held accountable for the value she adds in a year: "I don't mind being held accountable for my students' achievement for the year as long as that achievement for the year is being measured." Her state's accountability system does not produce the kind of information that accurately measures annual gains by individual students. She continues,

> I taught for years the elementary students other teachers didn't want. Most of them were two to three years behind in reading and had never gotten past basic addition in math. Most of them made up a year or two with me, but still might not be on grade level. Our tests today would have shown these students and me as failures when in actuality we would have had a very successful year.
>
> Most of the high-stakes testing we do is someone's idea of what the "normal" child should know by a certain age. Unfortunately I'm not dealing with a machine that can be assembled or programmed steadily. Developmental differences and outside influences contribute to different rates of learning that may not be captured by the standardized tests. If the increase in learning for the year could be tested then I'm all for being held accountable for that. Otherwise, I would have to say no thanks.

A number of teachers had a great deal to say about the content of the standardized tests themselves, which easily explained their reluctance to be judged solely by them. Some teachers critiqued Florida's elementary school math test because it asked young students to assess three-dimensional objects without having a chance to manipulate them. These expert teachers cited researchers who have studied "geometric and spatial reasoning readiness levels" and spoke to how many of the test items "fly in the face of everything we learned in educational psychology about children's cognitive development." Others teachers expressed concerns about writing tests that ignore how students' life circumstances or culture can seriously impair their understanding of the test prompts, and cause them to score poorly (even when they know how to write effectively).

Still others claimed that when students on test day "had just had a fight with a parent" or "did not get a good night's sleep" their performance can easily suffer and yield "false negative" scores. This is especially a concern to special education teachers who work with a smaller number of students, and where one low score can bias overall school results.

Susan, who works in one of Florida's low-performing schools (and is also an unpaid "data coach"), talked of a problem with the state's accountability system, which can label schools as failing, even when students are learning:

> I know how to collect and use student achievement results and I have the data to show that *all* the kids in my classrooms are really learning; I accept no less. But, several things work against schools like ours when Florida calculates our school grades. The worst is the dogged position that newly arrived Hispanic and Haitian students have only two years' grace before their performance must be equal to average native English speakers or be counted against us. Yes, some students can meet this goal, and it is wonderful when they do. This is most likely to occur when they were previously high-ability students, literate in their native language and when they also have family at home who are speaking/learning English. For the rest, hard work and remarkable gains are not enough; even astonishing gains are often "rewarded" with mandatory retention. Our school desperately needs quality teachers. I have been unable to convince a single one of my teacher friends to join me here. Why would they? Their jobs are easier.

This does not mean that these accomplished teachers do not want accountability. They may appear to be recalcitrant because they do not believe the current accountability systems are valid and reliable and are stacked against both students and teachers. They want to take matters into their own hands, but do not quite have the vehicle to do so. Linda, a teacher expert from Florida who also is leader in a national school improvement network, suggests that outsiders are rushing to hold teachers accountable because they do not see teachers publicly exploring their own successes and failures:

> We need to make our thinking *public*, so we are open about our struggles and our triumphs, like those in the legal and medical professions do as routine, embedded pieces of their culture. *This* is what we have to figure out how to do on a large scale. Because we know this will benefit us. I think the reason others are rushing to do this for us is the fact that we haven't done it so far. And our inaction looks like resistance to the idea of accountability, when in reality, we know we don't trust or believe in the accountability methods that are being used on our students, and don't know how to make them more meaningful when applied to ourselves.

However, these teachers are more than willing to be evaluated on the basis of student results if multiple and fair measures are used. Jeanne said she wanted an accountability system that accurately measured her students' growth, which needed to be over time (not just one year). They are attracted to plans, like the one developed in Denver, that measure student results on the basis of more customized goal setting and rewards reaching those goals.

They also want more time to collaborate with their colleagues. Linda talked about organizing teachers into small learning communities, who then are responsible for student learning results that they report to their community:

> This is only possible when teachers are meeting together in small learning communities, with the same people, over extended time, using processes for looking at both teacher and student work, and asking questions of ourselves and each other about our intentions, our processes, and how we know it's working, and also what else we can do when it doesn't work.

Anne, a former scientist turned teacher and NBCT (and now award-winning teacher coach), points out,

> Do you want to see teachers holding each other accountable? Find the principal who encourages teachers to think and try new ways of doing things; who provides time during the teachers' workday for them to work together to study and jointly increase their expertise. Give teachers opportunities to do the thing they've devoted their lives to doing—studying

> and practicing the art and science of instruction in order to help students reach their potential. A culture of collaboration can build a faculty of teachers who hold themselves and one another accountable. The real winners, of course, are the students.

What makes a good teacher? For accomplished teachers it is about content and teaching skills, but much more. Julie, a literacy teacher and coach in a large Southern California school district, describes the good teachers with whom she seeks to work: "Do they care about families? Do they speak the home language and/or know the home culture? Do they see impacting student achievement as the goal of everything they do?"

Often policymakers who let anyone enter the teaching profession discourage these accomplished teachers. But these teachers also want more than traditional teacher education, and see the need to provide opportunities for midcareer switchers to enter teaching. In fact, many of them entered teaching after careers in math, science, nursing, and engineering. They also are discouraged by "the lack of professionalism among (their) colleagues" and the "blue collar" responses of teacher unions. They are anxious for new forms of accountability. Deidre, who is involved in a peer review process, believes teachers must enforce teaching standards, because administrators do not or cannot do so themselves:

> I have been working with this one teacher and if he can't or won't adapt and learn then he should be out of the classroom. I don't have the final say, but as someone who will have worked with this person over a period of time I believe my observations are more valid than a 20-minute review by the administration. If we want to be viewed as professionals then we must hold ourselves and everyone else to a high standard.

Policymakers and policy wonks who do not know teaching and learning are the developers of most accountability policies. They often believe that teaching is simple work that one with a modest amount of content can do well. Carolann, an expert elementary science teacher and NBCT, noted,

> Because policymakers, administrators, and even many principals, keep sorting all teachers into two piles, effective or bad, many nonteachers

> seem to believe that the quality of a teacher can be measured the first day on the job—with finality. Yet just about every teacher in our Teacher Leaders Network will tell you that they weren't great teachers after two years, or even after five years, and that they are still getting better. It's very, very hard to teach very well, and hardest when you are working with students who are "disadvantaged."

Accomplished teachers are likely to see that they have not come up with alternatives to current student testing and accountability schemes, and that this is a problem. Bill, another NBCT and district Teacher of the Year, notes that

> it does seem like much of the energy that I see coming from classroom teachers (and their representatives to some degree) is spent on criticizing NCLB and teacher accountability as opposed to finding alternatives. But what is really strange is that as a classroom teacher, I would never have even thought it was my place to offer alternatives! I guess what I wonder is what place do classroom teachers play in the process? Where does our voice come from and how do we make it louder?

Bill continues,

> I think that teachers feel as if they've been alienated from the process of shaping school decisions and plans. We aren't seen as partners in the process of education. We're seen as "hired hands." Teachers have grown to see their relationships with decision-makers as adversarial because we're on the outside looking in. It's this adversarial relationship that causes so much skepticism among teachers, and prevents real change in our system of schooling.

Ellen, who works in a very difficult inner-city school, adds,

> There are certainly many ills in our profession, but they are not going to be cured by a politician who hasn't been inside a classroom (aside from photo-ops) since his senior year of high school. When policymakers and others outside the system set standards and criticize (not constructively) and stereotype teachers, they automatically set up an adversarial relationship. In the end, the teachers' groups (like the NEA and other organizations) and the politicians end up fighting, and the kids are lost in the battle.

CONCLUSION

In the early twenty-first century, American teachers continue to struggle in their efforts to earn status as professionals. The current teacher-quality debates over how to recruit, prepare, and reward teachers have not advanced the cause, and in many ways have limited progress. Researchers, policy wonks, administrators, and teacher union officials—who often have special interests and ideological bents—send a number of mixed signals to politicians who have had ultimate control over the profession. This should not be the case. The public wants to support a teaching profession. Recent polling data reveal the extent to which the public wants an accountable profession, but one that is not judged solely by high-stakes tests. The public wants a profession that prepares its members well, and it is willing to pay more in taxes to do so. "Blue state" voters are more likely to hold these beliefs, but "red state" voters support a teaching profession as well.

Why do the policymakers—who are holding the teaching profession's purse strings—not hear the public? One reason is that they are not paying attention to our nation's best teachers. Other reasons include both money and the lack of vision or commitment needed to change the status quo in our schools. Better-prepared teachers who meet higher standards will not only cost more, they will also demand more changes in the ways schools are organized and led. Redesigned schools, with more time for teachers to learn from one another and work more closely with students, will allow better-prepared teachers to be more effective.

The public wants teachers who know their students and who know the communities in which they work. As some researchers have noted, "The effective urban teacher cannot be skilled in the classroom [without] skills and commitment to equity, access, and democratic participation."[35] By examining the polling data, we can see that most of the public wants schools that reflect progressive values of civic responsibility, fairness, and economic opportunities, and recognizes that such schools require better-prepared professional teachers. What is called for is a new focus on creating a true teaching profession.

This notion of a true teaching profession is threatening to some market advocates, but it is reflected in values that are deeply rooted in the minds and hearts of the majority of the American electorate. Looking at the polling data it is clear Americans want their teachers to be well prepared, with all of them being held to high standards, and to prove that they know both content and how to teach it. The American public recognizes that holding teachers accountable solely on the basis of standardized test scores will undermine quality public education for all students.

Policymakers have simply not heard the right messages from the right messenger. So now it is time to mobilize some new messengers—the voices of our most accomplished teachers whom the public most admires—to reframe the debate over teaching quality and how best to close our nation's all-too-wide achievement gaps. Research and data are critical to this work. But research and data alone cannot be used to win the debate, only to reframe it.[36] The education community must now find ways to build new messages for new messengers who can speak to the majority of Americans, people who hold traditional progressive values of strength, safety, competency, quality, care, responsibility, and justice, and who recognize that only true teacher professionals can ensure that these values are represented in our public schools and imparted to our nation's children.

NOTES

1. A. Etzioni, *The semi-professions and their organization: Teachers, nurses, social workers* (New York: Free Press, 1969).
2. By the end of the 2005–2006 school year, all teachers need to be "highly qualified" by demonstrating subject matter mastery by either earning a major in his or her teaching field, passing a test in its content, or having full state certification.
3. K. Reid, Civil rights groups split over NCLB, *Education Week* (August 31, 2005).
4. L. Jacobson, States criticized on standards for veteran teachers, *Education Week* (January 5, 2005).
5. M. Petrilli, Improving teacher quality: Better luck next time, *Education Week* (August 31, 2005).
6. L. M. McDonnell, *The dilemma of teacher policy* (Santa Monica, Calif.: RAND Corporation, 1989).
7. J. Archer, Research: Focusing in on teachers, *Education Week* 21, no. 29 (2002), 36–39.

8. M. Cochran-Smith and M. Fries, The discourse of reform in teacher education: Extending the dialogue, *Educational Researcher* 31, no. 6 (2002), 26–28.

9. Fordham Foundation, *The teachers we want and how to get more of them: A manifesto* (Washington, D.C.: Author, 1999).

10. U.S. Department of Education, *Meeting the highly qualified teachers challenge: The Secretary's annual report on teacher quality* (Washington, D.C.: U.S. Department of Education, Office of Postsecondary Education, Office of Policy Planning and Innovation, 2002).

11. Education Commission of the States, *Two paths to teaching quality* (Denver: Author, 2000).

12. The National Academy of Education, *A good teacher in every classroom: Preparing the highly qualified teachers our children deserve* (San Francisco: Author, 2005).

13. National Academy of Education, *A good teacher in every classroom.*

14. S. G. Rivkin, E. A. Hanushek, and J. F. Kain, *Teachers, schools and academic achievement* (Dallas: University of Texas-Dallas Schools Project, 2002).

15. Education Trust, The real value of teachers: If good teachers matter, why don't we act like it? *Thinking K–16* 8, no. 1 (2004), 1–39.

16. Education Trust, The real value of teachers.

17. D. Ballou, Sizing up test scores, *Education Next* 2, no. 2 (summer 2002), available at www.educationnext.org/20022/10.html.

18. D. McCaffrey, J. R. Lockwood, D. M. Koretz, and L. S. Hamilton, *Evaluating value-added models for teacher accountability* (Santa Monica, Calif.: RAND Corporation, 2004).

19. I suggest that the NB process is expensive because its assessments cost teachers $2,300 while other typical teacher licensing exams often cost less than $100.

20. C. Danielson, New trends in teacher evaluation, *Educational Leadership* 14 (February 2001), 12–15.

21. Danielson, New trends in teacher evaluation.

22. C. T. Kerchner, J. E. Koppich, and J. G. Weeres, *United mind workers: Teachers and unions in the knowledge society* (San Francisco: Jossey-Bass, 1998).

23. R. A. Skinner, State of the states, *Education Week* 24, no. 17 (2005), 77, at www.edweek.org/ew/articles/2005/01/06/17sos.h24.html (accessed April 19, 2005).

24. B. Berry, Recruiting and retaining National Board Certified Teachers for hard-to-staff schools: Creating policies that will work, *Phi Delta Kappan* 87 (Dec. 2005), 290–297.

25. R. Ingersoll and T. Smith, The wrong solution to the teacher shortage, *Educational Leadership* 60, no. 8 (2003), 30–33.

26. K. H. Miles, A. Odden, M. Fermanich, and S. Archibald, *Inside the black box: School district spending on professional development in education* (Washington, D.C.: Finance Project, 2005).

27. M. Cochran-Smith, D. Davis, and M. K. Fries, Multicultural teacher education: Research, practice and policy, in *Handbook of research on multicultural education*, edited by J. Banks, 2nd ed. (San Francisco: Jossey-Bass, 2003).

28. American Federation of Teachers, 2003, AFT salary surveys, available at http://65.110.81.56/salary/index.htm (accessed April 7, 2005).

29. R. C. Neild, E. Useem, and E. Farley, *The quest for quality: Recruiting and retaining teachers in Philadelphia* (Philadelphia: Research for Action, 2005).

30. D. McGray, Working with the enemy, *New York Times* Education Life Supplement, January 16, 2005, available from www.nytimes.com/.

31. See the Hart-Harris polling results conducted for the Teaching Commission, available at www.theteachingcommission.org/press/pdfs/pollreport-final .pdf.

32. Established and chaired by Louis V. Gerstner Jr., the former chairman of IBM, the Teaching Commission proposes to improve student performance and close the student achievement gap by transforming the way in which America's public school teachers are prepared, recruited, retained, and rewarded. The commission's recommendations focus on paying teachers for performance, holding teacher education programs accountable, improving licensure and certification, and supporting new forms of school leadership. Although the commission speaks of professionalizing teachers, their implementation strategies include supporting programs like Teach for America and the American Board for the Certification of Teacher Excellence.

33. The Teaching Commission, *America's commitment to quality teaching in public schools* (New York: Author, 2005).

34 See www.teacherleaders.org/.

35. J. Oakes, M. L. Franke, K. H. Quartz, and J. Rogers, Research for high-quality teaching: Defining it, developing it, assessing it, *Journal of Teacher Education* 53, no. 3 (2002), 228–34.

36. G. Lakoff, *Moral politics: How liberals and conservatives think* (Chicago: University of Chicago Press, 2002).

5

SCHOOL CAPACITY: ORGANIZING FOR HIGH STANDARDS AND CONTINUOUS LEARNING

Melody J. Shank

Once you've spent time at New Suncook Elementary School and Poland Regional High School, you know something is distinctive about them. The energy at these schools is almost electric. The feeling of purpose is palpable and students are actively engaged in learning. Teachers are constantly in motion, as they interact with intention and concern for students and each other. They collaborate regularly about curriculum, instruction, goals for students, and aims of the school. They have high and universal expectations for student learning and behavior.

At New Suncook, students can be seen inside and outside the classroom learning alone, huddled with other students, or talking to a staff member. Their in-progress work may lie messily on classroom or hallway floors, as they contemplate next steps. Hallway walls are filled with finished student work: paintings, drawings, inquiry projects, stories, essays, and poems. Students connect with the community resources during interdisciplinary studies by visiting local and distant historical sites, welcoming parents and grandparents to be actors in their in-class social studies simulations, or working with local science educators on investigations. They join teachers at noontime, on their daily walk around the school grounds as part of the school's common theme of healthy living. And they learn about the goals successful students need through instruction and poster reminders: A successful student is a clear and effective communicator, a self-directed and lifelong learner, a collaborative and quality worker, an integrative and informed thinker, a creative and practical problem solver, and a responsible and involved citizen.[1]

Learning is paramount for New Suncook teachers. They move easily in and out of each others' classrooms, swapping ideas and using each others' expertise. Teachers of the same grade level may confer about the best ways to bring the American Revolutionary period alive for students, or they may deliberate about students' progress as they jointly plan the next instructional sequence in math. In their planning, they may discuss questions like these: Who understands what multiplication is? Who has a working command of the multiplication facts? Who is ready to move on? How will we group them? Which one of us will work with which students? Oh, and what about Joan? She's achieved all of the learning goals for fourth grade. How can we challenge her? Their learning about kids never stops.

At Poland, teachers also collaborate in pairs or small groups about students' learning on a daily basis. Freshman and sophomore team-teachers, housed together in faculty work spaces, often confer about students' needs or joint curricular projects. In their shared work space, they can easily drop everything to discuss an immediate concern about an individual or whole group of students. Interdisciplinary teaching teams or groups of like subject-area teachers talk frequently about their next class, upcoming unit, or project rubric. Teaching partners jointly score students' work and determine next steps for individual students. Across grade levels and subject areas, teachers consult about students' progress and aspirations as part of their role as student advisors.

Like New Suncook, Poland's goals for students are quite evident in visual displays and learning activities. Early in a recent school year, posters of seniors are exhibited on a lobby wall, outlining how each student is "college ready," a graduation goal for all students. Later in the year, a wall of success, picturing each senior and his or her post–high school plans, celebrates the increased number of seniors attending college. The slogan "Quality the First Time," a specific goal for student work, is visible at the school's main exit. Students' learning products are frequently displayed in hallways and school lobby, and students regularly demonstrate their learning in public presentations. The criteria for quality student work are spelled out in course syllabi and rubrics.

These two schools are characteristic of the kinds of schools organizational development experts and school reform scholars claim are needed to support the continuous renewal and improvement necessary for high levels of learning for all students. They have structured space, time, learning activities, curriculum, and organizational processes to support student and faculty engagement and achievement. On a deeper level, they have also created a culture of learning and collaboration by attending to beliefs and values that focus on student learning and relationships that foster shared understandings and meaningful professional development.

In this chapter, I use vignettes and examples from these two schools to illustrate the structural and cultural capacities that schools need to continuously engage in the kind of learning process that enables them to respond effectively to students' needs and capacities, as well as the economic and political concerns of their communities, and ultimately, help all students meet high learning standards. In doing so, I address two questions: What organizational capacities must schools develop and maintain in order to support a continuous process of renewal and improvement as they strive to ensure that all students are achieving at high levels? What do those capacities look like in practice?

PORTRAITS OF THE TWO SCHOOLS

New Suncook and Poland are both situated in the foothills of the White Mountains in southern Maine. They are rural schools in small districts. While they don't confront the challenges of large urban schools, they must, as rural schools, meet the needs of primarily working-class families. These needs often include negotiating the tensions caused by a shifting economy. In rural Maine specifically, jobs have historically been in land-based occupations (logging, farming, and fishing), manufacturing, and small business. The recent closing of paper and textile mills and disappearance of farms have decreased employment opportunities and have left many rural communities struggling to secure stable employment for their residents. At the same time, policymakers are calling for higher educational attainment of high school graduates as the economy shifts to more technologically sophisticated businesses.

Rural working-class families, however, tend to be committed to a strong work ethic based in manual and skilled labor, and value a sense of place and family connections. They may, therefore, not see the advantages of their children leaving the community to attend college. Furthermore, as more affluent, professionally employed people move from urban areas to enjoy the peace and beauty of the country, the socioeconomic diversity of rural schools increases. A tension between rural values and economic development through education becomes apparent. Increasing numbers of rural high school students are expected to be "college ready," but many resist the idea. This push for high achievement among teenagers also impacts the education of elementary students, as striving for higher standards for all students at all grade levels is the common expectation.

New Suncook Elementary School

New Suncook is one of four small elementary schools in a K–8 school district that serves fewer than 1,000 students from several small communities along the New Hampshire-Maine state line. It serves approximately 215 students in kindergarten through fifth grade, and has twelve classroom teachers and a number of support staff. The district also has one middle school, and contracts with an independent day and boarding school for the education of its high school students.

In the mid-1980s, New Suncook, with a visionary and empowering principal and a group of dedicated teachers, embarked on a restructuring process that resulted in organizational and instructional practices and structures that are hallmarks of the school today. As part of its reform process, the school community outlined a vision for the school that still grounds its teaching and learning practices to this day. Paraphrased, the vision emphasizes lifelong learning both inside and outside the school walls, with learning a shared responsibility between teachers, students, parents, and community. Teachers facilitate learning within the school by providing students ample choices about their learning within an integrated curriculum. Teachers, as learning professionals, set aside time to make decisions about curriculum and instruction based on sound research, common sense, and practical experience. All staff members are leaders and collaborate about their own learning. Strong, regular communication with parents is also valued.[2]

These beliefs are evident in the school's practices. For example, to support students' lifelong learning, teachers make every attempt to know students well. By grouping primary-aged students in multiaged, looped classrooms, teachers can observe students' development over time and build strong relationships with parents, thus increasing their ability to respond to students' learning needs. At the primary level, some classrooms are configured as K–1–2 classrooms, and others as K–1 classrooms. Two intermediate classrooms are also grouped in multiaged, looped arrangements, with the remaining upper level classes organized as single grades. In these classrooms, New Suncook teachers strive to develop all students' confidence as learners and help them understand each other's strengths by including students with special needs in all regular classrooms, rather than placing them in separate classrooms.

The faculty fosters positive learning environments and student responsibility by combining social learning with academic learning through several means. Faculty members are strong proponents of the Responsive Classroom program, which focuses on students' social skill development through an emphasis on responsibility, self-control, proactive parent communication, student choice, and discovery learning.[3] Students and teachers engage in a daily routine, called Morning Meetings, in which students learn how to interact constructively, solve problems, and have fun together. Classroom rules are collaboratively outlined in a classroom contract, and cases of misbehavior are handled either as a class, in supportive ways by the teacher, or by drafting a behavior change plan. During focused curricular studies, often interdisciplinary, students have the opportunity to choose a focus that sparks their interest. In addition to skill-based literacy instruction, ample opportunity is provided to read books of choice, and at the upper grades, engage in student-led literature groups.

In addition to the changes made at the school site during New Suncook's restructuring process, the district reorganized its schedule to include a weekly early release for students, so teachers across the district would have time for both building-based and cross-school collaboration. This common time enables faculties to alternately meet in horizontally and vertically organized groups to focus on common issues or projects, such as outlining common standards in literacy and mathematics and revising grade-level curricula. Thus, the work of teachers at New Suncook, while independent in some ways from the other district schools, is embedded in broader district goals and activities.

Poland Regional High School

Poland opened in 1999 with a philosophy and structure grounded in the best thinking and research about high schools.[4] A community planning group, representing three small adjacent K–8 districts that had previously sent their high school-aged students to neighboring schools, wanted a community high school that would foster higher educational aspirations and achievement for their children. The community group laid the philosophical groundwork for the practices subsequently designed by a trio of administrative leaders and innovative teachers. After an initial two years of phased-in enrollment, today Poland has 540 students, grades 9–12, and a faculty of 75.

The mission and beliefs of the school, published each year for students and parents in the school's Program of Studies, have created a consistent foundation for the practices in the school. The three components of the school community's mission include:

- To teach all students to use their minds well and to cultivate their particular talents;
- To establish a culture of respect, responsibility, service, and courage; and
- To demand excellence and to foster lifelong learning in a safe, welcoming environment.[5]

The belief statement addresses learning, the school environment, the needs and roles of students, the responsibilities of parents and the community for the education of their children, and the values, needs, and roles of teachers. In general, the belief statement asserts that:

- Learning, as a lifelong pursuit, must be focused on critical thinking and supported through integrated curriculum and responsive, active, problem-oriented, real-world instruction appropriate for individual students;
- Parents and the community, as part of much broader communities and essential for student learning, must lend their support to the school financially, morally, and socially;
- Highly qualified, committed, and continually learning teachers must collaborate to offer students opportunities to be creative and critical thinkers; and

- The school must be a safe, open environment that fosters active learning, individual achievements, and good citizenship.

The school's instructional and organizational practices that support this mission and belief statement include:

- Teaming for ninth and tenth graders;
- Integrated humanities, science, and mathematics curricula;
- Community service, job shadowing, internships, and individualized learning opportunities, including a special program for selected juniors and seniors;
- Standards-based grading;
- Advisory groups for all students and teachers;
- Required college application for all seniors;
- Public exhibitions of learning;
- An inclusive decision-making or governance model;
- Fifteen professional development days;
- Ongoing, site-based professional development for teachers through critical friends groups or professional learning communities, and learning-focused faculty meetings; and
- Peer review panels for merit-based salary increases.

CHARACTERISTICS OF COLLABORATIVE LEARNING ORGANIZATIONS

The foundational, structural, and pedagogical aspects of these two schools, as well as the energy for learning they exude, typify them as collaborative learning organizations. Both schools demonstrate a common purpose for student learning, share beliefs about their work, and have created processes and structures that enable faculty members to engage collaboratively in continuous learning and decision making. The literature on learning organizations, professional learning communities, and collaborative cultures consistently claim that the following features are central to a school's capacity to learn:[6]

- Shared responsibility for a set of beliefs about students, learning, teaching, and organizations;

- A culture of inquiry;
- Structures and processes that support collaboration, feedback, communication, and inclusive decision making;
- Transformational and distributed leadership; and
- Mechanisms for holding themselves accountable.

These features, which I examine in more detail in the following sections, do not exist in isolation from one another. Instead, they function together to create a school culture that supports continuous learning and self-design. The synergy that exists between the features is created through the ongoing process of putting values and beliefs into practice. The establishment of a school as a learning organization is therefore not a linear or mechanistic process or a series of hierarchical action steps. Instead the process may start, as it did at New Suncook, with a forward-thinking leader, who supports a group of teachers in examining their teaching together. Or, it might start, as at Poland, through a challenge undertaken by a group of community leaders to create a new high school by articulating their aspirations for their students in a set of beliefs. Regardless of the starting point, attention to the interplay between the features in an ongoing manner and the process as it unfolds is what pushes a school toward the establishment of a collaborative learning organization.

Shared Responsibility for Beliefs about Students, Learning, Teaching, and Organizations

Poland and New Suncook both have strongly stated and held sets of beliefs. Having and acting upon these beliefs is central to each school's capacity to continue improving. Their beliefs encompass not only the realm of the learning process or how to teach but also the roles of teachers and the community and how they will work together in their organizations.

Beliefs about Learning and Students As is clear in Poland's belief statement, a belief that all members of the school community—students, teachers, administrators, and community members alike—are lifelong learners is at the heart of their mission. This belief permeates New Suncook as well, and is the source of the energy that can be felt in both schools. Teachers at these schools embrace Senge's idea that learning is a fundamental human process:

> Through learning we re-create ourselves. Through learning we become able to do something we never were able to do. Through learning we re-perceive the world and our relationship to it. Through learning we extend our capacity to create, to be part of the generative process of life.[7]

Teachers in these schools are not just fulfilling the requirements of their job description. They express their curiosity and dedication to always learn about the content they teach, their students, and their capacity to teach. In turn, they foster a learning environment to support students' curiosity, interests, and aspirations.

In these schools, student learning is at the center of teachers' thinking and practice. This may seem like a common claim for schools to make, as schools almost always have this as part of their mission. But schools like Poland and New Suncook are striking in their declaration that their beliefs about learning pertain to *all* students—not just those who demonstrate immediate ability or whose parents have influence, but every student who walks through their doors.

They support this belief with pedagogical approaches that guide and support all students' learning, and a set of learning standards for which they hold themselves accountable. Their practices are not driven by pedagogical or structural traditions, students' exhibited levels of achievement or socioeconomic backgrounds, or bus schedules. Rather, their practices are grounded in a strong philosophical foundation about how learning takes place and what is good for their current groups of students. Learning is not seen as a simplistic transfer process from teacher or text to student, but rather an active and interactive hands-on process rooted in life-connecting problem-solving or inquiry projects. Therefore, group learning, project-based activities, and integrated curriculum are the norm, along with targeted skill and knowledge building.

Beliefs about Teaching With these beliefs about student learning and conceptions of how students learn, faculty members investigate possibilities for and make decisions about their own practices and the practices of the whole school, based on what will support students' capacity to learn. Teaching is viewed as the structured facilitation of learning engagements through which students develop skills, acquire knowledge, make sense of complex ideas, and develop thinking habits. Teachers meet diverse learning needs by knowing their students well and building relationships with them. They tailor learning for individuals and groups of students by analyzing students' strengths, accomplishments, and aspirations, as well as learning challenges. They constantly inquire about their students as learners and about the strategies and conditions that will support learning. They pose questions about students and devise ways to meet students' needs through individualized and whole class strategies. Teachers therefore are constantly expanding their pedagogical and curricular repertoire.

Cochran-Smith and Lytle claim that being an inquirer into one's own practice is best done in collaboration with other teachers.

> Working together in communities, [teachers can] pose problems, identify discrepancies between theories and practice, challenge common routines, draw on the work of others for generative frameworks, and attempt to make visible much of that which is taken for granted about teaching and learning. From this inquiry stance, teachers search for significant questions as much as they engage in problem-solving. They count on other teachers for alternative viewpoints on their work.[8]

Teachers at Poland and New Suncook ascribe to this belief, so teaching for them is both collaborative and public. In these schools, it is no longer only a question of what an individual teacher can do, but what teachers can do together to ensure that students are learning. Said differently, teaching is viewed as not only a capacity of individual teachers but also as a distributed property or capacity of the whole school.[9]

Vital to this conception of teaching is the validation of the professional knowledge and skill that teachers bring to bear in making decisions regarding student learning and the school, and support for their continued professional development through high quality learning experiences. As New Suncook teachers observed, a condition that their principal established early in their restructuring process and that they collectively continue to support is "the importance of teachers who think deeply about their educational purposes and who have the courage to act on their ideas, . . . [and] work with each other to stretch our ideas as well as our practices."[10] This sentiment is reinforced in the school's vision statement: "Teaching decisions are based on a combination of valid and reliable research, common sense, and practical experience. All school staff relate on a professional level, formally and informally, with the continued growth of the school in mind."[11] It is understood then that both individual judgments and teachers' collective responsibility are expected and honored.

Beliefs about Organizations Just as the teaching and learning process in collaborative learning schools is not viewed as a mechanistic process, neither is the school, as an organization, viewed as a machine, with separately functioning parts. Instead, teachers and administrators at New Suncook and Poland see the school as an organic social system that is constantly changing to respond flexibly to students and environmental shifts. More specifically, the school is seen as a web of relationships that is sustained through facilitative processes and structures. At both Poland and New Suncook, supporting relationships within the organization (between teachers, between teachers and students, among students, and between members of the school community and the larger community) is vitally important to the school's capacity to identify and solve problems, establish priorities, and support learning of all of its members. As the former principal of Poland notes, how teachers treat and work with each other is as important in their schools as how teachers treat and support students.[12]

But the importance of relationships goes a step further. Building strong professional relationships around a common purpose of student learning is vital for maintaining and revisiting common goals in everyday practices, for building teachers' capacity to proactively meet students' learning needs, for having a shared understanding of articulated learning outcomes for students in action, for upholding the commitment to ideals and the renewal process, and for sustaining inquiry about their practices and values. As McLaughlin and Talbert and others claim, taking collective responsibility for student learning is essential to helping students achieve at high levels, and for maintaining a culture of learning.[13] Sustaining a focus on student learning and sharing responsibility for student learning can only occur through collaborative relationships. At Poland and New Suncook, creating ample time and space for collaboration around shared tasks is a priority.

As learning organizations, schools like New Suncook and Poland are also open systems, interacting with the policy, local community, and professional contexts within their environment. They actively focus on possibilities, anticipate changes, and detect problems as they appear on the horizon. They constantly seek input or work collaboratively with their various constituents, and actively seek perspectives and input from external sources. Members of the school community, particularly leaders, anticipate policy changes or directly contribute to the policymaking, and think flexibly about the implications of the measures for their work as a teaching and learning community. This orientation shifts the locus of control related to processes, inputs, and outcomes from external agencies, such as federal or state educational agencies, to the school site itself. Members of school community assume the responsibility to make proactive choices about how to incorporate external influences or policies into their work, or when appropriate, challenge them.

Teacher Professional Development in a Culture of Inquiry

A crucial capacity in a collaborative learning organization is the expectation and support for teachers to learn as part of their everyday work with students and colleagues. As teachers work together to pose questions about what they will do next and how they will do it, and subsequently analyze how their plan went, their collaborative work constitutes a relevant and effective means of improving practice. Reflecting on their teaching becomes even more valuable when they also pose questions about the purposes of their plan; the assumptions underneath their thinking; the coherence between their plan, goals for students, and values about learning; the consequences of their actions for particular students' learning; alternative ways to think about their pedagogy; and ultimately, the results of the plans for the range of students with whom they are working.

Organizational learning experts make an important distinction between these two levels of reflection by distinguishing between single- and double-loop learning. The narrower and more instrumental approach, single-loop learning, is the result of a linear and controlled process in which actions are measured by whether the desired results were achieved. No questioning of underlying assumptions or use of broadly collected and credible information is incorporated in this learning process. In contrast, double-loop learning is an examination of not only what worked to achieve intended outcomes but also the assumptions and consequences of actions and additional possibilities.

> Double-loop learning involves careful reflection upon not only actions, but the appropriateness of the outcomes those actions are intended to achieve. Such reflection necessarily carries over into the values and norms upon which desired outcomes are founded, as well as the social structures that make them meaningful.[14]

When teachers engage in double-loop learning, they delve deeply into theoretical and philosophical grounds for their practices, and seek diverse and divergent ideas that may in fact challenge their existing theories and beliefs.

At both Poland and New Suncook, teachers approach their learning and understanding of students and their practices as part of a community of double-loop inquirers, thoughtfully facing the dilemmas and questions of their teaching. For example, the New Suncook teachers have continually sought to improve their practices by asking themselves two questions: What are we doing with students? And, more importantly, why are we doing it? As part of their restructuring process, they studied their practices and the best thinking about early childhood development to determine that multiage grouping was the best approach for students aged five to eight. Later, when they wanted to expand their connections with parents and the community, they investigated with parents how they could increase communication between parents and the school, and how community expertise could enhance the curriculum.

Similarly, teachers at Poland challenge their own assumptions and established structures, when evidence or new ideas warrant it, and make necessary changes in programs, structures, and processes. Let me illustrate their commitment to this inquiry process with this recent example. Since the opening of the school, critical friends groups have been a mandatory part of professional development for faculty members.[15] The principal viewed them as a means for teachers to develop the habits of reflection and collaborative problem solving, as well as for providing teachers a view of the teaching and learning process from the perspectives of both individual teachers and a broader cross-section of the whole school. These groups were both cross-disciplinary and cross-grade level. Based on several years of data collected on teachers' perceptions of the groups, and on recent thinking on the subject in the literature, a professional development task force concluded that the professional development needs of teachers would be better served through a choice of topically defined small professional learning communities. Critical friends groups would still continue, but action research groups, math study groups, and differentiation study groups all became acceptable options.

Collaborative Structures and Processes

Both New Suncook and Poland support their collaborative cultures through visible structures and processes. Because describing the full complexity of these processes and structures is not possible in this chapter, I will highlight four collaborative structures that make continuous attention to student learning and the renewal of the school possible: inclusive decision making, ample common planning time, shared work space, and joint tasks.

Inclusive Decision Making Both schools use an inclusive process to make significant decisions at the classroom, grade, and whole-school levels. Participating in the deliberation and decision process not only sustains shared understanding and commitment but also validates and empowers all participants and fosters ownership and action. Conflicts are more likely to be solved when all perspectives are honored.

At Poland, decision making occurs at many levels, with decisions about whole-school issues and programs facilitated through the Visionkeepers, a central governance group made up of administrators, teachers, students, and community members in charge of ensuring that proposed changes are congruent with the school's mission and belief statement. All policy issues are fed to the Visionkeepers through committee or individual proposals, with a vote of the full faculty taken when a critical issue arises. Whole-school decisions are also facilitated through regularly held faculty and smaller activity-specific meetings. The faculty meets every Tuesday after school, in an alternating meeting sequence of full faculty, learning area teams, grade-level advisors groups, and professional learning teams. Additionally, Poland's annual calendar includes fifteen teacher professional development days that are used for a variety of activities that enable the school to deliberate about all types of issues.

As a small school, New Suncook's governance structure involves the whole faculty in a consensus-based decision-making process. The guiding principle of the faculty is that those people who are affected by the decision should be involved in making the decision. Therefore, the intermediate teachers confer about the issues that affect their students and curriculum, as do the primary teachers. When issues are of a concern to the whole faculty, they are handled in faculty meetings. Furthermore, all staff members are encouraged to raise issues and make proposals for consideration.

Common Planning Time Finding time in teachers' regular workday to plan and consult together is a mainstay at both schools and is vital to making inclusive decisions, understanding curriculum and standards in action, and meeting students' learning needs. At New Suncook, teachers confer over lunchtime and during the planning time provided by the scheduling of back-to-back music, art, and physical education classes.

Poland's extra professional development time is coupled with ample planning time during the regular weekly schedule. Teachers at Poland have approximately thirteen hours per week of planning time, which can be used flexibly by individual teachers, teaching teams, and grade-level teams. Teachers spend this time designing curriculum, learning activities, and assessments; assessing student work; consulting about or with students; and contacting parents. Much of that time is spent in collaboration with teaching partners, fellow team members, or other educators throughout the building. This extra time is essential for completing the tasks that come with expanded teacher roles.

Shared Work Space Having a generous amount of planning time doesn't necessarily foster collaboration by itself. The planning time needs to be combined with two additional dimensions: shared space and joint tasks.[16] At Poland, teachers, with the exception of those in music, visual and performing arts, technology, and physical education, do not "own" their rooms. Instead classrooms are shared spaces, and teachers work in common offices, where they have individual desks, common meeting tables, and all needed support equipment (a telephone, copier, office supplies, etc.). The groupings of teachers in these spaces are very carefully considered to make sure teachers who collaborate on curriculum and other joint tasks are in close proximity to one another. Therefore, grade-level teams and teaching partners have work space in the shared offices. Often teachers of the same courses also have common work space. This proximity to work partners facilitates both in-depth and on-the-fly planning and assistance.

The physical arrangements of classrooms at New Suncook facilitate close collaboration. The primary classrooms are clustered at the end of a hallway, with the doors opening onto a common square hallway space. Collapsible walls between classrooms allows for additional collaborative ventures. Intermediate teachers, while not clustered so conveniently, do have classrooms with pass-through doors for easy movement of students from one room to the other. These teachers can also consult easily during and between classes.

Joint Work Judith Warren Little describes the highest form of collegiality as joint work, work that can't be accomplished unless teachers collaborate.[17] At Poland and New Suncook, in their efforts to ensure that all students learn at high levels, teachers assume that meeting students' learning needs is not individual work. At Poland the joint work of teachers is multilayered. Humanities teaching pairs collaborate on all aspects of curriculum and lesson planning for their groups of students. Teachers teaching the same courses in science, math, and world languages work together to outline assessments, projects, and learning activities. Grade-level teams jointly set expectations for their groups of students, consult about students, and plan interdisciplinary projects. Advisory group teachers meet regularly to design activities for their advisees, plan the sequence of curriculum for the particular grade-level focus, and fine-tune the assessments. Teachers also collaborate by focusing on each other's teaching and performance in critical friends groups and salary review panels. In fact, there is little at Poland that is not a collaborative venture.

At New Suncook, teachers who teach in multiage intermediate and self-contained fourth-grade classrooms collaborate closely to design engaging learning activities for students, and create relevant interdisciplinary units of study. For example, during a unit on the American Revolution, all fourth and fifth graders learn about the reasons for the uprising through a simulation about colonists' experience of England's taxation regulations. The simulation is a large logistical undertaking and requires collaborative planning and problem solving. Additionally, New Suncook teachers use the district's learning benchmarks for student progress in reading, writing, and mathematics to design, score, and norm assessments, and in turn inform students and parents about achievement and growth. To make a determination about a student's progress, it is important to have several perspectives on the evidence reviewed, so teachers work together to make judgments about student learning.

Distributed Transformational Leadership

For over two decades, the importance of positive school leadership has been acknowledged as an essential element of a school's capacity for continuous renewal and improvement. Over this time, however, the conception of the kind of leadership needed in schools has changed. The image of a charismatic, highly skilled, visionary, and authoritative savior, or "great man," riding in on a stallion to lead followers to a better place is not only riddled with gender stereotypes but is also no longer a viable conception of leadership in complex and changing organizations.[18] The power of strong individual leaders can't be dismissed. Such leaders play important roles in seeing possibilities, framing problems and processes for solving them, buffering others in the organization from undue stress and external obstacles, resolving conflicts, and being an advocate for the school. But the kind of leadership needed for high-performing schools has shifted from instructional leadership and management to a combination of transformational and distributed leadership.

According to Leithwood and Jantzi, a transformational leader has six primary roles:[19]

- Sustain the school's vision and goals;
- Provide opportunities for intellectual engagement;
- Provide individualized encouragement and assistance;
- Embody the professional practices and values ascribed to by the school community;

- Be an example of and uphold high standards of performance; and
- Create structures to support inclusive decision making.

These roles must be coupled with what the authors consider transactional or more managerial roles: filling staff positions, supporting instruction, overseeing school activities and functions, and making connections to the community. While these roles are indeed performed by building administrators, they can and should also be assumed by faculty members across the school. In fact, as Hargreaves and Fink argue, it is shortsighted to relegate leadership to an individual or small group.[20] Instead, leadership should be considered a capacity distributed across the members of the organization, as it takes the skills and knowledge of all members of the school to respond to the diverse challenges faced by schools today.

> Distributed leadership means creating a culture of initiative and opportunity, where teachers of all kinds propose new directions, start innovations, perhaps sometimes even challenging and creating difficulties for their principals in the overall interest of the students and the school.[21]

Central leaders would do well, then, to share the power and authority with teachers, other staff members, and ideally, parents and students. In schools where transformational and distributed leadership is honored, the school community supports the leadership potential of individuals by looking carefully at the skills and expertise of its many members.

At New Suncook and Poland, the expectation and support for distributed, transformational leadership is evident. Developing the leadership capacity of the school was a main focus at New Suncook when the restructuring effort was initiated. The story of the school's change process clearly portrays the principal as a central figure in sustaining the processes of visioning, goal setting, and conflict resolution, as well as encouraging the participating teachers as they studied and initiated instructional and curricular changes. But the teachers at New Suncook are remarkable leaders, too. Teachers did the research to decide to move to multiage groupings early in their restructuring evolution. Teachers drafted the literacy benchmarks for grades K–5. Teachers develop and implement engaging interdisciplinary projects with their students.

Teachers communicate weekly with parents through multiple means. Teachers share their expertise and wisdom in conference presentations, and with a new generation of teachers as mentors and course instructors in our university's teacher education program. New Suncook teachers also chair district curriculum and assessment committees. More than one of them has received national awards for their teaching and leadership expertise. Finally, when the principal left his principalship of twenty years to become the superintendent of the district, a veteran teacher at New Suncook stepped into the role of the school's central leader.

At Poland, the collaborative organizational structures, including team-teaching arrangements, grade-level groupings at the ninth- and tenth-grade levels, advisory groups, and an inclusive governance structure are built on the idea of distributed leadership. The three central administrators—the principal, dean of faculty, and dean of students—all have specific responsibilities to ensure that various aspects of the school organization are attended to, but teachers assume leadership for many facets of the school. Each grade-level team, for instance, takes leadership in making decisions about the best approaches to meeting the needs of its eighty students. Similarly, the advisors for students in particular grade levels plan and facilitate activities for their advisees, with a teacher-leader coordinating the efforts of each group of advisors. Subject area teachers have over the last several years drafted grade-level and subject-specific learning standards, summative assessments, and curricula. The facilitation of the Visionkeepers is shared by all committee members on a rotating basis. And lastly, the critical friends groups and small professional learning teams are organized and facilitated by teachers.

Assuming such leadership roles requires a much-expanded set of roles for teachers, and also fosters ownership of ideas and actions. Decision making can more readily occur at the point of action, a defining feature of a learning organization.

The Support and Influence of External Educational Networks and Agencies

While one of the conditions of a school-as-learning-organization is the autonomy to make decisions about resource allocation, programs, curriculum, and practices that best meet the needs of its students and teachers, membership in external networks and educational agencies can provide a school with much needed assistance and professional development opportunities. Fullan claims that schools need outside agencies to accomplish the difficult job of continuous improvement.[22] He challenges us to think of the relationships between schools and outside educational entities, especially central district administrations, state and federal education departments, and sometimes professional organizations, not as hierarchical or adversarial but reciprocal. As open systems with permeable boundaries, collaborative learning schools seeking to build capacity need to constantly attend to the external opportunities, obstacles, and emerging policies that will influence their goals. They need to seek collaborative learning opportunities with professionals outside their schools, so they do not become isolated from current thinking and policies. They need to interact with state and federal governments because these agencies greatly impact what schools can do, as do district administrations, local school boards, and communities. Professional organizations and intermediary educational service providers also play an increasingly important role in both framing and supporting a school's capacity for renewal.

The support and learning opportunities Poland and New Suncook have embraced through networking and collaboration with other professionals outside their school have been vital to their learning and development. Both schools have been active members of the Southern Maine Partnership, a university-school collaboration with over thirty-five member-schools, housed at the University of Southern Maine. The partnership has supported school and teacher development for twenty years in the southern Maine region through a range of teacher learning and school renewal projects. Through their affiliation with the partnership and other professional organizations, New Suncook faculty members were able to refine their goals, develop processes for studying their teaching, develop an understanding of the change process and how to manage it, and extend their thinking. Outside facilitators from the partnership helped them to face difficult questions.

Likewise, Poland Regional High School has been involved in more than one grant project with Southern Maine Partnership to support its continued effort to fine-tune expectations for students and personalize learning. The projects have helped Poland teachers create the individualized learning program for juniors and seniors, support all seniors in applying to postsecondary education institutions, and develop greater connections with the community through internships, job shadowing opportunities, and community-wide book discussion nights. The school is also a member of the Coalition of Essential Schools, a national school reform network, which enables them to learn through the ideas of distant others. Both schools are also active partners with the University of Southern Maine's Teacher Education Department in supporting teaching interns.

Mechanisms for Holding Themselves Accountable

In their study of schools' internal structures for accountability, Abelman et al. use the interplay between three dimensions of a school culture as a framework for determining whether schools have strong or weak accountability systems. The three dimensions include

- *Individual responsibility* assumed by teachers for students and the schools as part of their personal and professional value system.
- *Collective expectations* shared by faculty members. These expectations include the norms and values that teachers understand through relationships within the school culture.
- *Accountability mechanisms* through which individuals give an account of their work to someone in authority. They may be informal and formal mechanisms, and may be external or internal to the school.[23]

From their study, they conclude that when there is coherence and consistency between individual teachers' senses of responsibility, shared expectations, and the mechanisms of accountability, internal accountability is strong. More specifically, the authors suggest that internal accountability may be based on "the collective expectations gell[ing] into highly interactive, relatively coherent, informal and formal systems by which teachers and administrators [hold] each other accountable for their actions *vis-à-vis* students."[24] They go on to claim that collaborative structures are vital to establishing this coherence. In the schools they studied where individual responsibility reigned as the primary mechanism for accountability, the system of internal accountability was weak. In fact, when teachers work in isolation, "the school's conception of accountability collapses, by default, into individual teachers' conceptions of responsibility."[25] Without collective expectations and coherence, the authors claim, schools will not have the internal capacity to hold themselves accountable, nor will they be able to successfully participate in an externally driven system of accountability.

To illustrate how a school can incorporate both formal and informal mechanisms of accountability into the organizational structures and practices, I focus on two dimensions of Poland's culture through which the teachers hold themselves accountable for the expectations they have for students and themselves: curriculum and assessment development and evaluation, and the selection, evaluation, and support of teachers. But I must remind you that the collaborative structures described earlier in the chapter provide the tightly woven network of relationships that support the commitment to and practice of accountability in the school. It is through the inclusive decision making, collaborative planning and problem solving, and distributed leadership that teachers at both Poland and New Suncook continuously deliberate about expectations for student learning, their teaching practices, and their overall mission.

Curriculum and Assessment Development and Evaluation Poland opened after the state's learning standards, Maine Learning Results, and the local assessment system were mandated.[26] Therefore, from the outset teachers at Poland were able to base the curriculum on the state learning standards. A first step in holding themselves accountable for their expectations for students was the process of translating the state standards into their own words, and often into student-friendly terms, prioritizing the standards, and subsequently, making the standards real through the development of curriculum. In the ongoing development of curriculum, teachers translate these standards into clearly articulated learning outcomes and assessment for each course and unit. The expectations for success are shared with students and parents and are therefore public knowledge. Students are then held accountable to the standards through a standards-based grading system. In order to receive credit for the course, students must show evidence of meeting the standards, or they may be asked to do additional work or attend summer school.

Internal to this system of accountability is the collective responsibility of teachers for what they intend to accomplish with students. Teachers who teach the same courses or grade level work closely together to develop assessments, create scoring rubrics, double-score student products, and check for validity and reliability. The collaborative process that Poland teachers use to develop curriculum and assessments at both course and grade levels requires that they come to a shared understanding of what it means for students to meet or exceed the learning standards. Judgments about students' achievement are most frequently made collaboratively.

Selection, Evaluation, and Support of Teachers The second arena in which Poland faculty members hold themselves accountable is in the area of teacher hiring and evaluation. As in many other facets of the school, the hiring review and recommendation process is an inclusive and collaborative one. A hiring team consisting of administrators, teachers, and often students is assembled for the hiring of all positions. The makeup of the team depends on the position being filled, but usually the team is comprised of teachers from the applicant's content area and members of the team of which applicants may become a part. The hiring team reviews applications, selects applicants to interview, interviews candidates, and makes recommendations. This inclusive hiring process enables the faculty to choose their own colleagues and be involved in maintaining the quality of teaching.

Once teachers are hired at Poland, the professional review and support process continues. A mentor-guide, called an Obi-Wan, after the Jedi guide in *Star Wars*, is assigned to each new teacher and is responsible to meet periodically with the new colleague to offer personal support and guidance regarding the school's logistics and practices at the beginning of the year. To guide new teachers through the goal-setting and review process required by the state to move from provisional to professional, a mentor is assigned. An administrative evaluation process operates parallel to the certification process and includes annual reviews, goal setting, and classroom observations. Additionally, if a new faculty member is struggling with some aspect of his or her practice, a peer support team, consisting of an administrator and two teachers, is assembled to offer closer assistance to the teacher.

All of these support and evaluation processes engage at least some faculty members in the support and evaluation of their colleagues, but the most involved peer review process is the standards-based merit pay review process. As part of Poland's work agreement, merit-based salary increases are awarded based on peer review of teachers' demonstrated proficiency of specified performance standards. The professional standards were drafted by teachers as an adaptation of Charlotte Danielson's standards for teacher performance,[27] and include a developmental rubric for each of the following categories: planning and preparation, instruction, classroom environment, and professional responsibilities. Based on goals set in a Professional Growth Plan, faculty members applying for a salary raise compile evidence of their accomplishments in a portfolio, the Performance Archive Folder. Peer review panels, called Salary Review Panels, made up of three peers, review the portfolio and conduct classroom observations to determine if the presented evidence of professional practice warrants a pay increase. The collaboration that leads up to a teacher salary increase—sharing of artifact examples, reviewing early versions of the Professional Archive Folder, and reviewing and interpreting the standards in faculty meetings—adds an informal dimension to the more formal process. Together, all of these processes create a thick web of collegial support and review.

CONCLUDING THOUGHTS

Many years ago, when I was first working with schools as a reform coach, I remember a high school teacher reflecting on one of the most important insights she and others in her building had had as a part of rethinking expectations for students and structures of their school. She shared that prior to engaging collectively in their reform effort, they assumed that their colleagues, the teachers next door, held the same values about learning and high standards for students. But in fact she discovered that as a faculty they held quite dissimilar values or expectations for meeting the learning needs of all students, and to her it felt like a blemish on their school. I realized in her statement, and it has been confirmed many times since, that when we are determining the quality of students' work, we cannot and should not assume a common understanding of standards of performance or learning across a group of assessors, let alone a shared set of criteria, unless the assessors have spent ample time deliberating about evidence. Determining and substantiating the quality of any work is a joint enterprise, something that can't be accomplished by individuals working alone.

What distinguishes New Suncook Elementary School and Poland Regional High School is that they have organized themselves around a strong vision of success for all students, and have created the collaborative structures to ensure that they continue to grapple with the pedagogical and curricular challenges of supporting achievement of all students. They don't assume a shared understanding of the standards and values they hold, but rather engage with each other intensely on a daily basis to define and redefine what their values and standards mean in practice. They have organized time, space, and processes to provide the staff meaningful deliberation about the practices that facilitate student learning. In short, Poland Regional High School and New Suncook Elementary School have built into their culture and structures the collective will and capacities to engage quite purposefully in student-centered practices that support an internal accountability system.

But the process of creating and maintaining such capacities has not been easy for either of these schools. Both schools have met with resistance from dissenting voices either within or outside the school. These voices have challenged the schools' practices and, both intentionally and inadvertently, pushed for maintaining the status quo.

As a result, both schools have made every effort to articulate their beliefs and practices through the involvement of parents and community members, and to ground their beliefs and practices in sound research and professional judgment. They strive to accept diversity of thought and practice among faculty members within the range of ideas that support the school's mission and beliefs. They accept, under the umbrella of a common purpose, that good practice varies from teacher to teacher. Poland specifically realizes the importance of teachers developing their own individual identities and voices within the classrooms and the school community.

Maintaining constant attention to their mission, valued practices, and continuous collective and public learning is energy-intensive and time-consuming work, however. Even with extra professional planning and learning time, teachers at both schools work intensely. They are constantly pressing themselves to high professional standards, which can be both emotionally and intellectually taxing. It is therefore vital for them to have the professional involvement of external educational agencies and networks, like Southern Maine Partnership, that provide them valuable critical friendship and professional guidance through grant funding, coaching, network meetings, and visitations. Meeting with others who are struggling with similar change issues offers not only a mechanism for exchanging and challenging to ideas but also the necessary support for persisting during difficult times. External coaches and visitors provide a broad and impartial perspective that is important for both confirming and challenging practices. The external agencies also help the schools anticipate the policy changes and mandates on the horizon, and in some cases, challenge those policies.

State and federal education departments would do well to heed the lessons from schools like New Suncook and Poland, and provide high-quality professional support that both helps teachers and other school community members to create the structures and culture necessary to a collective focus on student learning and relationships of internal accountability. By partnering *with* schools, state education departments could collaboratively take on the difficult task of assuming collective responsibility for high standards. They could help schools improve their organizational capacity while developing their own capacity. Just as schools work best as collaborative learning organizations with their teachers, parents, and communities, so too would state departments of education with their client schools and districts.

As state departments of education endeavor to assist schools—and themselves—in the demanding task of developing organizational capacity for high standards and continuous learning, the following questions might serve as a common framework for reflection and action:

- Do our mission and beliefs center squarely on the learning of all students and suggest concrete professional practices?
- To what extent are our present practices coherent with our mission and beliefs? What changes do we need to aim for?

- Do we as professionals go beyond the instrumentality of our practice (What will I do? How will I do it? Did it work?) to pose questions about the assumptions of our practices and the potential consequences for students?
- Do we engage in the teaching and learning process—meeting the students' learning needs, designing curriculum, planning instructional strategies, and assessing students—through a joint means? Do we teach and deliberate in pairs and groups to make pedagogical decisions?
- Do our work times and spaces support collective responsibility for students and their learning? For each other's learning?
- Do our central administrators share their authority and leadership with teachers, and support teachers' authority to make decisions that affect their teacher and their students' learning?
- Is our governance structure inclusive of the range of diverse perspectives and voices? Is it structured to value individual voices as well as the school's articulated common purpose? Does the governance structure allow for leadership and decision making at all levels?
- Do we approach conflicts, issues, and possible changes through a thorough inquiry process, using research and practical wisdom?
- Do we articulate the standards for learning clearly at all levels of curriculum development and do we engage in collaborative practices through which we hold each other and our students accountable to these standards?
- Do we as leaders interact with outside educational agencies and organizations as partners in a reciprocal critical friend's relationship?

Reciprocal questioning and simultaneous planning about the school's capacity could guide any internal or external review process. By supporting such an approach, state education departments could replicate the systems that school reform networks, like the Coalition of Essential Schools, have established to connect schools as critical friends or supporters, and provide ongoing technical and professional assistance. Such systems combine periodic workshops for school-based analysis and inquiry, external peer review, and continuous on-site coaching into a powerful means of helping schools both develop and maintain their missions and practices. They also help schools stay accountable to their own missions and continuously develop the organizational capacities necessary to work collaboratively toward high standards and continuous improvement.

ACKNOWLEDGEMENTS

I acknowledge the incredible accomplishments and hard work of the faculties at Poland Regional High School and New Suncook Elementary School. They are exceptional professionals and colleagues. I thank them for sharing their dedication and practices with me for this chapter.

NOTES

1. These are the guiding principles outlined in Maine's learning standards for students, the Maine Learning Results, published by the Maine Department of Education in 1997.

2. The full text of the vision statement can be found in L. Goldsberry, A. Holt, K. Johnson, G. MacDonald, R. Poliquin, and L. Potter, The evolution of a restructuring school: The New Suncook case, in *The work of restructuring schools: Building from the ground up*, edited by A. Lieberman (New York: Teachers College Press, Columbia University, 1995), 143–43.

3. *The responsive classroom: Principles and practices* (July 16, 2005), available at www.responsiveclassroom.org/about/principles.html. For a general overview of the approach, read R. Charney, *Teaching children to care: Classroom management for ethical and academic group* (Turner Falls, Mass.: Northeast Foundation, 2002).

4. National Association of Secondary School Principals, *Breaking ranks: Changing an American Institution* (Reston, Va.: NASSP, 1996); Maine Department of Education, *Promising futures: A call to improve learning for Maine's secondary schools* (Bangor, Me.: Author, 1997); T. Sizer, *Horace's compromise: The dilemma of the American high school* (Boston: Houghton-Mifflin, 1984); T. Sizer, *Horace's school: Redesigning the American high school* (Boston: Houghton-Mifflin, 1992); T. Sizer, *Horace's hope: What works for the American high school* (Boston: Houghton-Mifflin, 1996); The Coalition of Essential Schools, available at www.essentialschools.org (accessed July 16, 2005).

5. Poland Regional High School, *Program of studies and course descriptions 2005–2006* (2005), 2.

6. J. Cilbulka, S. Coursey, M. Nakayama, J. Price, and S. Stewart, *Schools as learning organizations: A review of the literature—The creation of high-performance schools through organizational and individual learning*, Part 1 (Washington, D.C.: National Partnership of Excellence and Accountability in Teaching, 2000); R. DuFour, R. Eaker, and F. DuFour (Eds.), *On common ground: The power of professional learning communities* (Bloomington, Ind.: National Educational Service, 2005); S. Hord, *Professional learning communities: Communities of continuous inquiry and improvement*, Southwest Educational Development Laboratory, available at www.sedl.org/pubs/change34/ (accessed July 30, 2005); A. Lieberman (Ed.), *Schools as collaborative cultures: Creating the future now* (New York: Falmer Press, 1990); F. Newman, M. B. King, and M. Rigdon, Accountability and school performance: Implications from restructuring schools, *Harvard Educational Review* 76, no. 1 (1997), 41–74; Northeast and Islands Regional Laboratory, What it takes: 10 capacities for initiating and sustaining school improvement (Providence, R.I.: Brown University, 2000); H. Silins, S. Zarins, and B. Mulford, *What characteristics and processes define a school as a learning organization?* Paper presented at the Australian Association for Research in Education Conference, 1998; L. Lashway, *Creating a learning organization* (1998), Eric Digest No. 121, ED 420897, available at www.eric.ed.gov (accessed September 16, 2005).

7. P. Senge, *The fifth dimension: The art and practice of the learning organization* (New York: Doubleday, 1990), 14.

8. M. Cochran-Smith and S. Lytle, Relationships of knowledge and practice: Teacher learning in communities, in *Review of research in education,* Vol. 24, edited by A. Iran-Nejad and P. D. Pearson (Washington, D.C.: American Educational Research Association, 1999), 293.

9. J. MacDonald, *Redesigning school* (San Francisco: Jossey-Bass, 1996).

10. Goldsberry et al., The evolution of a restructuring school, 137.

11. Goldsberry et al., The evolution of a restructuring school, 143.

12. Interview, June 2003.

13. M. W. McLaughlin and J. Talbert, *Professional communities and the work of high school teaching* (Chicago: University of Chicago Press, 2001); Cilbulka et al., *Schools as learning organizations*; Newman et al., *Accountability and school performance.*

14. M. J. Paul, Double-loop diversity: Applying adult learning theory to the cultivation of diverse educational climates in higher education, *Innovative Higher Education* 28, no. 1 (2003), 39.

15. Critical friends groups are a professional development approach that engages teachers in examining their teaching practices and student learning in the company of a small group of colleagues. Conceived by leaders and teachers in the Coalition of Essential Schools and promoted by the National School Reform Faculty, the groups use protocols to frame the reflection process and group interactions. For more information about critical friends groups, see information at www.essentialschools.org, www.nsrfharmony.org/, and D. Bambino, Critical friends, *Educational Leadership* 59, no. 6 (2002), 25–27.

16. M. Shank, Common space, common time, common work, *Educational Leadership* 62, no. 8 (2005), 5–8.

17. J. W. Little, The persistence of privacy: Autonomy and initiative in teachers' professional relations, *Teachers College Record* 91, no. 4 (1990), 509–35.

18. K. Leithwood, School leadership in the context of accountability policies, *International Journal of Leadership in Education* 4, no. 3 (2000), 217–35.

19. K. Leithwood and D. Jautzi, The effects of transformational leadership on organizational conditions and student engagement. Paper presented at the annual meeting of the American Educational Research Association, 1999.

20. A. Hargreaves and D. Fink, Sustaining leadership, *Phi Delta Kappan* 84, no. 9 (May 2003).

21. Hargreaves and Fink, Sustaining leadership, 700.

22. M. Fullan, *Change forces: The sequel* (London: Falmer Press, 1999).

23. C. Abelman, R. Elmore, J. Even, S. Kenyon, and J. Marshall, *When accountability knocks, will anyone answer?* CPRE Research Report Series, RR-42. (Philadelphia: Consortium for Policy Research in Education, University of Pennsylvania, 1999).

24. Abelman et al., *When accountability knocks*, 39.

25. Abelman et al., *When accountability knocks*, 40–41.

26. A statewide standardized proficiency test is given at fourth, eighth, and eleventh grades, but, as mandated by legislation, the test scores can only make up 10 percent of the body of evidence used to determine whether students have met the standards. The remainder of the evidence must be based in multiple measures of students' achievement through a locally developed comprehensive assessment system. This approach places most of the responsibility and accountability for developing an assessment system and for determining whether students have met the standards in the hands of local school districts and teachers.

27. C. Danielson, *Enhancing professional practice: A framework for teaching* (Alexandria, Va.: Association of Supervision and Curriculum Development, 1996).

6

BOTTOM-UP ACCOUNTABILITY: AN URBAN PERSPECTIVE

Norm Fruchter and Kavitha Mediratta

In major cities across the United States, mayoral control of school systems is replacing the traditional governance of locally elected citizen school boards. This transformation of school system governance also transforms accountability, as New York City's Mayor Michael Bloomberg demonstrated when he urged the city's voters to deny him reelection if they judged the public schools' achievements as unsatisfactory. Bloomberg's example shows that governance and accountability functions are not easily separated when considering school system control, management, or effectiveness. Whoever wields ultimate power and control over schools also has the power to hold the school system accountable for its performance and outcomes.[1] That power in the United States has traditionally been lodged in systems of schooling governance.

Though governance and accountability are often closely linked, they are not functionally equivalent. Governance involves the power to control the operations of school systems, and particularly to control the critical functions of personnel, budget, curriculum, and instruction. Accountability involves the power to assess school and school system performance and outcomes, preferably against specified standards; to hold schools and school systems responsible for their performance and outcomes; to impose requirements for improvement when performance and outcomes are less than adequate; and to decide how to proceed when outcomes and performance do not improve.

In the nationally controlled education systems of western Europe, governance and accountability functions are often separable. Great Britain, for example, developed an inspectorate system of external accountability that was politically and functionally distinct from local and national systems of governance.[2] It has been harder to separate governance and accountability functions in the United States because locally elected or appointed school boards have traditionally played both the primary governance and the key accountability roles.

This unitary system is now in some transition. For much of the past half-century, states have been expanding their accountability roles, particularly by imposing performance assessment systems, based on standardized testing, on schools and districts. With the passage of No Child Left Behind in 2002, the federal government has used the leverage of Title I funding to assert a powerful national accountability role by imposing both grade-level assessments and punitive sanctions for poor performance, on states, districts, and schools.

Thus what used to be tightly linked functions of governance and accountability at the local school system level are being increasingly separated, as accountability functions gravitate to state and federal levels. Still, in thousands of local schooling units, governance and accountability remain closely linked. Elected school boards and the superintendents they appoint, or mayors in mayoral-controlled school systems and the superintendents they appoint, are the local entities held primarily accountable for school system performance.

BOTTOM-UP ACCOUNTABILITY AND IMPROVING POORLY PERFORMING SCHOOLS

The current wave of top-down reform through mayoral control and centralization of school system management is part of a national movement to establish rigorous student achievement standards for all schools, assess the extent of school and system achievement of those standards through universal testing, and drive improvement through centrally mandated programs. The underlying theory is that schools will improve and students will learn more if a politically accountable mayor leverages reform through a clearly delineated chain of command down to the schools. Thus mayoral control has replaced elected or appointed school boards in New York City, Chicago, Cleveland, Detroit, Baltimore, Boston, and other smaller cities.[3]

We argue that mayors and other schooling authorities that impose such top-down and external forms of accountability are failing to hold poorly performing schools and districts responsible for poor performance in most urban settings. Nor have top-down and external forms of accountability managed to significantly improve the education provided to poor students of color in most urban districts.

Top-down imposition of standards, testing, and mandated reforms are insufficient to change the limited capacities for effective classroom instruction, school organization, and teacher support that characterize poorly performing schools and districts.[4] The core functions of teaching and learning must be transformed in such settings, a transformation that requires a concentration of local investment in resources and capacity. Such a transformation involves replacing ineffective leadership with dynamic leadership, developing and supporting the skills of teaching staffs, and transforming dysfunctional professional cultures into learning communities focused on continuous improvement. In poorly performing schools that have been severed from their communities through decades of bureaucratic insulation and professional defensiveness, that transformation also requires the creation of new forms of relationships with parents and community constituencies that can support the linkages, transparency, and leverage necessary to make these schools serve their students effectively.

Top-down reforms may well create some immediate benefits. What seem to be emerging from the most recent wave of top-down reforms are first-level improvements in poorly performing urban school systems. The Chicago, Baltimore, Philadelphia, and New York City school systems have all registered gains in test-score performance at the elementary school level. But these gains still leave at least half, and in some cities more than half, of all elementary public school children reading below grade level. Outcomes in middle and high school grades are far worse; fewer than 60 percent of all entering ninth graders graduate from many of our large city school systems. Though top-down reforms seem to be jump-starting a process of necessary improvement in elementary schools in urban districts, it is not yet clear that those improvements can be sustained across time. Some evidence indicates that the gains flatten out after a few years, while other evidence suggests that the skills improvement necessary to master basic reading tasks do not necessarily translate into the more complex skills mature readers must employ.

This suggests that top-down governance reforms, by themselves, are insufficient to achieve the scale of transformation necessary to permanently improve the nation's poorly performing urban schools. As Tony Bryk and Barbara Schneider argue in their conclusion to *Trust in Schools*.

> Good schools are intrinsically social enterprises that depend heavily on cooperative endeavors among the varied participants who comprise the school community. Relational trust constitutes the connective tissue that binds these individuals together around advancing the education and welfare of children. Improving schools requires us to think harder about how best to organize the work of adults and students so that this connective tissue remains healthy and strong.[5]

Bryk and Schneider's analysis pinpoints the development of parent-teacher and parent-principal trust as critical elements of the relationships necessary to improve poorly performing schools. Our argument is that the development of bottom-up accountability in such schools is a key ingredient in building that relational trust. What we mean by bottom-up accountability is what Bryk and Schneider refer to as "organiz(ing) the work of adults and students so that this connective tissue remains healthy and strong." Our particular emphasis is on relationship building between the adults who provide schooling and the adults whose children and communities benefit, or should benefit, from that schooling. We see bottom-up accountability as the development of structured relationships, between parents/communities and school people, based on mechanisms of transparency, representation, power, and oversight. We develop a framework of how these bottom-up accountability mechanisms might operate later in this chapter. But consider an example of a transparency mechanism at work, as defined by an elementary school principal whose school was participating in the Bay Area School Reform Collaborative (BASRC).

> It all comes back to the fact that teachers have such a commitment to developing relationships with their [students'] parents. There's a lot of trust. And we also do a pretty good job about letting people know what we don't know, too, through our conversations. Again, what happens is . . . it's not what the *school* says or does . . . the power is in the relationship between the teacher and the parent. And if the teachers are on board and really understand, then that is communicated in every drop and drip of conversation.[6]

We argue that in poorly served urban districts, parents, families, neighborhood residents, and community organizations, all primarily poor constituents of color, need to become key participants in forms of bottom-up accountability like the BASRC example to ensure that their schools and school systems serve their children effectively.

The Limits of Current Opportunities for Bottom-Up Accountability

If bottom-up accountability is a necessary component of successful school reform, but if governance and accountability are so tightly merged in this country's schooling, how can the constituents whose children and whose neighborhoods public school serve exercise any bottom-up accountability when they possess no governance power?

Some experiments in changing the nation's traditional schooling structure have lodged some governance power, and consequently some accountability levers, at the urban school and neighborhood level. The Chicago school reform of 1988 established Local School Councils, elected at the school site, with the power to hire and fire principals, shape the school budget, and participate in developing the school's improvement plan. Though researchers and policymakers differ about the results, in terms of school-level academic achievement, of Chicago's school-based governance transformation, what is clear is that successive central administrations of the Chicago school system consistently worked to reduce the jurisdiction, powers, and capacities of the Local School Councils.[7]

A similar conflict characterizes the thirty-year history of decentralization in New York City schooling. In 1970 the New York State legislature engineered a decentralization scheme as a compromise to end the raging citywide conflict over demands for community control pursued by activists in African American and Latino neighborhoods. Flawed from its inception, decentralization allocated power to locally elected, neighborhood-based school boards in ways that produced overlaps in basic functions and massive confusion about accountability responsibilities.[8]

Although the thirty-year history of decentralization is traditionally characterized as a history of local subdistrict corruption, venality, and failure to focus on improving academic achievement, an alternative historical reading is beginning to suggest some of the successes of decentralization in particular local districts.[9] These new readings also argue that decentralization's potential was fatally limited by the central administration's role in reducing and inhibiting, as in Chicago, the local boards' capacity to exercise their governance functions and accountability responsibilities.[10] If bottom-up accountability in Chicago and New York are, at their best, only partial examples of the efficacy of locating accountability responsibilities at the school and community levels, part of their limitations may well flow from the central authorities' failure to permit the potentials of those experiments to emerge.

Aside from Chicago's Local School Councils and New York City's decentralized local subdistricts, as well as a statewide effort to mandate local school decision-making councils in Kentucky, few experiments in local control and accountability have challenged the dominance of centralized governance of the nation's school systems. Most urban constituencies, especially the poor constituencies of color that comprise most of the publics served by public school systems, have experienced neither structures of local control nor forms of local accountability.

How, then, can we begin to think of bottom-up accountability in such settings? Perhaps more importantly, why should we bother? If the few experiments in bottom-up governance and accountability have been so apparently problematic, why belabor the concept? Aren't the traditional forms of bottom-up participation and involvement—the formal parent organizations such as the Parent-Teacher Associations or the Home-School Associations—sufficient to engage, mobilize, and exercise the necessary accountability functions at the school level?

The Limits of Current Forms of Bottom-Up Participation and Involvement

Our nation's public schools have traditionally attempted to involve parents almost exclusively through school-based parent or parent teacher associations. One of the enduring paradoxes of parental involvement across the United States is that, in middle-class settings in which schools serve their students quite effectively, these formal parent groups are often quite strong, vibrant, and thriving. Yet in urban settings, schools that inadequately serve their predominantly poor students of color often have small, anemic, and ineffective parent organizations.

Principals and teachers in urban systems often complain about the reluctance of parents to get involved in schooling support.[11] Some school practitioners offer benign explanations for this limited involvement (parents are often single mothers, they work two or three jobs, they don't understand the language, they're too intimidated to come to school). Other practitioners indict students' families and their overarching cultural norms (they're apathetic, they don't think schooling matters, they're too lazy to come to school, they're drunk or on drugs). Both groups blame the parents and their home culture, rather than consider that the culture of the schools may be part of the problem. What often results is a reciprocal cycle of blame, resentment, and recrimination that exempts only those few parents who show up at school functions, volunteer for school support, and staff the usually supine parent organizations.

But suppose what schools do, or don't do, is at least as important in building trust relationships with parents and families as what parents do or don't do. Considerable research demonstrates that parents' relationships with schools are shaped by their class status and racial/ethnic and linguistic backgrounds. Several studies have established that middle-class parents are more likely to be actively involved in their children's education, and their efforts are more likely to lead to student success, than those of working-class or poor parents.[12] Although all parents, regardless of social class, have high aspirations for their children's education, middle-class parents are more likely to anticipate school expectations, and possess and deploy those cultural resources that schools value.[13] Annette Lareau and other researchers have demonstrated that, because of their class status, middle-class parents are able to transmit a kind of cultural capital to their children in the form of attitudes, preferences, behaviors, and credentials that facilitate children's inclusion, successful participation, and upward mobility in schools and other social institutions.[14]

The ways in which race shapes educators' low expectations for student achievement and, therefore, the quality of instruction they provide have also been shown to contribute to the distance between families of color and schools.

> Many black [and other minority] families, given the historical legacy of racial discrimination in schools, cannot presume or trust that their children will be treated fairly in school. Yet, they encounter rules of the game in which educators define desirable family-school relationships as based on trust, partnership, cooperation with and deference to white school officials. These rules are more difficult for black than white parents to comply with.[15]

In schools serving middle-class constituencies throughout the country, parents and school practitioners work within similar cultural contexts. In schools serving poor and working-class urban neighborhoods and communities of color, they do not. If schools are organized on middle-class (particularly white) social norms and cultural values, and middle-class children whose families inculcate those norms and values do better in school, how can schools respond effectively to the children of working class and poor families and communities of color who come to schools with a different set of social and cultural histories, norms, values, and assumptions?

A variety of parent involvement models have evolved to help educators try to bridge these sociocultural distances and connect the disparate worlds of home and school by creating meaningful ways for parents to support their children's achievement, from assisting with homework to participating in school improvement.[16] These models argue that, when parents are involved in school support activities and schools are involved in supporting parents' efforts to educate their children, congruence between the culture of the home and the school is increased, and these complementary efforts are likely to reinforce each other. Educators such as Asa Hilliard, Lisa Delpit, Sonia Nieto, Robert Moses, and Theresa Perry argue that for schools to be effective, they must base curriculum and instruction in the particular cultures children (and their parents) bring to schools, while helping children acquire the skills and knowledge of the mainstream culture they need to function in both worlds.[17]

These new formulations of parental involvement are critical to helping schools respond effectively to the academic and social needs of children from poor and working-class neighborhoods and communities of color. Helping parents become involved helps children develop the self-esteem and sense of self-efficacy that supports learning in school. Just as critically, involving parents in the school informs parents about the school's expectations for both parents and students, and helps educators construct culturally relevant and appropriate curriculum and instruction for their students. In successful schools serving poor and working-class neighborhoods and communities of color, the parent (or parent-teacher) association is often the base of efforts to connect schools and families.

But what happens in schools and districts in which few efforts are made to base instruction in what children bring to school, or to bridge home and school cultures? Where, instead, the school's overarching assumption is that cultural differences are irrelevant to curriculum and instruction, and that all children, whatever their backgrounds, must learn a prescribed curriculum in prescribed ways? Where parents are considered a hindrance, and incapable of helping their kids? And where schools have little capacity for effective instruction? The nation's poorly performing urban schools—schools with high levels of staff turnover, weak instructional leadership, and little sense of community connection or trust among adults or between adults and students—have seldom built common frameworks for bridging the differing assumptions, resources, skills, and expectations that too often separate home and school cultures.

Across the United States, poorly performing urban schools and districts support a professional culture that often serves the interests of adults, rather than students. By professional culture, we mean the aggregate of the reciprocal relationships that teachers, administrators, and other staff members create within a school. Such staff relationships often develop an insular language, a restrictive and elitist set of assumptions about what constitutes schooling knowledge and the authority of those who wield it, and a dismissive stance toward parents and community. When such relationships congeal into professional cultures, and the staff members who have created such cultures act on their assumptions about the limited capacities of students' families and how little they can contribute to student success, they often isolate schools from the parents and communities they serve, and attenuate the critical link between schooling and democratic participation.

When such schools define the few active parent members as the *good* parents, and socialize them into the schools' professional cultures, the active parents come to share the school's perspective. They ally themselves with the principal and staff, and join the school in placing the blame for school failure on other, less involved parents. Thus many poorly performing schools maintain a tiny parent association, composed of a few stalwarts, who bemoan the apathy of the rest of the school's parent cohort, and define parental failure to adequately support their children as the cause of poor student performance.

Professionalized cultures exist in all schools, and in many schools these cultures make major contributions to schools' instructional effectiveness. Much less cultural distance, for example, separates middle-class parents and educators in racially, socioculturally, and linguistically homogenous communities. Educators in these communities expect parents to engage with them; moreover, many of those parents are professionals, and many others have considerable experience in dealing with professional behavior. Rather than being intimidated by the superior knowledge and qualifications of educators, parents in middle-class communities are often more educated than the school practitioners. In such settings, accountability relationships often develop organically. White middle-class parents' relationships with schools start from the assumption that they are entitled to access to their children's schools and that their participation is legitimate. These assumptions shape an implicit—and sometimes explicit—parent power that ensures schools' receptivity, and helps develop relationships based on the trust that all parties are committed to aiding the maximal academic development of the child. Moreover, school validation of parental assumptions about the legitimacy of their involvement supports the exercise of democratic participation in school governance, and helps to demonstrate, to the school's students, the importance of such participation in the governance of local institutions.

In contrast, poor parents simply seeking involvement, let alone accountability, in their children's schools often must contend with school defensiveness, hostility, and rejection. The norms of democratic participation in school governance are not part of the professional cultures in many schools in poor urban neighborhoods. Too often, poor parents must fight to gain access to such schools by turning out large numbers of neighborhood constituents; producing knowledgeable, sophisticated leaders who can forcefully articulate their vision; and forming strategic alliances with more powerful allies. Attempts to exercise democratic rights are often forced to become efforts to organize neighborhood power.

Parents and communities inadequately served by poorly performing schools need to leverage power similar to what middle-class constituencies can wield. But when parents in poorly performing schools challenge educators across class and racial lines, without the power that middle-class parents can employ, school practitioners and district administrators often react by mobilizing a professional culture in which parents are criticized, dismissed, ridiculed, and even treated as threats to school safety. In such environments, traditional parent involvement through the parent association is an instrument for socializing parents to comply with school norms and for keeping nonconforming parents out.

In too many poorly performing urban schools and districts, the official parent organizations are more an avenue of cooptation than a means of genuine involvement. They provide no platform for the exercise of any form of bottom-up accountability or democratic participation. In an era in which testing and the dissemination of test score results increasingly monopolize accountability functions, many formal parent organizations never receive their school's test results or are asked to evaluate their school's performance. In some middle-class communities, parents complain that their schools and districts define parent involvement solely as school support rather than as accountability. Yet parents in thousands of poorly performing urban schools and districts are never invited to exercise any accountability functions. Since, as argued above, such parents have less power to confront the school system than middle-class parent constituencies, they have limited leverage to demand participation in forms of bottom-up accountability.[18]

Formal parent organizations in poorly performing urban schools and districts offer limited venues for bottom-up exercise of accountability. Even the simplest forms of parent involvement are structured on the school's terms, and offer little meaningful participation in school assessment and critique, or in processes of school improvement. If parents in poorly performing schools are to be involved in bottom-up accountability that is meaningful and has leverage, new forms of relationship and structural participation must be developed. These efforts must begin by developing the trust necessary to overcome the layers of suspicion, cynicism, and despair accumulated through decades of distance separating home, community, and school.[19]

A BOTTOM-UP ACCOUNTABILITY FRAMEWORK

What follows is a framework for bottom-up accountability that can encourage new forms of parent-community-school and school district relationship and joint participation. We define the critical components of this new accountability framework as transparency, representation, power, and oversight. Although we would much prefer to see bottom-up accountability lodged within a governance framework that combines top-down and bottom-up measures of power and control, our accountability framework is not dependent on such a governance transformation. Instead, the framework can be implemented under current forms of school governance, whether mayoral control or school boards.

What we are proposing are frameworks that can bring about new forms of reciprocal accountability between parent and community constituencies and schools and school districts. We acknowledge that these frameworks would be far more powerful, and effective, if they were situated within bottom-up as well as top-down forms of school system accountability. Still, we think that instituting such new forms of relationship and participation, even within current top-down and centralized governance mechanisms, would make significant contributions to improving the relational trust at the core of successful school improvement efforts.

Transparency

Transparency is our term for a school or system's ability to produce and disseminate data and information that describe student and school-level educational inputs and outcomes. Transparency includes providing data that identify annual school-level student indicators and student performance results, as well as critical school-level inputs (for example, data on teacher and administrator experience, school expenditures, and facilities conditions).

Transparency that contributes to helping parents and community constituencies understand how well or how poorly schools are educating their children involves more than simply making data available in hard copy or on the Web, as many school systems currently do. Instead, transparency requires comprehensive school- and district-level reports that cover a wide range of indicators, that are visually presented so that each indicator is clearly definable and easily understood, and that provide indicators in comparison formats so that school and district outcomes can be assessed in comparable contexts.

Transparency also requires major efforts to disseminate those school- and district-level reports to the widest possible set of constituencies. Web-based reporting, for example, is only as effective as the dissemination of the school system's website so that anyone with Internet access can easily access it. For the many constituencies without Internet access, hard copy dissemination, and intensive media dissemination are necessary. Effective use of radio, television, and newspaper coverage can begin to compensate for limited Internet access in many communities.

But transparency also requires that Internet, hard copy, and media dissemination of outcome reporting be complemented by intensive face-to-face efforts between school practitioners and parents. Because the most important component of transparency is parental understanding of children's outcomes and performance, parents need opportunities for detailed discussion with children's teachers to examine student work, analyze student progress, and consider strategies for learning improvement. The current parent-teacher conferences most school systems organize rarely provide sufficient time, privacy, preparation, or focus to meet these opportunities. Structural changes in school organization, scheduling, professional development and staff support are necessary to provide the kinds of parent-teacher dialogue about improving student achievement that are essential elements of transparency, and that also build critical parent-teacher trust.

Transparency in bottom-up accountability cannot function only at the parent-teacher level. Improving school-level performance also requires new structures for communication, dialogue about effectiveness, and discussion of strategies for improvement at the school site. Such dialogue should bring together school administrators, school staffs, parents, neighborhood organizations, and community constituencies. Through such dialogues, school and district administrators should report on the State of the School, share data defining school performance and instructional practice, identify school strengths and shortcomings, and discuss strategies for improvement.

Examples of such school-level dialogue are the accountability events developed by the BASRC. BASRC's events brought together school and parent constituencies to review data about school outcomes, examine teacher instructional practices, and discuss school improvement strategies. As a participating BASRC teacher observed,

> The accountability events have been really fabulous for us. I mean, I think we've had four of them now, and each one has been really insightful. And I think the parents have truly enjoyed and learned a lot (from these events). We've shared the hard data with them. We've shown them that we're doing a great job for some kids and not for others. . . . We're not doing as well narrowing the gap for our African-American kids and Latino students, and we've been very clear about it and asking (parents) how they think they can help, both for their own students and then for other students.[20]

Community organizing groups in the Industrial Areas Foundation network in Texas have helped school administrators convene and host similar sessions in schools participating in the Alliance Schools network.[21]

Transparency also requires district-level dialogues about performance, outcomes, and directions for systemic improvement. Superintendents should make semiannual presentations about the State of the District, propose improvement strategies, and discuss their presentations with parents and community constituencies in open forums. Many suburban and rural school boards have developed effective community-wide accountability dialogues focused on data-rich examinations of district performance and discussions of strategies for improvement. Several local public education foundations, in Wake County, North Carolina, and Mobile, Alabama, among others, have developed public forums that bring school practitioners, parents, service organizations, and community constituencies together for extended dialogues analyzing district performance and developing strategies for improvement.[22]

Representation

Formal parent associations provide structured forms of representation for parents at the school level. Because poorly performing schools harbor barely existing, under-resourced and often collusive parent organizations, the educational interests of the school's parent population are rarely effectively represented. Moreover, the interests of the school's neighborhood organizations and community constituencies are almost never represented.[23] Yet these groups have continuing commitments to the academic achievement and school success of their neighborhood's children. One way to approach this problem is to develop new and broader forms of parent and community representation.

Suppose the status of the formal organizations that currently represent parents were annually or biannually contestable. If, as we argue, most poorly performing schools have poorly performing parent organizations, why not allow community groups to contest elections for the right to represent parents at particular schools, much as unions contest to represent a plant's workers through a National Labor Relations Board-mediated election? An annual election could determine whether the school's parents will be represented by one of the local community-based organizations that serve the school's children and families, or by the existing parent organization. A committed community group might do a far better job of holding the school accountable for its performance and outcomes than a traditional parent organization.

We offer this suggestion as an example of the new forms of representation necessary for bottom-up accountability in poorly performing schools, and acknowledge that it is problematic. Perhaps few community groups would be willing to assume the school support roles that many traditional parent organizations play. Perhaps the prospect of contesting annual elections would lead community groups to use their resources to employ influential parent leaders or promise benefits to prospective voters.

A complementary solution might be to configure specific accountability roles, rather than overall parent representation and management, for community groups with a strong stake in helping schools improve their performance. But to transcend the current inability of traditional parent organizations to play any role in school-level accountability, creating effective representation involves identifying roles for community groups in new bottom-up accountability relationships. In almost every urban neighborhood, a far wider range of stakeholder groups has a strong interest in helping schools do better for their children than we currently engage.

Across the country, several districts have developed analogous bottom-up collaborations among elected officials, service providers, community organizations, and school systems designed to improve student and school outcomes. Examples of school improvement collaboratives in El Paso, Providence, the south Bronx in New York City, Charlotte-Mecklenburg, and other urban districts suggest some new directions for how to explore the linkages between effective accountability and new forms of representation.

BEYOND THE PA: ORGANIZING FOR SCHOOL IMPROVEMENT

New Settlement Apartments (NSA) began organizing parents in 1997 in response to widespread concern about the quality of neighborhood schools among public school parents living in the NSA housing development in the South Bronx. Parents formed the NSA Parent Action Committee (PAC) and began by looking at the Annual School Report of a nearby elementary school. They found less than a fifth of the students could read at grade level, and yet the school was removed from the New York State's list of low performing schools (SURR).

Parents invited a district representative to address their concerns about their children's low reading scores. But when the district representative ignored their questions and dismissed their data presentation, parents decided to launch a campaign to improve the school. They gathered petitions from parents, met with local institutions and churches to enlist their support, held meetings with Board of Education officials, and staged demonstrations and press conferences to call for school improvement. These efforts ultimately led to the resignation of the school's principal, whom both parents and teachers believed was ineffective.

Local school and district officials repeatedly used the parent association as an excuse to turn away the NSA parents for not being "the official parent organization." Parent association members felt loyal to the school's principal and were hostile to NSA parents. A 2001 study of school reform organizing conducted by the NYU Institute for Education reveals that parent leaders in most community organizations are refused essential school documents like the school's improvement plan and annual performance review, and berated by school administrators for not participating in the parent association.[24] Ironically, the entity created to strengthen parent involvement in low performing schools has become a way for the school system to deflect parent-led school improvement efforts.

Imagine if the parent activism conducted by PAC were the norm in urban schools serving poor and working-class neighborhoods and communities of color. What if there were an alternative to the parent association in all failing schools? What if parents could choose the organization that would represent them in holding school and district officials accountable?

Through a clearly defined process, perhaps articulated and monitored by the New York State Department of Education, parents in failing schools could choose to have a traditional parent association or one organized and facilitated by one of the neighborhood's community organizations working with families served by the school. Once selected, the organization would serve as the legitimate representative of parents with the authority to negotiate on their behalf. School and district staff and administrators would be mandated to recognize, legitimate, and meet with the community group, to make available a variety of information and data about school performance and instructional programs, and to discuss priorities and negotiate school improvement goals. The official parent association would then be disbanded until the next electoral cycle, perhaps in three years, when it could compete with the community organization to represent parent interests.

Power

The new structures to achieve transparency and representation that we suggest above are mostly based on dialogue and discussion about student and school performance and how to improve their outcomes. But such new forms don't adequately deal with the unequal power relationships in most poor neighborhoods of color. Suppose, for example, district and school administrators attempt to dominate these new forms of dialogue, by exercising their traditional modes of professional expertise. Suppose, as a result, they re-create traditional forms of intimidation, exclusion, and obfuscation. Or suppose district and school administrators ignore their responsibility to participate in those dialogues, and dismiss the opportunities to create these new bottom-up accountability relationships. What structures can grant sufficient authority to parents and community groups, at school and district levels, to ensure that schools develop these new forms of bottom-up accountability?

One possibility is to mandate the development of these new accountability structures and hold principals and superintendents responsible for their implementation. Failures to implement could be appealed, through existing grievance procedures, to the superintendent, the school board, and the state education agency.

Another possibility is to create a much broader districtwide forum, in which representatives of parent associations, community groups, and other constituencies are mandated to conduct annual school performance evaluations and to discuss the results, in public sessions, with the superintendent. Such districtwide forums could also have the power to annually evaluate local school principals and make recommendations to the superintendent and the school board for continuance or termination. A similarly composed group at the district level could be mandated to evaluate the superintendent's performance and make its recommendations to the school board.

All these new structures have the potential to create new forms of bottom-up accountability that generate new relationships among parents, community groups and constituencies, and schools and districts. The ultimate goal of all these efforts is improved student and school achievement.

Oversight

Whatever new forms of transparency, representation, and power are eventually enacted, we see a need for oversight to ensure that the new structures are implemented effectively. An oversight structure, external to schools and districts and independent of the school system and the mayor, will be required to sustain any form of bottom-up accountability in most school systems' top-down governance arrangements. Such an external, independent accountability structure could provide a forum for investigation, venues for redress of grievance, and the power to enforce change, particularly in poorly performing schools and districts that continue to resist parent and community accountability.

Such an oversight function might be structured on models of *ombuds* oversight for public services in western European countries, particularly in Scandinavia and the Netherlands. Such an *ombuds* structure could be established as an independent city agency, with sufficient authority and funding so that oversight, investigation, and the authority to mandate solutions can be carried out, across the city school system. At a minimum, such an *Ombuds Office* could be charged to oversee the implementation of whatever new accountability structures are created.

We have imagined the *ombuds* role primarily as a local district responsibility. But many states have legislated a nascent *ombuds* role by empowering their state education commissioner to hear and rule on appeals by citizens of local school board or superintendent decisions. This appeals process is often very lengthy, quite formal and bureaucratic, and usually affirms the decisions of local jurisdictions. But nothing prevents states from structuring an *ombuds* process with considerable power to support and ensure the operation of effective bottom-up accountability at local levels.

CONCLUSION

The bottom-up accountability framework we have suggested would contribute to building relational trust, a more supportive school climate, and overall academic improvement in all the nation's schools. But our primary focus is on how to improve the poorly performing schools in urban districts. Our argument is that mandates and interventions driven by top-down forms of management and control will not ultimately improve student achievement in such schools. We argue that forms of bottom-up accountability, through the frameworks we propose, are necessary to achieve the scale of school transformation required.

In his conclusion to *The New Accountability*, Richard Elmore argues that "schools construct their own systems of accountability," and that "different schools solve the accountability problem in very different ways."[25] The critical problem, for the children, parents, and neighborhood constituencies poorly served by too many urban schools, is that these schools have solved the accountability problem in ways that work for the school's practitioner adults but not for their students. Bottom-up accountability presents a way to include parents and neighborhood constituencies in the school's definition of accountability—essentially to broaden that definition to include the voices, and the roles, of parents and neighborhood constituents—to ensure that accountability contributes to school improvement. As Elmore argues, "educational accountability systems work—when they work—by calling forth the energy, motivation, commitment, knowledge, and skills of the people who work in schools and the systems that are supposed to support them."[26] Making accountability work in poorly performing schools in urban district requires including the energy, motivation, commitment, knowledge, and skills of the people whose children and neighborhoods are served by those schools, through new forms of bottom-up accountability.

NOTES

1. We use the term *external accountability* to mean the formal accountability exercised by entities external to schools or school systems, in acknowledg-

ment of Richard Elmore's important argument that schools develop "conceptions of accountability" that help them adjust their practices to external forms of accountability. See R. Elmore, Accountability and capacity, in *The new accountability: High schools and high-stakes testing*, edited by M. Carnoy, R. Elmore, and L. S. Siskin (New York: Routledge/Falmer, 2003).

2. T. A. Wilson, *Reaching for a better standard: English school inspection and the dilemma of accountability for American public schools* (New York: Teachers College Press, 1996).

3. L. Cuban and M. Usdan, *Powerful reforms with shallow roots* (New York: Teachers College Press, 2003).

4. R. Elmore, Testing trap: The single largest and possibly most destructive federal intrusion into America's public schools, *Harvard Magazine* 105, no. 1 (September–October 2002).

5. A. S. Bryk and B. Schneider, *Trust in schools* (New York: Russell Sage Foundation, 2002), 144.

6. M. A. Copeland, Leadership of inquiry: Building and sustaining capacity for school improvement, *Educational Evaluation and Policy Analysis* 25, no. 4 (winter 2003), 390.

7. J. Simmons, Lessons from Chicago school reform, in *Breaking through: How to transform the results of urban school districts*, edited by J. Simmons (New York: Teachers College Press, 2005); D. Moore, *Major gains in 186 Chicago schools* (Chicago: Designs for Change, 2003); A. S. Bryk, P. B. Sebring, D. Kerbow, S. Rollow, and J. Q. Easton, *Chicago school reform: Democratic localism as a lever for change* (Boulder, Colo.: Westview Press, 1998).

8. In 2002, New York City Mayor Michael Bloomberg succeeded in persuading the state legislature to end the decentralization experiment and lodge control of the city system in the mayor's office.

9. R. Elmore, School decentralization: Who gains? Who loses? in *Decentralization and school improvement: Can we fulfill the promise?* edited by J. Hannaway and M. Carnoy (San Francisco: Jossey-Bass, 1993); D. Ravitch, *The great school wars: A history of the New York City public school wars*, rev. ed. (Baltimore: Johns Hopkins Press, 2000); F. Siegel, *The future once happened here: New York, D.C., L.A., and the fate of America's big cities* (New York: Free Press, 1997).

10. D. Rogers and N. H. Chung, *110 Livingston Street revisited: Decentralization in action* (New York: New York University Press, 1983); J. P. Viteritti, *Across the river: Politics and education in the city* (New York: Holmes and Meier, 1983); H. Lewis, *Aftermath stories: Community control and its continuities*, Ph.D. diss. in progress, New York University, History of Education Department.

11. The 2005 MetLife Survey of the American Teacher reported that new teachers felt that "communicating with and involving parents is their biggest challenge." L. Jacobson, Survey finds teachers' biggest challenge is parents, *Education Week* 24, no. 41 (June 22, 2005).

12. L. Beneviste, M. Carnoy, and R. Rothstein, *All else equal: Are public and private schools different?* (New York: Routledge/Falmer, 2003).

13. A. Lareau, Social class differences in family-school relationships: The importance of cultural capital, *Sociology of Education* 60 (April 1987), 73–85.

14. M. Lamont and A. Lareau, Cultural capital: Allusions, gaps and glissandos in recent theoretical developments, *Sociological Theory* 6 (1998), 153–68; P. Bourdieu, *Outline to a theory of practice* (London: Cambridge University Press, 1977); P. Bourdieu and J. C. Passeron, *Reproduction in education, society and culture* (Beverly Hills, Calif.: Sage, 1977).

15. A. Lareau and E. M. Horvat, Moments of social inclusion and exclusion: Race, class and cultural capital in family-school relationships, *Sociology of Education* 72 (1999), 42.

16. J. Comer, Home-school relationships as they affect the academic success of children, *Education and Urban Society*, 16, no. 3 (1994), 323–37; J. Epstein, Parent involvement: What research says to administrators, *Education and Urban Society* 19, no. 2 (1987), 119–36; J. Epstein, School/family/community partnerships: Caring for the children we share, *Phi Delta Kappan* (1995), 701–12.

17. A. G. Hilliard III, No mystery: Closing the achievement gap between Africans and excellence, in *Young, gifted and black*, edited by T. Perry, C. Steele, and A. G. Hilliard III (Boston: Beacon Press, 2003); L. Delpit, *Other people's children* (New York: Morrow, 1995); S. Nieto, *Affirming diversity: The sociopolitical context of multicultural education* (White Plains, N.Y.: Longmans, 1993); T. Perry, Up from the parched earth: Toward a theory of African-American achievement, in *Young, gifted and black*, edited by T. Perry, C. Steele, and A. G. Hilliard III (Boston: Beacon Press, 2003).

18. In poorly served urban settings, one way to generate the equivalent of the power that middle-class communities wield is to build independent organizations of parents, youth, and other community stakeholders with the resources, knowledge, and capacity to uncover poor school and district performance, organize widespread community support for change, and develop a shared vision of how the school should effectively educate their children. Many such independent, community-based organizations committed to organizing to improve their local schools have recently emerged across the country. For overviews of this emerging activity, see K. Mediratta, N. Fruchter, and A. Lewis, *Organizing for school reform: How communities are finding their voice*

and reclaiming their public schools (New York: NYU Institute for Education & Social Policy, 2002); K. Mediratta, *Constituents of change: Community organizations and public education reform* (New York: NYU Institute for Education & Social Policy, 2004).

19. See Bryk and Schneider, *Trust in schools*, for an extended analysis of the role that parent-teacher and parent-principal trust plays in shaping school climate and academic effectiveness.

20. Copeland, Leadership of inquiry.

21. S. Dennis, *Community organizing for urban school reform* (Austin: University of Texas Press, 1997).

22. Wake Education Partnership, 2003, *Beyond 2003: Voices and choices*, available at www.wakeducates.org/*voices choices*/index.html (accessed May 23, 2003).

23. The 1988 Chicago School reform included seats for three elected community representatives on Local School Councils.

24. Mediratta, Fruchter, and Lewis, *Organizing for school reform*.

25. Elmore, Accountability and capacity.

26. Elmore, Accountability and capacity, 195.

7

THE ACCREDITATION PROCESS: AN INSIDE/OUTSIDE SCHOOL QUALITY REVIEW SYSTEM

Katharine Pence

> There is no power greater than a community discovering what it cares about. Be brave enough to start a conversation that matters. Our goal is to ask, What's possible? not What's wrong?
>
> —Margaret J. Wheatley

In his 2004 publication *Accountability for Learning: How Teachers and School Leaders Can Take Charge*, Douglas Reeves describes student-centered accountability, or holistic accountability, as

> a system that includes not only academic achievement scores, but also specific information on curriculum, teaching practices, and leadership practices. In addition, a student-centered system includes a balance of quantitative and qualitative indicators . . . the story behind the numbers. Finally, student-centered accountability focuses on the progress of individual students and does not rely exclusively on averages of large groups of students who may or may not share similar learning needs, teaching strategies, attendance patterns and other variables that influence test performance.[1]

Educators today could only wish that Reeves had been a part of the conversation when the controversial federal law No Child Left Behind was being developed, proposed, and implemented nationwide.

A system such as the one described by Reeves is certainly different from that enforced by current state and federal policies, which relies almost exclusively on test results, compares and ranks very diverse school populations, and focuses on sanctions as opposed to support. A student-centered accountability system considers the totality of schooling, is balanced in its approach, and views test scores in context. It is also not a new phenomenon. A student-centered, or holistic, accountability system known as *educational accreditation* has been in place since 1885.

The message in the opening quote by well-known organizational consultant Margaret J. Wheatley should be at the heart of any educational accountability system, and is at the heart of current educational accreditation. The accreditation process commits the school community to identifying commonly held beliefs, sharing in-depth conversations about how those beliefs are demonstrated in the daily life of the school and in relation to educational standards, and focusing on specific strengths and needs of the school, with a view toward the implementation of organizational improvements designed to move the school forward. This is a process, with the inevitable flaws that all processes present, that nonetheless offers schools the opportunity for both internal and external evaluation, is based on a holistic view of the organization, holds schools to a predetermined set of high standards, and results in a comprehensive plan for improvement.

Long before school accountability became a national catch phrase, accrediting associations across the country were providing quality reviews of educational systems and processes, one school at a time. I have been associated with one such association for the past thirteen years, the New England Association of Schools and Colleges (NEASC). I have a fairly unique perspective: I have chaired numerous visiting teams for other schools; with our steering committee I led our own school through the process; and I have served on the Commission for Public Elementary and Middle Schools for the past six years, the last two as chair. In this chapter, I focus on the NEASC process as a possible model for a quality review mechanism in a new system of school accountability.

Founded in 1858, NEASC is the nation's oldest accrediting association and governs the accreditation experience in the six-state region of New England, and in over 120 American/International schools around the world. NEASC's mission as an accrediting body is to serve "the public and educational community by developing and applying standards and assessing the educational effectiveness of elementary, secondary, and collegiate educational institutions."[2] The association carries out its mission through the work of several thousand trained volunteers who give their time and energy to participating on visiting teams as part of the external accountability system that accreditation requires.

NEASC accreditation is a system of accountability that is ongoing, voluntary, and comprehensive in scope. It respects differences in educational populations, missions, and cultures, and fosters institutional change grounded in the judgment of practicing educators. It is based on standards that are developed and regularly reviewed by the members and that define the characteristics of good schools. The system is structured in a continuous ten-year cycle of self-study, peer review, and follow-up. Because the process is standards based, it bears some similarity to reform initiatives emerging nationwide that also contribute to systematic improvement and renewal. However, NEASC accreditation does not guarantee the experience of individual students or the quality of specific programs within the institutional structure, nor does it utilize the process to compare or rank institutions.[3]

Although the association includes institutions of higher education, independent schools, and technical and career institutions, the focus of this chapter with regard to educational accountability will be on the public institutions served by NEASC, specifically those at the elementary and middle levels.

During the past twenty years, the process of school accreditation has been expanded to include both elementary and middle levels, prekindergarten through grade 8. The public perception of accreditation may be most closely associated with the accreditation of secondary schools and institutes of higher education. However, in 1984 NEASC appointed an ad hoc committee to begin the process of establishing a program for the evaluation of separately administered public elementary schools.[4] This action was in response to a nationwide call by the National Association of Elementary School Principals for all elementary schools to undergo an evaluation process designed to improve education. A fifteen-person Committee on Elementary School Evaluation and Accreditation was created, with the goals of developing standards, establishing procedures, coordinating activities with various state departments, seeking support from superintendents and school boards, and studying the recommendations of the ad hoc committee. In 1987 the Commission on Public Elementary Schools (CPES) was formally created with over four hundred charter affiliates and/or candidates.

The next eighteen years saw the development of a mission statement; changes in leadership; three revisions of the elementary standards; the implementation of new safety standards; the creation of updated materials, processes, and procedures; and more. A significant change was the creation of a set of separate standards for middle-level schools, which ultimately led to a major restructuring and, in 2002, the establishment of the Commission on Public Elementary and Middle Schools (CPEMS). The mission statement of the newly restructured commission is to "foster continuous school improvement through a standards-based accreditation process."[5]

Additionally, the commission received a major challenge and opportunity when the state of Connecticut determined that all underperforming schools in the city of Hartford seek accreditation. For the first time, accreditation was not a completely voluntary process, and the ongoing tension between a guaranteed increase in student achievement and the overall purpose of accreditation, that of school improvement, became a reality for the commission.

THE ACCREDITATION PROCESS

The process a school embarks upon when it has been determined, usually by a superintendent or school board, that accreditation is the system that will provide a holistic approach to school accountability is not an easy one. Similar to most processes designed to ultimately promote change, it is lengthy, intense, and, at times, both frustrating and rewarding. For example, for the staff to discuss the strengths that identify the school as a good place for students, as well as taking an honest look at the needs that all schools have, can be both positive and validating. The process of coming to consensus, which is often daunting, does ensure a level of agreement among the staff and has the potential to strengthen the staff as a whole. On the other hand, creating the positive climate necessary to support the process and finding the time to ensure the quality of the many tasks required throughout the eighteen-month process can be quite difficult.

One important component of this system is that participation in the accreditation process provides schools extensive opportunities for both internal and external accountability. While present accountability systems focus almost exclusively on the use of external authority, accreditation requires an in-depth internal process of self-reflection, the results of which are then the basis for the external process of peer review. Interestingly enough, despite the focus on external systems of accountability, the internal process may actually be the component most supportive of school improvement over time, especially if the internal review is an honest and straightforward look at the school, and the external review is in agreement with the school's own findings.

Initially, when our kindergarten through sixth grade school began the process in 1998, the overall focus and concern for us was the fact that seven educators would be coming in to the school to "evaluate" us. This was a frightening thought. At the beginning, we paid little attention to the importance of the self-study process, except to recognize that the visiting team would be receiving a copy of the final work, and we wanted to be sure it looked good. Much time and energy was spent around the logistics. For example: What kind of binders should we use? Should we have student artwork at the beginning of each section? What should be on the cover? Should it be printed in the district print shop, or would it be better to take it to a professional printer?

As we dug into the process, we began to realize that what we were doing together as a staff was actually making a difference in our school *as it was happening*. We didn't have to wait for the visiting team to identify our strengths and needs; we were doing that, and at times it was both a validating and a painful process. Because we finally figured out what was important and invested time and energy in this phase of the process, improvement, for our school, began at that point. The arrival of the visiting team, although still somewhat intimidating, was then seen as a vehicle that, we hoped, would endorse the work that we had accomplished.

Internal Self-Study

An internal self-study is the first phase of the accreditation process, and takes place over an eighteen-month period while the school participates in an introspective review, assessing the school as a whole in relation to its mission and also in relation to the qualitative standards determined by the commission. To quote Margaret Wheatley, this is "the conversation that matters."

The internal process is guided by a school-based steering committee whose members coordinate the work of as many as fifteen subcommittees, usually made up of three or four members, each of which addresses one of the seven standards and the school's identified learning areas. The result of this is the school's accreditation self-study, a comprehensive and detailed document, similar to a portfolio, and based on the standards, that for the purpose of this process serves as the visiting team's introduction and guide to the school. The self-study, even apart from this process, is the gathering of important evidentiary documentation regarding all aspects of the school, which can be used for a variety of purposes as long as the information remains current.

Typically, all staff members are involved to some degree in the work of self-study. In some cases, parents, students, and community members also participate as members of the steering committee or on specific subcommittees. The role of the principal is sometimes problematic in that accreditation needs to clearly be a whole-school, staff-driven process. Ideally, the principal should participate as one staff member. However, this is sometimes not the case, and too much involvement and control on the part of the principal or building administrative team can have a negative effect on the process of internal assessment.

All work accomplished in each of the subcommittees must be presented to, and accepted by the entire school staff before being finalized. Subcommittee members have an opportunity to share their findings, and explain their rationale for their specific answers to the guiding questions. The subcommittee also states its perceptions of the school's strengths and needs in its particular area of review, and, if there are disagreements among the staff, both groups need to come to consensus. Finally, the staff, again through consensus, assesses the school as a whole on a rating continuum for each standard. Guiding this important part of the process is one of the tasks of the members of the steering committee.

The result of this period of internal accountability is much more than the detailed and comprehensive self-study; it can also be an equally important period of self-discovery. Possibly this is the first in-depth look at itself that the school has undertaken, and the benefits of participation in a process of reflection, discussion, and consensus building can be immense.[6]

I had been principal for nine years when our school began the accreditation process. This was a small school, close to three hundred students, the only school in town, and we were closely connected with each other and with the community. Prior to beginning the internal phase, I would have described us as a staff that could talk about anything fairly comfortably, and that this happened routinely in the faculty room, at staff meetings, and at social gatherings throughout the year. Essentially, this description was accurate, but the depth and the breadth of the conversations that occurred during our accreditation process, and the resulting dissonance, surprised all of us. One teacher commented. "We were a tight staff, and expected that we were pretty much in sync with each other, especially about issues that directly affected teaching and learning. We found that this was not always the case, and, regarding some issues, we were poles apart."

Although we had participated in school improvement teams, goal-setting groups, and annual retreats for staff, the experience of internal self-study was somehow more personal and intense. There were several thorny issues, including a library that was not well maintained, and a dichotomy between the more seasoned staff members and those who were new, that caused the staff to approach the consensus-building meetings with real trepidation. We were committed to ensuring that the self-study be an honest look at our school, and that all staff members have a voice in the process. Therefore, all discussions needed to be open and frank, while trying to maintain a level of support, tact, and diplomacy.

These were not easy sessions. However, through the facilitation of the steering committee, and by taking the process one step at a time, we were able to work through it successfully. "As a group, we talked about things that we realized we had never really talked about. Ultimately, we all grew as a result, the staff became stronger, and that strength seemed more genuine and real," was one teacher's comment upon completion of the self-study process. Despite the challenges, from our experience, and those of many other schools, the internal process of self-study, based on the standards, can be viewed as beneficial, especially in the long term.

External Review

External review takes place at the conclusion of the self-study phase, when a team of educators—teachers, support staff, building administrators, and central office administrators from across the six-state region—spend three and one-half days with the school in peer review, validation, and evaluation. The importance of peer review deserves some note. The makeup of the visiting teams, and membership on the commission, as well, reflects a belief that classroom practitioners must play a major role for this to truly be "peer review." For a visiting team to consist solely of administrators sends a very different message, and one that, I believe, would minimize the effectiveness of the process. Much like the Critical Friends process, members of the visiting teams should be seen as equals, not experts.

Usually the team chair conducts a preliminary visit a few weeks in advance of the visiting team's arrival. The purpose of this is to ensure that the school is indeed ready for the visit, to meet with and sometimes reassure the staff, to arrange all the logistics of the visit, and to provide any other assistance that the school may need. Prior to their arrival, the team has had an opportunity to read the self-study and accompanying documentation provided by the school, and to have specific questions answered. When the team arrives at the school, it has a sense of the community in which the school functions, the beliefs of the school, and the school's own perception of its status with regard to the accreditation standards, as well as specific areas of strengths and needs generated through the process of self-study.

In order to ensure a high level of consistency from one school to the next, the visiting team's experience in the school follows a fairly detailed protocol. While each team chair imposes his or her own personality on the process to some degree, training sessions conducted several times during the year provide team chairs and team members with critical information designed to guarantee that all accreditation visits are conducted in a similar manner, and include all relevant components.

This is an intense period of time for both the school and the visiting team. The school has spent eighteen months collaboratively working on their self-study, internally assessing strengths and needs, and, in essence, holding themselves accountable to the accreditation standards. It now becomes the responsibility of the team, through the leadership of the chairperson, to ensure that the on-site visit is conducted professionally, that all aspects of the accreditation protocol are followed, and that the school, regardless of its ultimate status with regard to the accreditation decision, experience a visit that is focused, effective, and supportive as well as challenging.

Perhaps one of the most important aspects of the visit is the visibility and availability of the team, usually seven members for an elementary school, and twelve to fifteen for a middle school, depending upon the size of the school. All members of the school community should have some level of access to the team during the three-and-one-half-day visit. Through scheduled meetings, all school personnel, central office administration, students, parents, community members, and board members have the opportunity to talk with the visiting team about the school's strengths and weaknesses, issues and concerns. Both formal and informal discussions are held that may focus on, for example, how the mission of the school is congruent with its educational decisions, how the school relates to each of the commission standards, and what the school, and its community, feels that it must do to meet the challenges of the future.

In assessing the school's adherence to each of the seven standards, described below, members of the visiting team have in-depth and specific conversations with those staff members serving on the subcommittee that developed the self-study section on that standard. This provides an opportunity for the school to expand on the information presented in the self-study and offers the team a chance to ask clarifying questions. It is important that the team perceive a high level of congruence with the information provided in the self-study and what they actually observe in the school. "Are they who they say they are?" is the often unspoken question. Continually the team refers back to the mission statement of the school, seeking those connections between the beliefs of the school and its daily practice. Being cognizant of the specific indicators of the standards while observing all classrooms and programs and talking with all staff members enables the visiting team to collect both tangible and intangible evidence necessary to support its perceptions of the school's status with regard to each of the standards.

The internal self-study and external review mesh when the members of the visiting team work together to develop a comprehensive report for the school community that outlines how each standard is exemplified in the school, the team's perceptions of how effectively the school adheres to each standard, and specific commendations and recommendations designed to recognize strengths and point out areas in need of change or improvement. The report addresses both the qualitative and quantitative aspects of the school, "the story behind the numbers," which is one of the important points in Reeves's description of a student-centered accountability system.

It is important that the information presented in the report be factually accurate, and that the perceptions of the team be supported by very specific evidence. Both commendations and recommendations must be clear, have a foundation in the report, and provide substantive information.[7] After review and editing, the visiting team's report to the school community is a public document and serves as a blueprint for positive change. Through its deliberate and thoughtful responses to the recommendations, the school is able to move toward Wheatley's goal of asking "What's possible?" not "What's wrong?"

The follow-up phase of the accreditation process is the time for changes and improvements to all aspects of the school and may occur over a five-year period. This period in the process is benchmarked by continued involvement with the commission, both to ensure accountability and to provide support. Internally, an accreditation follow-up committee is responsible for facilitation of this process. This committee may be made up of members of the original steering committee that guided the school through the process of self-study. The school is required to submit reports to document the follow-up process, including specific Special Progress Reports, which deal with any issues on which the commission requires more information; a Two-Year Progress Report explaining the status of progress made addressing each of the recommendations cited in the visiting team report; and a Five-Year Follow-Up Report, which should conclude the work the school has accomplished on the recommendations. Accountability, both internal and external, continues to mark the follow-up phase of the process.

While the actual "being accredited" is certainly both positive and important, it may not be as vital as the process in which the school participates to obtain and maintain that distinction. Further, while the granting of accreditation is a one-time event, the positive effects of the process can be ongoing and long term.

Standards

Any accountability system must offer measurement against a set of criteria, and the accreditation process has developed very specific standards designed to provide a comprehensive look at a school. The belief that a good school is more than the results of its most recent test scores demands opportunities to demonstrate organizational and educational effectiveness against a range of criteria, assessed by multiple measures in a variety of settings. Essentially, the standards-based accreditation approach views all aspects of schooling—the total health of the organization—and operates on the premise that both outcomes and operations must be measured to allow for actual improvements to take place.

The NEASC process has identified two types of standards: teaching and learning standards, which include Mission and Expectations, Curriculum, Instruction, and Assessment; and support standards, which include Leadership and Organization, School Resources for Student Learning, and Community Resources for Student Learning. The description of the standards below is taken from the NEASC publication *Standards for Accreditation for Elementary Schools: A Comprehensive School Improvement Process*, which was revised in 2005. The standards for middle schools are currently under revision.

Although all seven standards are seen as equally important to the overall health of the organization, when a school enters into this process, it all begins with the mission, what Wheatley describes as a school community "discovering what it cares about." The mission statement of the school serves as the framework for the remaining standards, and the manner in which the school adheres to the other six standards is expected to support the mission and expectations. If the school does not already have a mission statement in place, the first conversations that the staff will have are attempts to articulate what makes their school what it is, and what they truly believe about teaching and learning.

From the school's perspective, these conversations, and there are always many of them over time before a final mission statement emerges, can be rich and powerful, as well as being frustrating and difficult. Consider that an intelligent and diverse group of people, with all the strong feelings of those committed to their profession, needs to come together to identify that kernel of educational individuality that sets their work apart from that of others. Not only do they need to agree philosophically but they must also agree semantically. "It would be so much easier for one person to go into a room and write this thing," commented one staff member when her school was developing their mission statement. Of course, she was correct. However, the accreditation process requires whole-staff involvement and consensus at all levels, possibly none more important than when developing the mission statement, which is the basis of the self-study and is utilized throughout the process to assist in measuring the school against the remaining standards.

The *Mission and Expectations* standard describes what the school intends to achieve, and gives purpose and direction to all aspects of the educational process. Measurable academic and social expectations are required, are designed to promote high standards, and are used to assess the success of the mission statement. Additionally, a level of congruence among the beliefs of the school, the district, and the wider community should be evident, as well as tangible acceptance and support of the mission on the part of all members of the school community. The mission of the school guides long-term planning and decision making regarding policies, procedures, and programming. Finally, a clearly defined process for review and revision to ensure ongoing validity should be in place.

The remaining teaching and learning standards, Curriculum, Instruction, and Assessment, are considered in isolation as well as component parts of the school's overall effectiveness. The curriculum links the school's expectations for student learning to instructional and assessment practices. Specifically, the *Curriculum* standard addresses the importance of a written curriculum that is effectively coordinated and articulated, both horizontally as well as vertically. The curriculum must be seen as intellectually challenging, developmentally appropriate, and allowing for the authentic application of knowledge and skills.

The *Instruction* standard is the means by which the curriculum is implemented and the stated expectations of the school are realized. Instructional practices, materials, and resources should include aspects that are exploratory, individualized, self-directed, authentically based, and integrated, and promote the development of higher order thinking skills and problem-solving approaches. Instruction should focus not only on the acquisition of knowledge but also on the development of appropriate social skills and responsible citizenship.

Although the standards define good schooling, there is recognition that the document must be dynamic and reflective of changes in educational research. As the standards are periodically revised, the focus of a particular standard may broaden to include indicators previously not considered, or accorded less importance. While the essence of the standard remains, programs and practices observed in member and candidate schools, along with current educational needs, shifts, and trends, may influence the manner in which a standard is viewed. The inclusion of social skill development and responsible citizenship are good examples of this type of change. As schools became more directly responsible to ensure that students not only acquired knowledge and skills but also grew ethically and socially, the focus of instruction, as well as curriculum development, school climate, support services, and more, changed to accommodate this need. In general, visiting teams agree that most schools have more than met this updated standard.

An additional aspect of the standard on instruction is the importance of ensuring that all learners have equal access to educational opportunities. This is not easily determined, and certainly cannot be limited to the results of state and federal testing programs, but must be observed in classrooms and documented through both qualitative and quantitative data. The wide variety of learning styles and the range of intellectual and academic capabilities present in any school necessitate instructional programs and practices designed to ensure that each student, regardless of where he or she may be placed on any continuum, can and will have an opportunity to successfully progress. Thus, the standard on instruction states that effectiveness in this area should accommodate the individual needs and learning differences of students and engage all students in a variety of ways.

The standard on *Assessment* measures the progress of the students toward the stated expectations and requires that data be used to review and revise curriculum and to modify and improve instructional practice.

A wide variety of assessment data, whether classroom assessments, grade-level common assessments, or whole-school standardized testing, may be used to determine the effectiveness of programming. Assessment strategies need to be varied, reflective of current research, and integrated with instructional practice. Methods of communicating assessment results within and beyond the educational setting must be clearly defined and effective.

The three teaching and learning standards have commonalities that not only address support of the mission and expectations of the school but also address additional areas such as effective utilization of support services, professional development, allocation of time, fiscal and material resources, and a clearly defined review and revision process. These commonalities are extended in varying degrees to the final three support standards, which include Leadership and Organization, School Resources for Student Learning, and Community Resources for Student Learning.

In its role as a support standard, *Leadership and Organization* focuses on determining whether the school functions as a viable and effective organizational system. The NEASC process views leadership as the collaborative responsibility of the administration, faculty and support staff. This process is designed, nurtured, and facilitated by the building administration. The school's structure and culture—the manner in which a school organizes itself, makes decisions, and treats its members—affects the atmosphere in which teaching and learning take place. It should foster mutual respect, provide opportunities for reflection and growth among both students and staff, and actively seek the meaningful involvement of parents and the wider community. Specific programs such as orientation for new staff; ongoing professional development; a clear supervision and evaluation process; established rules, expectations, and consequences; and crisis response and emergency planning ensure that the school is providing the structures necessary for organizational effectiveness. Clear, consistent, and meaningful communication within and beyond the school itself is an accepted hallmark of both positive leadership and successful organizations.

The two standards describing *School and Community Resources for Student Learning* provide a framework for the internal and external support system necessary for a school to meet the needs of students effectively and thrive as a viable educational institution. Internally, the school should provide an effective range of integrated resources, programs, and services designed to enable all students to participate in and benefit from their educational experience. This standard supports the expectation stated in Instruction that all students have access to an equal opportunity to learn and achieve.

The important issue of opportunity to learn is carried beyond the school in this standard that addresses the role and responsibility of the community. Through its elected school board, the community also demonstrates support for the school by providing consistent and sufficient educational funding. Qualified teachers, appropriate programming, adequate instructional materials and supplies, and facilities that support a positive and safe learning environment should be the expectation.

Overall, there is an interesting tension at work in this standards-based system. In essence, the school is being measured against a set of externally developed criteria, but it is also held accountable for its own mission, beliefs, and priorities within its internal self-study. It is in finding a balance between these two perspectives that the accreditation process seeks to be both standardized and consistent as well as distinct and individualized. The breadth of the standards is reminiscent of Reeves's description of the broad-based view of a student-centered, or holistic, accountability system.

A PRINCIPAL'S PERSPECTIVE

Inherent in the breadth and depth of the accreditation process are significant challenges and opportunities, as well as specific issues, that appear to be endemic to the current political climate, the structure of schools today, and the process as it now exists. It appears safe to say that all schools going through this process have experienced both opportunities and challenges during the process. As a principal attempting to lead a school through the process, I found that how well the challenges were managed directly impacted how effectively the opportunities were grasped.

The initial challenge in our school was attitudinal, and from my experience with other schools, this is not unusual. Accountability today, whatever the process, is often not seen in a positive light. Most systems are external, based on a single measure that compares differing groups of students, includes unfair expectations (such as those surrounding the special needs population), and focuses on sanctions as opposed to support. Further, to seek accreditation is often a decision not made entirely at the building level and may be seen as imposed upon the school rather than a positive choice determined by the staff. Superintendents and school boards may decide that school effectiveness should be determined by a credible, formalized, standards-based system and choose accreditation as the system that best meets their needs. Other reasons for their choice may include individual school recognition, validation to the community, or leverage for needed change.

A related concern in our school focused on the rewards of accreditation, and whether or not the process was worth the result. "What do we get out of this?" and "So we get accredited—so what? What does it mean for us?" were legitimate questions that needed to be answered. When the idea of an external review and the risk of not being accredited were factored in, it was fairly understandable that our school staff initially viewed the accreditation process if not negatively, then at least with a certain degree of skepticism.

Effectively presenting the values inherent in the accreditation process, and then obtaining, and maintaining, the school's commitment to the process throughout the eighteen-month self-study, the team visit, and the follow-up phase were clear challenges for me as the principal.

How to deal with these attitudinal issues was the first major hurdle, and I had strong support from the commission staff in this effort. However, as the building principal, I was the one who needed to make this work. I also knew that the manner in which we started the process was vital to a positive result. Knowing my staff fairly well, I decided that the most critical component for success in converting negative attitudes to positive ones was the selection of the chair, or, in our case, cochairs, of the steering committee. I thought a long time about this, considering the qualities and skills that would be needed to guide us through the process. Organization, follow-though, interpersonal skills, knowledge, and understanding of the process, grade level, and program representation were important, but more important were the position and influence of the cochairs in the building.

I recruited two teachers who, first of all, could work together and with the as-yet unnamed members of the steering committee, who possessed the required skills, and who had pivotal roles in the building. Neither of the cochairs were cheerleaders for accreditation, one was seen as outspokenly critical of change, and both were highly professional and well-respected staff members. This was the most important decision I made, and it is the one, in retrospect, that had the most significant impact on the success of the process for our school.

Once the cochairs and the steering committee were in place, I had to think seriously about the challenge of defining the parameters of my role as principal. Having been a building administrator for many years, control was not easy to give up, and I was in a unique position in that I knew the accreditation process well after having chaired many teams. However, I also knew that the self-study must be the work of the total staff and cannot be micromanaged by any one person or small group.

I decided that the most helpful thing I could do was already accomplished: the careful, thoughtful selection of the cochairs. For the rest of the time I needed to be an active participant—as one staff member, not as the principal. Certainly I needed to use my position to provide as much logistical support as possible, but I also needed to allow the process to play itself out in whatever way the staff determined. This was very difficult, and in talking with other principals, it was reassuring to discover that my desire to control the whole thing was not unique.

When the principal does overcontrol the process, which is rare, the results are most often negative: the total staff has no real ownership in the process, the information is sometimes skewed or invalid, and the resulting self-study document can have very limited value to the visiting team. In one case where the principal did exert excessive influence, even to the extent of rewriting portions of the self-study as they were submitted, the staff shared with the visiting team that the process, about which they were positive and supportive, was compromised. Although this school was accredited, with some obvious recommendations around the issue of leadership, the real benefits were lost.

Without question, the greatest logistical challenge we faced, along with probably every other school attempting the process, was time. It is apparent from the description of the process that the self-study is time-intensive on the part of the school. When one adds the accreditation process to the myriad of other demands, both internal and external, that continue to be part of the school day, it is clear that some specifically allocated time must be found. Most of the tasks demanded by the process are multistep: the creation of the mission statement, the work of the many subcommittees, and the important work of whole-staff reflection and consensus building, just to mention a few.

Schools, in some cases with the support of superintendents, have found creative ways to support the work of accreditation by allocating a certain amount of time specifically for this purpose. Strategies include focusing professional development time, putting other initiatives temporarily on hold, finding ways for subcommittee members to meet during the school day, using substitutes, creating short-term blocks of time such as an early release day monthly during the process, and using staff meeting time.

In our case, unfortunately, we experienced a change in leadership early on in the process. From a superintendent who was a strong advocate for accreditation as a viable accountability system, we experienced one who never understood the complexities of the process and, therefore, was not inclined to provide the needed time. This was difficult, not only because of the lack of time but also because of the lack of understanding and support on the part of district leadership. It was somewhat disconcerting to be working as hard as we were at the building level when we knew that the superintendent would be inclined to derail the process if it were not for that fact that our school board had voted to do it prior to his arrival. Our experience speaks to the importance of district leadership that takes an active and supportive role, not necessarily being responsible for solving all logistical problems, but demonstrating a commitment to the process and the willingness to work with the school to ensure its success.

In our case, the only time we had to work on this process was building based, which was limited to staff meetings held bimonthly. For the eighteen months that we spent on our self-study, all staff meeting time was given to subcommittee meetings on standards and learning areas and the subsequent consensus-building meetings, when portions of the self-study were ready to be shared. This worked, but not terribly well. Everything else needed to be dealt with by memo, and these were the days before we were fully networked for e-mail. Because of that, I felt building communication suffered to some degree, and I also found that it was difficult to always be talking about some aspect of accreditation when we came together as a staff. That seemed to lend itself to a heightened level of frustration and burnout as we worked our way through the process.

I am not sure how I would do this differently today if circumstances were similar. Certainly the advances in technology would greatly assist the communication issue—much of those informational items can now be effectively accomplished over e-mail. Changes in the accreditation protocol and a more streamlined approach, developed and implemented since our school participated in the process, would also reduce the amount of time required. The current political climate, with its increased focus on school accountability, might serve as an impetus for districts to provide better support for accreditation both philosophically and logistically. From our experience, it seems clear that, for the process to be successful, the issue of providing time must be accomplished in whatever manner works effectively for the school.

Once this problem has been solved, and the staff has been provided adequate time, the real work and the challenge of the self-study presents itself. For our staff, and many others as well, coming together first in subcommittees, and then as a whole staff, to reflect, to openly debate and discuss, and to arrive at consensus on the important and wide-ranging issues raised by the standards was a daunting task. This required strong facilitation skills on the part of the cochairs and steering committee members, an open and supportive climate in which disagreements can be seen as positive and productive, and viable personal and professional relationships among staff members that generate opportunities for all staff to be heard and valued.

While there is no question that ensuring this open atmosphere for staff dialogue is a challenge, it is also the most valuable opportunity of the internal process for the school. This is the chance for all members of the school to participate in in-depth conversations that truly have the capacity to change the nature of the school as an educational entity.

In our school, we found that the efforts of the staff to effectively work had far-reaching positive effects on the relationships between and among staff members. Future staff initiatives, such as finding ways to implement the recommendations in the follow-up phase of accreditation, working on curriculum revision, developing our local assessment system, and implementing the district Code of Conduct, were accomplished much more easily as a result of the time, effort, and hard work the staff had committed to the internal process of self-study.

Another aspect of our school's process that proved to be both opportunity and challenge for us stemmed from the steering committee's decision regarding the role and involvement of parents and the community in the process. Reeves's concept of holistic accountability presupposes that this process take place, not in isolation, but in collaboration with members of the wider school community. We felt that the perspective of noneducators should be sought and valued as a different lens through which to view the school, from its core beliefs to the many processes and procedures that make up its culture.

We knew that our parents would be involved during the external accountability phase of the process through a formal meeting, usually with the entire visiting team, but we felt strongly that we wanted parents, and community members, if possible, involved at the steering committee level, the subcommittee level, and throughout the process. This idea was generated first because the issue of community was very important to us—our philosophy statement begins with the words: "Community is the foundation on which our school is built." Accountability through self-study did not seem to make sense without the inclusion of individuals who might have had a more objective view of the school than we did, and as great, or greater, stake in the results. We had the sense that the final product would be richer, deeper, and ultimately better for the school, the students, and the community.

Although the inclusion of parents and community members meant some logistical maneuvering with regard to scheduling and meeting times, the advantages far outweighed the problems. This provided the opportunity to involve members of the wider school community in a grassroots process of school accountability, and to connect the school with the parents and the community in a substantive and meaningful way. It was also a positive method of sharing information about the school and resulted in increased interest in and support for the school within the community.

This played out in several ways. The local support for our budget improved, as more members of the community became aware of the work of the school. Two of the parents and community members who were actively involved in self-study with us went on to become members of our school board, and the parent who was an integral member of our steering committee became involved with the accreditation process for the high school. From the connections with our local Senior Center, we established a Foster Grandparent Program that has had up to eighteen members. Through a service learning grant and community connections, two grade levels have worked with a local organization in the area of science. Inclusion in the accreditation process opened doors, established new relationships, and helped us to be more aware of the mutual benefits of school and community interactions.

When our school received its visiting team report, there was great interest on the part of parents and the community to know and discuss the contents, to see "how we did" and what an objective view of our school would look like. There was a desire to both celebrate the commendations and assist with the recommendations, and a clear sense of ownership with us in the final product. Because we all worked together throughout the process, the resulting report was "ours," not just the school's.

Finally, it is important to note that the accreditation process can lead directly to improvements in the school through the power of outside influence. Schools often rely on the visiting team's objective evaluation of the situation to help solve a problem. The visiting team, representing the commission, brings a certain amount of leverage that, unfortunately, members of the school community often do not possess. This leverage can also be an advantage for a superintendent desiring to make specific changes within the school. In other words, an accreditation visit can have an impact not only on the way a school operates but also in obtaining needed resources. It happened in our school with respect to our facility, and I have seen it happen for other schools as well.

A SCHOOL QUALITY REVIEW

Based on the core beliefs of the school, held to high standards, supported by quantitative and qualitative data, and demanding both a comprehensive internal accountability process as well as an intense external review, educational accreditation espouses many of the characteristics of the holistic accountability system described by Reeves. Educators, researchers, and others have spoken strongly against the current practice of identifying successful schools based only on quantitative measures, recognizing that a standardized test score cannot define the effectiveness of schools. Reeves points out that there is a valid place for test scores, and that is within the context of the school itself. But how can the context of the school be effectively evaluated? There must be a process for directly observing the school as a complex system, and a set of agreed-upon criteria defining good schooling, against which the school can be measured. Educational accreditation, or other types of school quality review focused on these contextual and process-oriented aspects of accountability, offers a more authentic look at schools than the test-based system currently in place.

Should this be the process that is the norm rather than the exception? If an accreditation-like process were an essential element in the determination of accountability for all schools, where would education be in five years? Ten years? How would curriculum change? What would be the role of test scores? Would we see continuous improvement, increased capacity building, greater professional dialogue about teaching and learning? Would there be sanctions, or support, for schools not meeting standards? How would parents and the community respond to the process? Would accreditation become one more top-down, imposed initiative, losing some of its current value and benefit?

Accreditation is a voluntary process. Schools that choose educational accreditation are schools that are holding themselves accountable for more than an annual test score. Recognizing that the "story behind the numbers" must also be told, they have attempted an honest internal appraisal and opened their doors to external review. These are schools that have been "brave enough to start a conversation that matters."

All accountability systems have their issues, opportunities, constraints, and advantages. Educational accreditation is no exception. NEASC faces many such issues: ensuring viability in a changing political climate while remaining committed to standards, depending heavily on trained volunteers, exhibiting a high level of process consistency, and reconciling the role of testing as the primary basis for current educational accountability. However, the experiences of accrediting agencies such as NEASC offer a promising vehicle for establishing a new model of school accountability. If school improvement is truly the basis of the demand for accountability in education today, establishing a school quality review process, one that demands both internal and external scrutiny and places the work of teachers and students within the context of the educational system, would be a positive step toward fulfilling that goal.

NOTES

1. D. B. Reeves, *Accountability for learning: How teachers and school leaders can take charge* (Alexandria, Va.: Association for Supervision and Curriculum Development, 2004).
2. NEASC, *New England Association of Schools and Colleges Policy Handbook*, rev. ed. (Bedford, Mass.: Author, 2004).
3. NEASC, *A Guide to the Process* (Bedford, Mass.: Author, 1992).
4. NEASC, *An Unpublished History of the New England Association of Schools and Colleges* (Bedford, Mass.: Author, 2004).
5. NEASC, *An Unpublished History*.
6. NEASC, *A Guide to the Process*.
7. NEASC, *The Chair's Manual* (Bedford, Mass.: Author, 2002).

8

A LOCAL ACCOUNTABILITY SYSTEM IN PROGRESS

George Entwistle

I am a relative newcomer to the job of public school superintendent. The journey leading me to this job was surely not by way of the path more traditionally taken by other superintendents. With a background in applied and organizational psychology and with my most recent experience being in corporate human resources management roles, I am in only my third year of paid, public school employment. Before becoming the superintendent for the Falmouth Public Schools in 2004, I had worked as assistant superintendent in another Maine district for one year and had, just prior to that, served two three-year terms on the school board in my hometown. Now, at the beginning of my second year here in Falmouth, as I reflect back on my brief tenure, it is becoming clearer to see how much my passion for organizational development work and my private-sector experience—particularly my early learning in a Fortune 500 company that was committed to Total Quality Management (TQM)—has influenced my thinking about how to improve schools.

I joined Weyerhaeuser—a giant in the forest products industry—in the late 1980s. The company had adopted the principles and practices of the Total Quality movement and, at that time, was in the process of integrating them into the company's culture by way of a program called

Quality in Action. In some ways, I suppose, they wished to establish their own cultural imprint on TQM and, at the same time, not appear to be jumping on the same TQM bandwagon as everyone else. Adopting a new way of doing business came about, according to company lore, from a wake-up call received from one of the company's largest national customers. The good news was that Weyerhaeuser was one of this customer's top-rated suppliers. The bad news was that the customer was soon to reduce its number of key suppliers to two and Weyerhaeuser, when measured against the same quality standards as the other suppliers, was ranked in the number three position.

For me, there was an almost instantaneous connection to the tenets of an organizational orientation to quality principles. Intuitively and intellectually it all just plain *made sense.* Who could argue with the value of taking a thoughtful and analytical look into the future (or argue with the danger and liabilities of not planning for the future)? What better way could there be to identify opportunities to improve products or processes than using cold, hard, indisputable data? And how could we talk about improvement if we could not somehow point to a measurable change? The whole concept of measurable improvement awakened the statistician in me. Targeting incremental improvements to measures of product quality and learning from process changes that produce better quality products seemed almost second nature.

The human component of the quality improvement dynamic is what fascinated me the most. The TQM philosophy placed great importance on the role of the organizational members. Sustaining continuous improvement and/or improvement breakthroughs required focused thinking that was creative and innovative. The organizational culture would determine the extent to which individuals would contribute their energy and ideas, their level of interest in becoming meaningfully engaged and involved, and their willingness to rethink the status quo and to embrace change. Diversity in perspective became not only tolerated but viewed as essential to developing a competitive edge. Customers became real people with opinions and feelings and needs that required genuine interest and quick responses. Not only were customers always right but they were recognized as the life's blood of a company's existence; without the customer, we recognized that our company would have no purpose and would perish.

THE PUBLIC SCHOOL STAKEHOLDER AS CUSTOMER

As a gift from the incoming superintendent to his soon-to-be leadership team members, I gave each of my new colleagues a copy of Michael Fullan's book, *Leading in a Culture of Change*.[1] I like this book for the many insights Fullan offers as he examines leadership practices in the business sector and explores their applicability in managing schools. Throughout the year, as a regular agenda item for our bimonthly Leadership Council meetings, we would each pick a slip of paper from an assembled collection of slips of paper with Fullan quotes on them (to which we had all, earlier, contributed). The discussion of the Fullan "pearls," as we called them, was always a great tone-setter for what followed—it helped us to reestablish ourselves in our roles of district leaders regardless of the hat we were wearing the moment before we stepped into the room. Toward the end of the school year, we attended a national conference at which Michael Fullan was presenting. It was during that presentation that he offered what has since become my favorite Fullan quote: "It's not that business models don't work in education, it's just bad business models that don't work." In my very brief experience of attempting to match some practical, reliable, and what proved to be *effective* business models to our school organization's challenges, this Fullan pearl seems to be holding true.

In business, I learned that your crankiest customer—the one with the most persistent and, at least on the surface, seemingly most petty complaints—is a gem, a gift. By really listening to this customer, one can often uncover opportunities to strengthen the business. This customer needs to be appreciated and honored for the valuable insights he or she brings—the improvement opportunities he or she sees, the same ones that likely would not be so obvious or might be overlooked or dismissed within the organization. I learned that the behavior of this assertive customer is quite unusual because he or she actually takes the time to complain directly to those with control over the source of the problem. The commitment of this customer is unusual because most dissatisfied customers never say a word to you. They just never ever purchase your service or product again. They do, however, generally have lots to say about you to their associates, family, and neighbors. Granted, businesses and schools do have some fundamental differences in terms of the customers each one tries to please. Complaints, nonetheless, unlock the door to opportunities for improvement.

In the wake that followed the previous superintendent's exit from this district was some unrest created from issues that, as seen in at least some portion of the public's eye, were never resolved. Certain segments of the community had been polarized by the lengthy (often heated, I hear) debates of these issues. At center stage was a controversial change to the high school curriculum resulting in the elimination of what had been a long-standing, lower-level, college preparatory student track. This detracking assigned what had been previously upper- and lower-track students into blended groups and created "learning laboratories" offering additional instructional support to struggling students. Another issue that sparked debate was the implementation of a self-contained, multiage classroom designed as a safety net (at a high per-student cost) for students at risk of dropping out of school. These were divisive, high-profile matters for the district at the time, though recent programmatic reviews/analyses of these same issues seem to indicate that much of the fervor was in response to the *process* used in decision making more than to the substantive aspects (purpose and value) of these initiatives.

Thankfully, there were vocal individuals who sustained their passion about these issues (and others) and they wanted their time with the new superintendent. They wanted to have a chance to convince the new guy that their position on this issue or that issue was the most defensible.

Weeks before I started my new job, I requested my future administrative assistant to begin scheduling one-on-one interviews with individuals whose names were on lists submitted by school principals. Principals had received an earlier request from me to create a list of faculty members and staff, of parents and community members, and for grades 7–12, of students whom they recommended for me to interview. Of most importance to me was that the collective group invited to meet with the new superintendent represent the diversity of opinion about the school district (and about the "hot" issues) widely held by the community at large.

It was my desire to listen to successful students as well as students who felt their lack of success was directly attributable to the district's performance (or lack thereof). I wanted to listen to the parents who loved our schools and those who chose the option of either private or home schooling because of what they perceived to be our inability to meet their child's needs. It was crucial to hear from teachers and staff, those who loved their employment experience and those others who were much less satisfied about their work relationship with the district. Add to this growing list: school board members (current and past), town councilors, local state senators and representatives, the police chief, local clergy, and anyone else who requested. Quite a lineup of meetings had been created. More than seventy interviews were eventually scheduled and conducted, with each individual meeting lasting between forty-five and ninety minutes.

AN ACTION PLANNING PROCESS

Other valuable learning that I gained from the private sector relates to strategic planning—what works and what doesn't work. My experience taught me that the more complicated the planning process, the less energy there is to actually tackle the tough work of "working the plan." Too often, at the end of a strategic planning process, there seemed to be many individuals who thought that with the plan done, their work was done. School organizations, at least from my perspective, seem almost innately postured to maintain organizational status quo. When I took the job of superintendent, one of my major commitments to the school board that hired me was to develop a future-focused plan, one that was living and breathing and not collecting dust on a shelf. Specifically, I promised to create a plan of action for continuous improvement of the organization, one that was comprehensive in scope, simple in design, clear with regard to focus, easily measurable and data driven, instrumental in guiding future work, and authentically representative (of those individuals with a vested interest in the future of our schools). Quite a promise! Using a fairly straightforward and stakeholder-centered approach, I developed a simple diagram of the roadmap of what would guide our action planning process.

Simple, accelerated, and action oriented—that was the promise. While there were a whole heap of details still missing, I was sure that with the benefit of the energy and creativity of the very smart people on my team, filling in the details was really just a matter of time. Essentially,

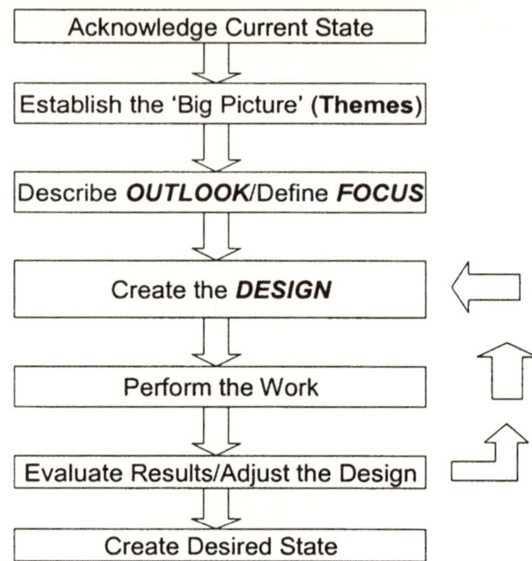

Figure 8.1. Action Planning Process.

utilizing a variation on a simple change model (acknowledging the current state, initiating and monitoring an intervention, and ultimately creating the desired state), the first two steps in the action planning process would be determined by the stakeholder interviews (see figure 8.1). It was from this input that the current state of the organization would be profiled. The profile would consist simply of both the organization's identified assets and the major areas (themes) identified as holding the most promise for, and most warranting, attention and improvement.

It would be later, in the larger community dialogue setting, that stakeholders collectively would define the organizational outlook (answering the question, "What do we want the future to look like?") and the focus (answering the question, "What should be our most important considerations, and why?") for each topic selected for dialogue. In each dialogue group, as well, stakeholders would be asked to capture any design recommendations (answering the question, "Are there tactical considerations—timing, sequencing, resources needed, research requirements—that surfaced during the dialogue?"). Creation of the design (the actual action plan itself) would be left to the Leadership Council in regular consultation with school leadership teams and faculty, the school board, and our invited, distinguished educators.[2] Following the road map toward the desired state of the organization, the action plan would be implemented and results would be evaluated. The plan would be revisited and adjusted and, ideally, the organization would, over time, become higher performing and more successful at achieving its goals.

Assets and Opportunities for Improvement

Some distinct themes began to emerge even as less than 25 percent of the stakeholder interviews were conducted. Each interviewee was asked to identify both the strengths and the areas of improvement opportunity for our K–12 organization. Participants were very forthcoming about both. What pleased me, as a new superintendent, was the incredible consistency demonstrated by stakeholders, in all categories, as they identified the district's assets. Much to my delight, at the very top of the list was what they described as the incredibly dedicated and professional faculty and staff employed by the district. Cited over and over were the district's high academic standards, the high-performing reputation of the schools, the curriculum/programs/learning opportunities available to students, the welcoming and safe environment in our schools and, our students—often described as being respectful and hardworking.

The community itself was frequently identified as a major asset to the school district. Often it was faculty members who touted the incredible commitment to education demonstrated by community members—not only by those who are parents of school children but also by those not involved (or no longer involved) with the schools. I was told that a true sense of community and of genuine caring among community members existed in the town. It is a growing town but one that nevertheless retains a small-town feel. This was often offered as the reason why lifelong or longtime residents decided to raise their families here and why others chose to bring their families here. A strong regard for solid family values prevails. Parental involvement in the schools was most often cited as a strength for the district—there was general agreement that the district gained great benefits from the time and talents contributed to the schools by parents and by way of the generosity of the community at large.

But the purpose of the interviews, after all, was to take advantage of the opportunity to talk about those areas within the organization that could use some attention, those that required improvement. Here again, in our conversations these areas quickly became apparent and were identified with a good deal of consistency. When we talked about students (which fortunately and most often we did), parents, students, and faculty shared their high level of concern about the amount of stress experienced. There was great worry expressed to me about parents overscheduling their children into school and other outside activities (afterschool clubs, competitive sports leagues, music lessons, tutoring, dance, etc.). In the higher grades when students were given the choice, many of them tended to overschedule themselves. Students and parents identified excessive and complicated homework and home projects assigned by teachers as contributing to students' time crunch and to their high stress levels.

What began to emerge from our discussions was a picture of a very high-pressured and competitive culture for students in our district. What I began to hear more and more about was the student response, particularly from our teenagers, to that culture: engaging in risky and/or self-abusive behavior (including abuse of alcohol and drugs) and/or exhibiting depressive or defiant behavior. Not surprisingly, there was some finger-pointing that went on. Students complained that parents and, in some cases, teachers did not really listen. In general, older students indicated that they did not have a real voice in school matters that pertained to them. There were indications that many families experienced disconnects in their family time—frequent interruptions to their ability to spend time together because of the hectic schedules kept by family members.

When we spoke about students, some aspect of student learning and achievement inevitably entered into the conversation. It was generally agreed by those interviewed that our school district did a good job meeting the needs of our special education students. Opportunity for improvement, however, existed pretty much everywhere else, I was told. Some parents and students had particular concerns about a specific course, teacher, new curriculum adopted, or new approach to teaching in a particular content area. A more generalized concern focused on the perceived gaps and/or redundancies that existed in the curriculum across grade levels in many subject areas. There were individuals who believed that we were not doing a good enough job for those students who were academically "gifted" while others believed we were short-changing those students ""flying under the radar"—being identified as a member of neither the very high performing nor the special needs groups.

Satisfaction with our district's ability to meet academic and student-support needs seemed to be inversely related to grade level. There was dissatisfaction at the high school level, for example, about guidance and counseling services offered to students, with a lack of clarity about where school guidance responsibility left off and parent/family responsibility picked up, or vice versa. With 90-plus percent of students heading off to college, there was a discernable dissatisfaction with the services we offered around postsecondary planning and the guidance and support offered to students and parents in the college application process. Though sounding a bit clichéd, the high school students were sincere in relating a sense of frustration with some of the adults around them for not really listening to what they had to say—even about school matters that most directly affected students.

Primarily from faculty members, I heard about anxiety created by the seemingly myopic focus placed on student assessment. For the past several years, district in-service or professional learning time had been fully occupied with creating a local assessment system (or LAS, designed on a local level to assess student learning with respect to the state learning standards—in Maine, called the Maine Learning Results). Philosophically well grounded, well intended as an alternative to high-stakes testing but, at the same time, quite prescriptive and overly technically complex, the state's LAS requirements of districts have left time and resources for little else. There were students and parents who believed that students were being assessed at the expense of instructional time. Clearly, a strong message emerged from the interviews: the district's apparent total preoccupation with assessing student achievement was "way over the top."

While most teachers with whom I spoke shared their concern about the detrimental effect that an exclusive focus on local assessment system development was having on the scope, variety, and value of their professional learning time, many also acknowledged that the collaborative nature of some of the assessment development work was stimulating and contributed positively to their professional growth as teachers. They hoped for more time, however, to collaborate with their colleagues on other substantive matters and they wanted to engage in professional development activities specific to their individualized needs and passions as educators. Faculty members and others were concerned that we might be "missing the boat" in terms of keeping our teachers current and thus, potentially negatively impacting the quality of teachers for which the district had become so well known.

Along these same lines, concern was voiced about the perceived mounting risk that appeared to be impacting the district's ability to retain the highly qualified professionals that we had worked so hard to attract to the district and to develop. Teachers respectfully, without drama and almost unanimously, articulated a desire for more meaningful involvement in charting the future course of their schools. They also shared a hope for seeing more evidence from the rest of the school community that would speak to a higher level of appreciation for them both as skilled professionals and as valued individuals.

As I met with stakeholders, I shared with them my belief that the school district, as a public organization owned by the people of the town, needed to ensure that it was, indeed, responsive to the needs of the students, parents, and other owners (community members). There was no disagreement with this premise and often, there was enthusiastic reception voiced by interviewees. Work (as I learned much later on, a tremendous amount of work) had been done in earlier years to define a foundation of common core values upon which the community could build a clearer vision for the future of their schools. Many that met with me expressed disappointment that despite the energy and effort invested in this work, there was little evidence that much of a foundation or common ground had been established. If there was a future vision or a plan, I was told, not many people knew about it. I was not shy about sharing my own view that "without a plan, anywhere we end up is okay." And I knew, as did each of the stakeholders, that that was not okay for us.

As I made my way through the first third of the scheduled stakeholder interviews, I was able to identify the key components of the themes that were on many people's minds. Through the next third and then, even better, through the final one-third of the meetings, by memory I was able to list the six to eight broad topics that served to organize all those notes taken over weeks of interviews. My review of assets and opportunities I have just presented emerged gradually. Good, bad, or indifferent, I am one of those individuals who needs process time to mull through data and to make sense of it. Although I experimented with a few different schemes to help me logically organize the data (generally finding most success when I employ outlines with drawings of boxes and relational arrows), I had not yet quite been able to fully make sense of how these key components fit when taken all together. That's when I came across the model for school accountability being presented in this book.

RETHINKING SCHOOL ACCOUNTABILITY

In an effort to try to make more manageable the very complex job of creating a local assessment system, the Maine Department of Education designed a four-part series entitled Rethinking Accountability. The series had as its targeted audience school administrators and teacher leaders charged with the responsibility of facilitating the development of an LAS in their home districts. Somewhat reluctantly, I attended, along with a team of school leaders from our district. I had long since decided that the only possible way to successfully implement a local assessment system was to keep it simple, make it practical, and to ensure that the work involved had meaning for participants (teachers), ensuring that teachers could see that the expenditure of time and effort was having some payoffs for them and for students. My view was that local leadership had as a primary role the job of making the tough calls necessary to sustain forward organizational movement and progress. In fact, on the first teacher day of the school year, during my very first address to the district faculty and staff, I advised them that they had my permission to stop engaging in any LAS-related work that they felt was not meaningfully improving either teaching or student learning. I was willing to take responsibility for making the tough calls, for bending rules when it would benefit student learning, and for taking any of the resulting heat that might follow. I had a high level of confidence that we were in a solid, even enviable, position in terms of our LAS development work and our ability to create valid and reliable local assessments to certify that our students were meeting state standards. We had both the technical and leadership capacity to keep our forward momentum. Other than to keep current with the latest news coming out of the state's education department, I anticipated that collectively we would leave the session with little other benefit.

Ken Jones was the featured speaker at the meeting. His article, "A Balanced School Accountability Model: An Alternative to High-Stakes Testing," had just recently been published and he was highlighting its central ideas. As Dr. Jones proceeded through his presentation of slides that day, it took very little time for me to see that he had been able to create a structure that would effectively function as a tool to sort the data I had collected from my stakeholders—the data that, up until that point in time, I had been clumsily trying to make sense of and to organize. Jones was redefining a way of thinking about school accountability that resonated with my own thinking. He had articulated a list for what schools should be minimally held accountable that matched up to the needs expressed in my own district (table 8.1).

Jones's proposed model for accountability made sense from both a practical and intuitive perspective. We did need to be using "a different set of assumptions and understandings about school realities and approaches to power;" we desperately needed to move away from bureaucratic systems of accountability to one "focused on the needs of learners and on the goals of having high expectations for all."[3]

My belief was that it all originated and depended upon developing a local and authentic school accountability system—accountability to students, faculty, parents, and taxpayers. The proposed model and structure suggested a reexamination of our beliefs about just exactly what schools needed to be held accountable for. It offered a template to help organize and make better sense of how the data collected in the interviews fit together. It provided a vehicle to be able to talk about what stakeholders had to say during those many hours of conversation.

As the members of the district's Leadership Council (in other school systems often referred to as Administrative Team or A Team), using the Accountability Components and Themes (see figure 8.2), helped me sort the findings from interviews, we were able to consolidate our findings to three themes that would best provide the structure for our upcoming Community Dialogue. We felt that we could subsume the re-

Table 8.1. Accountability Components and Themes

Themes from Interviews

- Physical and Emotional Well-Being of Students
  - Stress, cultural pressure (alcohol/drugs), "overscheduled"
  - Family "disconnects"/guidance and school counseling role
  - Listening to "student voice"
- Student Learning
  - Curriculum, assessment
  - Core values
- Teacher Learning
  - Retaining teachers, maintain quality, professional growth, time for collaboration
  - Appreciation, involvement
- Equity and Access
  - Meeting the needs of all students
- Improvement
  - Having a "plan" for the future
  - Defining our purpose
  - Responsiveness to students, parents, community

New Accountability Model

- Physical & Emotional Well-being of Students
  - Caring school climate
  - Nurturing, positive relationships
- Student Learning
  - Knowledge, thinking, and disposition
- Teacher Learning
  - Knowledgeable (content)
  - Skilled (instruction)
  - Relationship builders
- Equity and Access
  - Fair opportunity for all students to learn to high standards
- Improvement
  - Schools as "learning organizations"

sponsibility related to equity and access under the general accountability theme of Student Learning. As well, recognizing our accountability related to Improvement (becoming a learning organization) was, we believed, apparent in our ongoing investment and commitment to locally developing an improvement or action plan for the district. The themes then, using Jones's accountability language, which came to frame the large-scale, future-focused dialogue with stakeholders were:

- Student Learning (All students acquiring the knowledge, thinking skills and disposition needed in a modern democratic society)

- Emotional and Physical Well-Being of Students (Safe, caring schools and tending to student affective as well as cognitive needs)
- Teacher Learning (Enabling teachers to improve their knowledge and skills according to professional teaching standards)

The Community Dialogue

The name selected for our large-scale community event was deliberate. We did not intend the group to engage in a discussion, but rather in a Community *Dialogue*. Borrowing from the work of Peter Senge,[4] we framed our event as a collection of dialogues rather than break-out sessions, encouraging all participants to suspend their assumptions (and their tendencies to jump to conclusions), to regard one another as colleagues and partners, and to try to maintain a focus on the topic at hand (the dialogue facilitator was to gently provide some leadership in this effort as well). Too often focused on yielding winners and losers, discussions place too little emphasis on active listening and on bringing all participants to a higher level of understanding. Our purpose in the day was for participants (many of the seventy stakeholders interviewed were in attendance) to come together to help lay a foundation for a future-focused, action-oriented plan for improving our schools. On the invitation, the purpose of the day was presented in this way:

> The purpose of the Community Dialogue is to create an opportunity for a large, representative group of stakeholders (all those with a vested interest in the quality of the Falmouth Public Schools) to examine and offer comment/input on themes that are critical to the future planning for our schools. The themes that will be examined are those that have emerged from the many stakeholder interviews conducted by the Superintendent during July and August of 2004. Students, teachers and education technicians, parents, staff, school leaders, school board members, elected officials, community members and community leaders will join together for a day on October 8, 2004 and will engage in self-directed dialogues focused on important educational and organizational matters. The proceedings (data captured) from the day will be utilized in defining the future OUTLOOK for the Falmouth Public Schools, establishing a clear FOCUS for how we will spend our time, energy and resources and creating a DESIGN that identifies the specific action we will take to achieve our short- and long-term improvement goals for our district.

As it happened, what was most unique about the day and what surprised many of the nearly two hundred participants was the lack of a predetermined agenda for the day. Using a modified Open Space Technology[5] model, the three themes identified from the stakeholder interviews provided the only imposed context for the day. An invited, distinguished educator introduced the theme for the session (the day was broken into three sessions—morning, late morning, and afternoon—concentrating on only one theme in each session). Around the room and available to all participants were large sheets of poster paper and markers. After a very brief framing of the theme, the distinguished educator would invite anyone who felt that he or she had an important topic related to the theme to bring that topic forward. He or she would capture the topic on the poster paper and, in turn, move to the front of the room, introduce himself or herself and announce the topic for a dialogue. By offering a dialogue topic, that individual understood that he or she was also consenting to take responsibility for facilitating a dialogue with others who shared an interest in that topic.

Although the use of technology plays an important role in Open Space Technology sessions, our approach to using technology was unique. Owen's suggested protocol attempts to ensure that every participant leaves at the end of the day (or the multiple-day event) with a copy of the event's proceedings (notes generated). In each of our dialogue meeting areas there were tables, chairs, and a laptop computer for note taking. It was not unusual, at our event, for students to volunteer for the note-taker assignment. Immediately following the conclusion of the group's dialogue, the notes, saved onto a pen drive, would be taken to a central technology area and uploaded to a Community Dialogue site on our district's Web page. The Community Dialogue proceedings were accessible to participants as well as to others within our school community for review and/or immediate comment. Inclusion of the rest of the school community in the Community Dialogue was instantaneous. For event participants, the day's proceedings were available that evening upon their return home, via the website.

During the one-day Community Dialogue event, there were a total of forty-two topic dialogues conducted. Some dialogues drew as few as five participants while others drew more than thirty participants. More than sixty pages of proceedings were loaded onto the Community Dialogue link from the district's website. Our next task was to tease out the long- and short-term improvement priorities for the district from this collection of data. The Leadership Council members were asked, individually and then collectively, to carefully review the proceedings and to identify the larger organizational goals embedded in the data. A number of work sessions were spent pulling the proceedings apart and subsequently regrouping topics, themes, priorities, and goals in a fashion that seemed to most efficiently represent the wealth of creative thought and input contained in the data. Through this rather tedious process, we examined the data from every conceivable perspective, until it became clear that the long-term goals and shorter-term priorities consistently surfaced no matter which way we sorted the proceedings. Five district goals were established:

Goal 1: Establish a culture of wellness that supports the physical, social and emotional well-being of all members of our school community (students, faculty, staff).

Goal 2: Acknowledge and respect the wide range of student ability and offer diverse and appropriate learning opportunities for all.

Goal 3: Remain committed to building a supportive, professional learning community for the teaching staff.

Goal 4: Prioritize organizational needs and reallocate time accordingly.

Goal 5: Recognize and optimize the role of community resources in student partnerships.

Eighteen-Month Plan

One of the fundamental flaws I perceived in the strategic planning efforts I was a part of during my time in the private sector was the strong (read: *over*) emphasis on establishing an extremely long-range (three- to five-year) plan. Such attempts truly challenged the individuals involved, regardless of their collective capacity to anticipate long-range threats and opportunities, and distracted them from the important work that was awaiting their immediate attention. While there is certainly value derived from maintaining an eye on the distant horizon, an overemphasis on looking way out ahead creates the risk of either getting overwhelmed by the unknown or spending too little time on addressing the issues that could afford more control in shaping that future state. A Peter Drucker quote offered our team just the advice I was looking for:

> It is rarely possible—or even particularly fruitful—to look too far ahead. A plan can usually cover no more than eighteen months and still be reasonably clear and specific. So the question in most cases should be, where and how can I [we] achieve results that will make a difference within the next year and a half? The answer must balance several things. First, the results should be hard to achieve—they should require "stretching" to use the current buzzword. But also, they should be within reach. To aim at results that cannot be achieved—or that can be only under most unlikely circumstances—is not being ambitious, it is being foolish. Second, the results should be meaningful. They should make a difference. Finally, results should be visible and, if at all possible, measurable. From this will come a course of action: what to do, where and how to start, and what goals and deadlines to set[6] (Fig. 8.2).

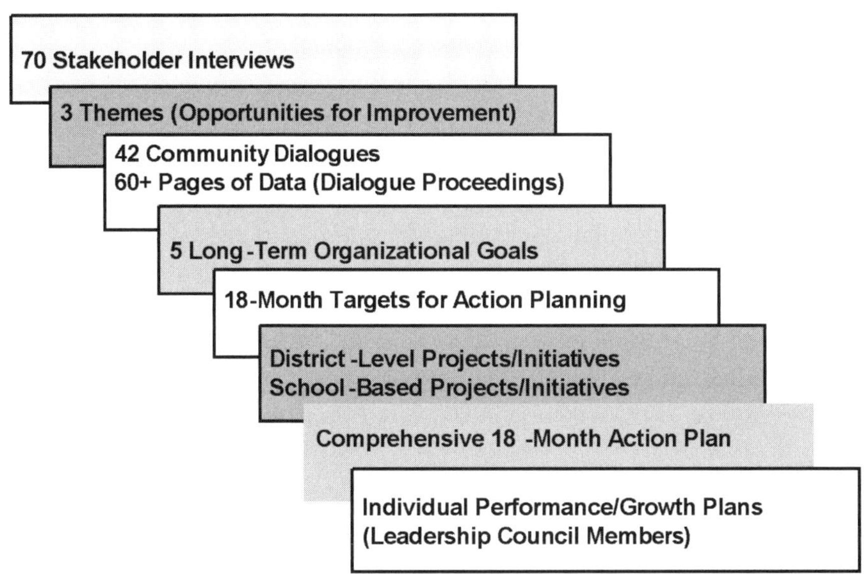

Figure 8.2. Building Blocks of a Local School Accountability System.

Building a local school accountability system was uncharted territory for our team. We found ourselves defining pieces of the process as we went along, adding what we believed to be the next logical link in the sequence of developing a plan that would retain an authentic connection to the stakeholder voice (see figure 8.3). Heeding Drucker's advice, we established eighteen months as our planning timeframe and we closely examined the priority areas for work (what we call targets) that surfaced from the Community Dialogue. It became clear that, contributing to the achievement of each of the long-term goals, there were many smaller, incremental steps (projects and initiatives) that could be taken in the shorter term—for our purposes, over the course of the eighteen months that followed the Community Dialogue.

At the school level, principals were encouraged to examine, along with their building leadership teams, the work that was already going on in their schools and to evaluate the relevance of those efforts to the eighteen-month targets and to achieving our ultimate long-term goals. Recognizing that they were assuming individual accountability to execute their school-specific plans, they were encouraged to push off any project that could not pass the "relevance test." Further, they were encouraged to replace abandoned projects with new initiatives that would have greater likelihood for success and for moving their schools (and the district, as a whole) to achieving our eighteen-month targets.

Another pitfall of those strategic planning efforts with which I was familiar was that the new strategic plan was often simply regarded as an "add-on" to the work already going on. Recognizing that we were already working with full plates, we consciously tried to ensure that we did not make this same mistake. Both at the school and district levels we refined existing efforts to be better aligned and supportive of our newly defined targets and goals. Where we could take on new projects or initiatives, we tried to do so cautiously and with the recognition that overfilling our plates with work would ultimately diminish our ability to create the outcomes for students that we so desperately desired to achieve.

BENEFITS OF A LOCAL SCHOOL ACCOUNTABILITY SYSTEM

So what changed as a result of all of this effort? As I write, it is almost eleven months after the Community Dialogue of 2004; the next Community Dialogue is already scheduled for March, 2006. Given the time invested to synthesize the proceedings from October 2004 and the time taken to develop the plan, we have been formally at work on the Eighteen-Month Action Plan for about nine months—seven months of which school has been in session.

In reality, however, the impact of the dialogue was felt almost immediately. We heard from students, parents, staff, and community members that the much-needed opportunity for expression of opinion and for exchanging ideas about important topics refreshed their sense of ownership in the schools. When news from the dialogue day hit the streets, there was regret expressed by many about the missed opportunity for participation. We believe we will double the number of participants, for the 2006 Community Dialogue, including a tripling of the number of students involved.

At Falmouth Middle School, Mrs. Greene's student participants were offered the option to substitute a Community Dialogue essay in place of some regular classroom assignments. The essay assignment was quite prescriptive in terms of structure and form. Interestingly enough, all of the students opted for the essay assignment. Here are some excerpts from their writing.

> One thing I thoroughly enjoyed about that day was the fact that even though there was quite an age difference between the adults and me, they thought of me and treated me like an equal, listening intently to what I said. Hopefully we can do this sort of thing again in the near future, where we can check in on the progress of issues and address new ones, so little by little, Falmouth schools will become a place of learning, comfort and enjoyment. [Jack C.]

> When listening to the many opinions in this conversation, I concluded that having a relationship with a teacher to the point where you feel as though you are on the same level, benefits on both ends equally. Each topic exudes a ripple effect, when combined they justify that even if the subject doesn't relate to you directly, in the long run, it impacts you in the whole picture. So if you don't help, even if it means just listening, you are only hurting yourself. That is what the Community Dialogue was all about. [Emily K.]

> Throughout the day I had a fun time talking about what students wanted changed and what could be done to change it. . . . For once the teachers

> had to listen to our opinions on the subject. They didn't get to choose what they want without hearing the students' opinions. I think that all the students and the teachers will benefit from Friday, Oct. 8th. [Robert F.]

> Friday, October 8th was a mind-boggling day for me as well as for all the other participants in the dialogue. I felt like I was no longer just some thirteen-year-old eighth grader in Falmouth, Maine; I now felt as though I were an adult, perchance an equal to all the other people in the building. I felt that what I said, because I was one of the people it affected most, was important and that everyone wanted to hear what I said. I felt that I gave my two cents' worth and that I was important. I understood also that maybe the teachers do not know everything and they do not know what we think or what we feel, maybe they need a little help in understanding the students here. From now on I will be a student who is trustworthy, who is important, and who is going to do everything in her power to allow the teachers to learn, help us learn, and trust everyone. [Sarah B.]

One of the greatest impacts I have seen from this entire process has been the development of a collective sense of clarity about our organizational priorities. This became first evident as we engaged ourselves in the process of building the district's budget for the 2005–2006 school year, immediately following the Community Dialogue. In a year of a pending and very real tax-cap initiative in Maine, and following a year during which budget development was most remembered for the contentiousness surrounding public debates and budget forums, our ability to credibly link our proposed budget with organizational priorities created a distinctly different tone and climate for budget discussions. This year's budget discussions were clearly distinguishable from those of previous years as reflected in the evaluative descriptions articulated by school board members and town councilors, including: "more focused," "more student centered," "more convincing," "more collaborative and cooperative," and, bottom line, "more efficient."

Across the district, we have continued to see and feel the positive impact of the Community Dialogue particularly in the way that it has allowed us to better focus commitment of our resources, including energy, effort, and time. The district's five goals and eighteen-month target areas have created a context and common language for us as we do our work and as we examine the relative importance of competing demands on our energy, effort and time—of which there tend to be many. I have made significant moves to redefine the roles of two of my nine Leadership Council positions in order to align talent and skills to more effectively execute our eighteen-month plan.

We have concentrated effort and resources to build district structures and systems to fill big voids in our organization. We have created a three-tiered structure for better meeting the professional development needs of our teaching staff: individualized development planning (including an in-depth orientation and mentoring program for new teachers); school-initiated professional learning (designed and implemented independently at the school level in coordination with ongoing, districtwide work); and district-sponsored professional development programs and events. The standards used by the National Board for Professional Teaching Standards have been adopted to serve as the foundation for a new evaluation and individual development planning process for our veteran staff, incorporating self-evaluations, leadership input, and individualized goal-setting components. New also as a result of the Community Dialogue is an online resource directory that connects resources of community members (knowledge, specialized skills, and/or life experiences) with students whose learning can be enhanced by the availability of those resources. The searchable Online Community Resources/Professional Learning Directory also serves as a vehicle for professional staff members of the district to access community resources or to share their own professional expertise, materials, or information with other district professionals.

Each school's adoption of projects and initiatives—all aligned with the organization's goals and midterm (eighteen-month) targets—have directly resulted in benefits for our students. Whether it was a Wellness Adventure taken on at the elementary school to increase exercise and healthy food choices (challenging both students and staff to make improvements), a Teen Issues Day (a student-designed program of teen-centered workshops), a Wellness Fair for our fifth and sixth graders, or a Civil Rights Day for our entire middle school student body, a new emphasis on each individual's physical, social, and emotional well-being has been created across the board. Codes of conduct are being revamped at each of our schools with particular care being paid to the very active involvement of students in the process. Comprehensive Emergency

Response Plans to ensure the safety of students, staff, and visitors have been developed for each of our schools.

Other projects and initiatives directly resulting from the dialogue attempt to redesign or expand existing services to meet the very diverse needs of our student population. The resources assigned to our high school guidance office, for example, have been restructured so that there now is a dedicated, full-time college/postsecondary planning counselor. A former college admissions officer has filled the position. This not only bumps up the caliber of professional expertise available to the majority of our students (and their parents) but it also leaves the other comprehensive guidance counselors unencumbered by postsecondary planning demands—allowing them to better attend to student needs for academic monitoring and to take a more proactive stance in supporting our high school students through the many other challenges of adolescence.

As a result of the Community Dialogue, we are now devoting much more time and additional resources to transition planning for our incoming high school freshman. We have, for the first time, designed and sponsored a summer academy for middle and high school students with offerings that address targeted needs for additional academic support (writing, math, and study skills workshops) alongside enrichment courses in art, photography, and creative writing for students who might otherwise not be able to fit these courses into their regular school-year schedule. We have committed to having in place, by the end of this new school year, a plan and efforts underway to expand our current literacy education into a comprehensive, coordinated literacy program spanning all grades, K–12.

By no means have we checked-off all of the "to do" items from our eighteen-month plan. There are still some initiatives in the plan for which we have not yet made any discernible progress. I suspect, for example, that we will not have solutions implemented (maybe not even identified) any time soon to scheduling challenges needed to enhance teaching and learning at our middle and high schools. Despite the great pride we take in our extensive and sophisticated system for collection and analysis of student performance data, our strategy and tools for formally measuring the positive impact on student learning are still a work in progress. We have come to realize that we really need more of a community-friendly district report card that will incorporate multiple measures and clearly demonstrate the effects of our adoption of a local school accountability system on student learning. Despite the solid progress that we have been able to make and items that have been checked off the "to do" list, our plates remain full.

SOME FINAL THOUGHTS

In our little coastal community in Maine, the Community Dialogue, our long-term goals, and our eighteen-month plan have retained a level of vibrancy over the course of the past eleven months that, quite frankly, has been amazing. The Community Dialogue continues to live and breathe in our school and district conversations and in the more expansive communication exchanges between the schools and the greater Falmouth community. I hear and see, on a regular basis, references to "the dialogue" and or "the action plan" in correspondences from our school leaders to parents and to staff and in our local newspapers. Our attempts to redefine accountability at the very local community level have added a dimension of richness to our conversations that had not quite been imagined as we embarked on this journey. The student learning improvements and organizational enhancements that have been made as a result of the Community Dialogue are outcomes in which we take great pleasure and satisfaction. But even as we continue building and responding to our local school accountability system, the value derived by the district's stakeholders becomes more and more evident.

Involvement of stakeholders has meant allowing them in as welcomed and active participants to the very complicated business of improving public schools. This has created a whole new level of exposure for them beyond that ordinarily offered by reports of SAT, PSAT, or MEA (Maine Educational Assessment) scores. What is being gained is a deeper stakeholder understanding of what is truly involved in the educational, managerial, and organizational realms of schools and a more genuine appreciation for the complexity of the interaction between these dynamic realms. It is this level of understanding that is essential in order to move beyond quantitative measures of high-stakes tests to a recognition that these scores, in fact, do not tell all that much about a school district. The complexity of the education business requires a savvy and sophisticated consumer, one who can see that the quality of a school or school district can only be evaluated by incorporating and considering multiple measures—both quantitative and qualitative. Qualitative data is crucial and important. Maybe that is one fault of the Total Quality model: an almost complete infatuation with the statistics, percentages, and variance measures and too little emphasis on the dual measures of quality.

Much of what we did borrow and apply from a broadly interpreted Total Quality business model, however, did bring clarity to our work in Falmouth Public Schools. I believe that these same ingredients, incorporated into the process of building a local school accountability system, could also work for other districts, regardless of size and/or location. The process would undoubtedly need to be revised to fit differing circumstances, but the building blocks would essentially remain the same.

Meaningful engagement of stakeholders—students, parents, and community members—must take center stage. A credible and unwavering acknowledgment of their central role in the process is required to set the climate for productive dialogue. The professional educators sitting at the table have to be willing to appreciate that our training and expertise does not always lead us to the answers we need. In fact, sometimes it is because of our training that we do not know that we even have a problem. Diversity of perspective adds strength. Truly collaborative and cooperative partnerships take advantage of all available resources and all communities, it seems to me, do have resources to be shared. Individual agendas are welcome, but there can be no room for hidden agendas in this process. Disbelief may need to be suspended—participants have to trust that high-quality outcomes for students are possible.

Unfortunately, strategic planning has given a bit of a bad name to both strategy building and to plan development. Having a plan, however, and identifying strategies for doing what needs to be done is critical to improving schools. As the saying goes, without a road map, anywhere you end up is fine. But creating local accountability systems has nothing in common with a recreational road trip. While there may be some "low-hanging fruit" (obvious, quick fixes) to be plucked, the most reliable method for making positive improvement and sustainable change is in continuous and incremental steps. Our eighteen-month plan, quite certainly, is not perfect. We do know, however, that it is not bad—in fact, we think it is pretty good. One learning that has been reinforced for me over these past eleven months is this: if you have a pretty good plan, stick with it! Laserlike focus, consistency, a sense of stability, and yes, even comfort have come from staying this course.

What about my hopes for the future? Remember, what is being shared in this chapter is a glimpse at a work in progress. My first hope is that when I reread this chapter two years from now, I do so even more assured that we were on the right track. My second hope is that others who are so inclined now—the risk takers, perhaps—will be convinced enough by either the intuitive appeal of our overall strategy or by our results so far to try their hands at this interesting business of developing a local school accountability system. Those who jump on board can help us write the rest of the story about what impact this approach has on improving student learning in public schools.

NOTES

1. M. Fullan, *Leading in a culture of change* (San Francisco: Jossey-Bass, 2001).
2. Distinguished educators working with the Falmouth Public Schools on the Community Dialogue project include Dr. Thomas Forcella, Superintendent of Schools (Essex, Chester, and Deep River, Connecticut), Dr. Ken Jones, Director and Associate Professor, Teacher Education (University of Southern Maine), Dr. Lynne Miller, Professor of Educational Leadership (University of Southern Maine) and Co-Executive Director, Southern Maine Partnership; Cindy O'Shea, Executive Director of the Casco Bay Educational Alliance; and Dr. Stacy Smith, Associate Professor of Education and Department Chair (Bates College).
3. K. Jones, A balanced school accountability model: An alternative to high-stakes testing, *Phi Delta Kappan* 85, no. 8 (2004): 584–90.
4. P. Senge, *The fifth discipline: The art and practice of the learning organization* (New York: Doubleday, 1990).
5. H. Owen, *Open space technology: A user's guide* (San Francisco: Berrett-Koehler, 1997).
6. P. F. Drucker, Managing oneself, *Harvard Business Review* (March–April): 65–74.

9

A QUESTION OF BALANCE: STATE OVERSIGHT VS. LOCAL OWNERSHIP

Patrick R. Phillips

In the first phase of the standards-based reform movement, during the last decade of the twentieth century, the central organizing policy goal was to achieve both excellence and equity—high standards for all students. Now with both feet firmly planted in the next decade—not to mention a new millennium—educators face a more complex and multidimensional policy landscape. The policy goals of excellence and equity remain high priorities, but added to the landscape five years into the twenty-first century, I have come to believe, is the need to reconcile an increasing emphasis on accountability for outcomes at the state and national levels with what is rapidly becoming the essential challenge for all organizations, businesses, states, and nations: adapt to rapidly changing conditions or face becoming irrelevant.

The currency of the twenty-first century will be, arguably, the ability of both individuals and organizations to apply knowledge in novel problem-solving situations, to mobilize innovation and creativity to respond effectively to new technological, social, environmental, economic, and political realities. As Tom Friedman has suggested, the key to success in a flattened world will be to inspire both adult and young learners to become voracious and passionate about their own learning.[1] These individuals, inhabiting our institutions and economic enterprises, will become the engine for effectively responding to technological, economic, and social forces whose cycles of change are accelerating as never before. Or to carry forward what businesses learned after a decade or more in the quality movement: that only through maximizing personalization, creativity, engagement, and ownership at all levels of the organization is there any hope of achieving excellence and rapid responsiveness to change. (For purposes of this argument, let the term "innovation" stand for this personal and organizational characteristic.)

MAINE'S COMMITMENT TO LOCAL ASSESSMENT AND ACCOUNTABILITY

In ways both overt and subtle, however, the push for accountability for achieving excellence and equity—symbolized by the No Child Left Behind Act of 2001 (NCLB)—has introduced new challenges to those interested in developing organizations deeply imbued with the spirit of innovation. Maine's journey is a case in point. Since the early 1990s, education reform in Maine has followed, for the most part, a pattern largely true across the country. The state has developed a set of rigorous content standards, supported schools and districts in aligning curriculum and instruction with the standards, strengthened graduation requirements, and addressed long-standing financial inequities by introducing a new school funding formula based on providing all districts with sufficient financial support for essential programs and services to achieve the standards.

Where Maine has departed from the vast majority of other states is in our approach to assessment. Rather than base high-stakes accountability decisions for students on the state test, the Maine Educational Assessment (MEA), Maine has invested heavily in building a system of local classroom performance tasks, our Local Assessment System (LAS). This broad approach to accountability for student-level outcomes, however, and Maine's emphasis on local ownership of the tools of accountability, have run headlong into NCLB.

Like many states, Maine has struggled to reconcile existing reform structures with NCLB, in particular the strikingly different approaches to accountability. The overall impact of NCLB's increased emphasis on state identification of low-performing schools, complex rewards and sanctions, and subgroup achievement reporting has been a subtle but profoundly significant externalization of the local sense of accountability. Maine's LAS, though not a *school* accountability device, has embedded in it a number of implicit beliefs about the appropriate balance of external and local authority. Through NCLB, the federal government has taken unprecedented power by requiring even more of a testing regimen and laying out rules for what constitutes "adequate yearly progress" (AYP), a highly qualified teacher, and sanctions for schools in need of improvement. The locus of power and decision making has moved further away from schools and communities. The combination of such federal influence, combined with existing state structures of testing and accountability, has resulted in organizational behavior that is the antithesis of innovation. Indeed, our drive to build accountability structures for achieving state standards has created conditions in schools, school districts, and state agencies that appear to be moving us in the direction of standardization, compliance mentality, and declining optimism that our goals are achievable.

Though much of the rhetoric during the standards-based reform movement has asserted that the presence of standards should not restrict locally based decision making about curriculum and instruction—"common ends, uncommon means," as we have said here in Maine—the reality is that the impact of standards and increasingly complex systems of testing and accountability has made it a daunting task indeed for local educators to resist the overwhelming force of the actions of state education agencies and the federal government. By centralizing the testing system and making it high stakes, external governmental influence has become the deciding factor in curriculum decisions and has had a huge impact in matters of instruction, teacher professionalism, and the classroom environment itself.

Moreover, the tradition of local control of public schools, a form of democracy that has made the United States' system of public education different from most other industrialized countries, is clearly at risk. What is so important about local control of schools? The answer has to do with the purposes of public education in a democracy. As discussed in chapter 1, schools in this country play a significant role in accommodating and welcoming diversity and in providing equitable access to learning for all. The more decisions are made remotely from above, however, the less schools are able to adapt practices to meet the needs of their own special contexts, clients, and circumstances. In order to preserve both the democratic traditions of local control and to enhance client responsiveness, significant control over decisions must remain at the local level.

MAINE STRENGTHENS THE STATE ROLE

Having emphasized the importance of local control, however, one must also acknowledge that great injustices and inequities can be carried out in the name of local control. Witness the Civil Rights Movement of the 1960s, when school segregation, among other things, needed to be overcome by federal intervention. Consider, as well, frequent decisions to track poor and minority students into lower-level classes. Clearly, if our policy goal includes both excellence and equity, some degree of external accountability must be in place to assure that inequities are not permitted to exist without being challenged.

The new challenge, then, for education policymakers and educators from classrooms to district offices is to support the development of conditions in which accountability, local control, and innovation can exist in the same organizational environment. But as the impact of external testing and accountability structures on educators—and the schools and districts in which they work—becomes increasingly clear, it will be necessary to reexamine the intergovernmental power relationships that have resulted in the loss of control and innovation, and construct a new accountability paradigm for policy development and local action. This new paradigm must include a framework for action that addresses each of the key levels of the educational hierarchy: school, district, and the state education agency.

Here in Maine, a first step in engaging local school districts in discussions about a new paradigm for accountability took place during the 2004–2005 school year with a series of workshops titled "Rethinking Accountability." Organized by the Maine Department of Education, with extensive support from the New England Comprehensive Assistance Center in Newton, Massachusetts, the three-part series of daylong workshops sought to establish both a conceptual understanding of the need for a new vision for accountability and a set of practical tools designed to help local districts examine their own existing internal accountability structures and develop more effective ones.

Participants in the Rethinking Accountability series, who had come, for the most part, in district teams consisting of the superintendent, a school board member, a school administrator, a teacher, and a parent, were introduced to a model for locally based, balanced accountability in Session I (summer 2004), along with extensive historical and legal perspectives from a panel of school law attorneys. Most importantly, however, district teams began to examine their own beliefs, practices, and district-level structures in the light of new information gained through workshop presentations and prior reading.

Session II (late fall 2004) shifted the focus from the conceptual to the practical, as teams were provided with several data-analysis tools and corresponding case studies of how districts in Maine are applying such tools. In Session III (spring 2005), participants conducted a self-assessment on the status of key aspects of a balanced model of accountability and developed action plans based on their findings. Evaluations of the workshops indicated that teams found the self-assessment tool a useful bridge between the conceptual model and its practical application. By the end of the three-part series, district teams were better positioned to be effective partners in a broader and reconceptualized accountability network.

Set against the background of a shifting sense of accountability at the local level, a second cornerstone for building a new accountability framework in Maine came about not through direct action by the Maine Department of Education but indirectly through a contentious and often passionate legislative discussion of the implementation of Maine's own system of standards and assessments, the *Learning Results*, and our primary means for accountability, the Local Assessment System (LAS). Since the standards were adopted into law in 1996, state agency staff and local educators have invested thousands of hours and considerable financial resources constructing a locally based system of classroom performance tasks to provide formative data to improve teaching and learning, and as a more formal basis for documenting student achievement of the standards. That summative requirement has resulted in a technical dimension of the LAS, considered essential to build a system with validity and reliability sufficient to withstand potential challenges to denying a student a diploma or other high-stakes decisions during a student's education.

The combined impact of NCLB and the considerable stress on educators stemming from *Learning Results* and LAS implementation led to the introduction of numerous bills in the 2005 legislative session, many of which called for the simplification or outright elimination of the LAS. Another laid the groundwork for the Maine Attorney General to file suit if adequate funds for NCLB are not provided by the federal government. Clearly, the overall impact of state and federal accountability structures resulted in significant resistance to any further implementation efforts without first addressing the problems that had emerged in the first phase of the work.

During the testimony before the Joint Standing Committee on Education and Cultural Affairs of the Maine Legislature on the bills having to do with the *Learning Results*, it became clear that the impact at the district level of implementing the LAS, and other aspects of the system of *Learning Results*, has been far from uniform. Indeed, by the end of the testimony and Education Committee deliberation, the inconsistency of the implementation became an issue unto itself. Teachers from some schools reported having great difficulty in building assessment and accountability structures that were coherent and integrated. New assessments were being dropped into existing units of instruction, with little or no thought about whether students were prepared to demonstrate achievement of the standards. In other districts, however, school officials reported that implementation was proceeding in a logical and coherent manner and encouraged the Education Committee to refrain from taking actions that would take the state in a different direction.

In the end, all of the significant modifications to existing law were contained in a single bill, L.D. 1424, "An Act to Simplify Implementation of Maine's *Learning Results*." In addition to simplifications to the LAS, and delays in implementation timeline for diploma requirements based on achievement of the standards, the bill required the Department of Education to gather information school administrative units (SAUs) on the status of their implementation efforts, a charge that led to the development of the SAU Review Process.

Prior to the changes brought about in 2005 legislative session, accountability for student achievement of the standards rested on the ability of local school units to effectively, and with strong comparability across school units, implement the LAS. This was to be based on interpretation of written guidance provided by the Maine Department of Education and with some degree of technical assistance from both the state and regional professional development service providers. But as the testimony during the session revealed, Maine was far from achieving a standards-based reform system on an equitable or comparable basis across all school units. The SAU Review Process was designed to both gather data on the status of implementation and strengthen capacity at both state and local levels for realizing the core elements of standards-based accountability systems.

Beginning in September 2005, four-person teams, consisting of two Department of Education staff members and two external reviewers from either local school units or professional development service providers, began visits to Maine SAUs to engage in daylong conversations on the status of implementing Maine's Learning Results, using as a guide a self-assessment tool which describe in concrete detail core aspects of effective standards-based learning and accountability systems. The process, which included a visit to all 164 local school units in Maine by January 2006, was primarily formative, designed to build local capacity for self-directed continuous improvement.

Michael Fullan's vision for balanced accountability centers in his notion of "tri-level" development.[2] Each of three distinct levels of the educational infrastructure—school, district, and state—must have capacity to fulfill its role. The Maine Department of Education intends to build internal capacity for monitoring and supporting local districts, on the belief that, as Fullan suggests, a missing piece of our reform structures is updating of the role of the state for the challenges of this new era. If it's about all students, it has to be about all districts. For all districts to be included in a meaningful way, the state is obliged to ensure that appropriate capacity exists for monitoring the implementation status of all districts, and for intervention in those districts that need assistance. In developing greater capacity at the state level, Maine is asserting again that equity is a fundamental principle of standards-based reform. If the SAU Review Process continues, however, it will be crucially important to carry out this state monitoring and intervention process in such a way that promotes and nurtures district level ownership for Maine's educational vision.

The Maine Department of Education, as recently as the early 1990s, was able to conduct periodic (once every five years) school approval visitations to each district in the state. However, due to budget cuts and government efficiency efforts during economic hard times, the department lost the staffing positions that had made such a periodic district review possible. In its absence, the department has emphasized lower-cost strategies that, while commendable in their own right, have proven to be less effective in ensuring consistent implementation. These lower-cost strategies have involved publishing extensive guidance on developing valid and reliable assessment systems, establishing aggressive timelines for shifting to a standards-based high school diploma, and providing one-day, drive-in regional technical assistance events over the past several years. But as the legislative session illustrated, these efforts were no substitute for department involvement in each district. True accountability must be balanced with support.

Richard Elmore developed the idea that accountability systems must be reciprocal—every increment of increased accountability must be balanced with an equal increment of support.[3] Without this fundamental balance, large-scale accountability systems are both unstable and unjust.

The SAU Review Process holds the potential to mark a significant evolutionary step in Maine educational policy, from a system with high expectations and excellent values—but with an accountability system with missing pieces—to a more balanced and effective system that takes into account capacity that must exist at *all* levels of the educational infrastructure. As Fullan argues, the role of the state in addressing inequities across districts cannot be forgotten. By gathering richer data on statewide implementation efforts, the Maine Department of Education and state policymakers will be able to more effectively align resources and technical assistance strategies so as to better ensure equitable and comparable district-level development.

THE NEED FOR BALANCE

Maine's emerging review system will also rest on the premise that external accountability systems must be developed with a clear understanding of what is lost when local ownership of goals and outcomes becomes secondary to national or state control. If the standards-based reform movement of the late twentieth and early twenty-first centuries is to evolve and incorporate influences from the flattened world of Tom Friedman and others who argue that the individual learner must learn how to learn, and *love* to learn how to learn, what, then, can states do to enhance the likelihood that local educational units produce *that* kind of outcome?

Are we seeing the twilight of the standards-based reform era, a construct that, because it has produced too much compliance mentality and too little of the organizational characteristics necessary to produce teachers and students who are enthralled by the learning process, must evolve into a system that strikes a better balance between standardization and innovation? I would argue in the affirmative, that in a similar way to Friedman's realization that while he had been paying attention to the economic and cultural aspects of the early 2000s, the world has suddenly thrust upon us a fundamentally different set of challenges. The problem, of course, is that many of our existing challenges will remain with us, most notably the urgent necessity of achieving greater equity in outcomes to ensure that a much larger percentage of our young people are sufficiently well prepared for the twin challenges of globalization and the unprecedented pace of technological change.

Over the past year, I have been working on a simple mental construct that almost always produces a sense of resonance and recognition among those with whom I have shared the idea. The interaction shown in figure 9.1 is my attempt at articulating the tension between policies founded on our commitment to equity and the urgent need to push our systems toward individualization and innovation.

As we struggle to integrate features of the world as it is rapidly coming to be, this tension between what we do in the name of equity and what we do in the name of individual customization, I believe, will form the next great challenge for local, state, and national policymakers. Seen in a somewhat different light, I believe that if we do not maximize aspects of the system on the right side of the graphic shown in figure 9.1, we have no hope of achieving the equity envisioned as the goal of the standards-based reform depicted on the left.

Against this background, the discussion of balanced accountability takes on new significance. In an era when the emerging paradigm for

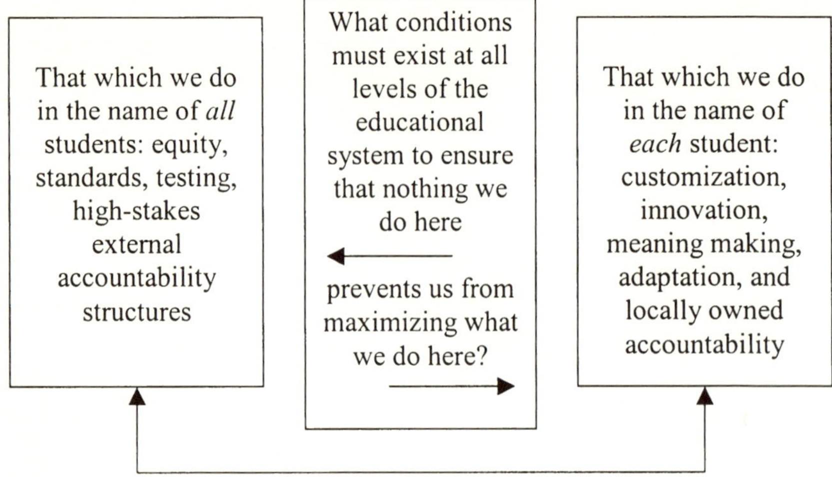

Figure 9.1. Tension between Policies.

personal and organizational success revolves around learning and innovation, accountability structures must remain primarily as close as possible to the point of contact with individual students. Moreover, the roles of state and federal levels must be evaluated in the light of how they might or might not enhance innovation at the local level. The actions of policymakers to hold schools and districts accountable for achieving state and federal educational goals must reconsider the unintended outcomes of existing structures that in recent years have tipped the balance away from the local level. Sharing accountability in ways that restrict actions at higher levels of government to those that are necessary to ensure the development of district-level capacity for serving the needs of all students, those that maximize the likelihood that accountability for equitable outcomes will emerge from local educators, represents the path forward.

For this approach to shared accountability to succeed, where our current top-down methods have failed, several key capacities must be strengthened at the local level. First, local school leaders, from school boards and superintendents to principals and teacher-leaders, must articulate a shared commitment to building more responsive and data-driven practices that place continuous improvement of outcomes as a first-order priority. In addition to the identification and articulation of the idea, leaders must then ensure that effective practices are put in place to carry out this vision. Data systems will need to be strengthened and the skills necessary for their effective use enhanced. Communications programs, particularly those that permit parent, student, and public interaction with school officials around outcomes, must evolve well beyond what currently exists in most districts. Though the list of critical features necessary for truly shared accountability at the local level would certainly be longer than the elements noted here, a final feature for this argument cannot go without mention. If the culture in schools among professional staff does not embody an authentic commitment to collective reflection and action in support of all students achieving learning targets, then all else that happens—at any level of the educational enterprise—is destined for minimal impact or failure.

As the Maine Department of Education prepares to confront, and we hope embrace, the next set of evolutionary challenges to prepare our students for a flattened world, our first goal must be to do no harm. As we seek to build greater understanding and commitment among local educators, the crucial question we must ask ourselves is: Will our actions make it more or less likely that passionate teaching and engaged learning, sufficient to the challenges of a flattened world, will take place in Maine classrooms?

POSTSCRIPT

During his State of the State Address in early January 2006, Governor John E. Baldacci directed Education Commissioner Susan A. Gendron to carry out a moratorium on Maine's Local Assessment System, thus adding an abrupt shift in direction to events described in this chapter. Also in mid-January 2006, the Maine Department of Education completed its School Administrative Unit Review Process involving day-long visits by four-member teams to over 160 school units. At the time this manuscript was entering the final editing stages, Commissioner Gendron was preparing a comprehensive report to the Education Committee of the Maine Legislature on the status of implementation of the Learning Results and the Local Assessment System.

NOTES

1. T. Friedman, *The world is flat: A brief history of the 21st century* (New York: Farrar, Straus and Giroux, 2005).

2. M. Fullan, *Leadership and sustainability: Systems thinkers in action* (Thousand Oaks, Calif.: Corwin Press, 2005).

3. R. Elmore, *Bridging the gap between standards and achievement: Imperative for professional development in education* (Washington, D.C.: Albert Shanker Institute, 2002).

10

THINKING AHEAD

Ken Jones

"Just because it hasn't happened yet, doesn't mean it isn't true." A colleague offered this piece of wisdom to me recently as we discussed various possibilities for school reform and renewal. I took heart in that, as I sometimes lose hope that things will change for the better. I get struck with how we seem to lack not only the will and the investment to significantly renew our schools but also the imagination. It's as if we are locked into what we have known and can't get free to try something entirely new. At least this seems true on the large-scale level. As this book and many others illustrate, there are many excellent and promising efforts being made on the small-scale and local levels.

What is disturbing is that many of the school and district innovations that have been created over the past few years stand a good chance of being squelched by what is playing out on the larger scale. As state and national governments define school accountability in very standardized and coercive ways, the opportunities to learn from local innovations are lost. This is clearly bad strategy. One might hope that policymakers would understand the need to avoid overcontrolling local initiative and decision making, for this has been at the root of the business-led quality movement for years. Why do they not apply some of the same thinking to schools, as Superintendent George Entwistle does (chapter 8)? Why does the present test-based system of school accountability continue to have such a hold on our thinking when there are better alternatives already in play, as seen, for example, in the Nebraska local assessment system (chapter 2), school visitations such as those used in NEASC (chapter 7), and the organized oversight of nongovernmental community agencies around the country (chapter 6)? The testing industry seems to have an unthinking monopoly on defining what a quality school is.

Perhaps the overreliance on standardized tests is due to the fact that our society has developed an almost religious belief in the methods of "science" as an objective means of arriving at the truth. But such scientism belies the fact that even scientific knowledge is always tentative, growing, and changing with new discoveries and understandings. The recent popular movie *What the Bleep Do We Know?* makes it clear that as scientists explore the subatomic world of quantum physics and the celestial world of astrophysics, they are more and more confronted with mysteries and nonlogical realities that cannot always be explained.[1] In fact, it appears that the deeper scientists go with their organized and logical systems of inquiry, the more they encounter commonalities with other ways of knowing, including intuitive, interpretive, and spiritual. Yet in our Western world, we hold these other ways of knowing suspect, too subjective and idiosyncratic to warrant credibility. Perhaps this mind-set underlies the continued belief in standardized testing as an "objective" methodology.[2]

While policymakers tend to trust testing, they also seem to mistrust teachers. This, even though, as Barnett Berry shows in chapter 4, the public solidly supports the teaching profession. To be sure, we have all had teachers who didn't live up to the schooling responsibility entrusted to them, whether that be academic, professional, or interpersonal. We know that the teaching profession must be continuously fed and nurtured, like a garden, in order to be vital—and trustworthy. But this is not a reason to believe in the pejorative characterization so often given to teachers as a whole—that they are not committed to student learning and need to be prodded with manipulative accountability mechanisms. This mistrust and negative image does not come, as Phi Delta Kappa/Gallup polls consistently show, from those who have children in the schools.[3] Parents tend to believe in their children's teachers.

While other professions such as law and medicine are given the societal respect and license—and trust—to establish and monitor standards for accountability, the teaching profession is not. Of course, schools are in a different position than law and medical offices—they are tax-supported public institutions. This means that the public, not just parents, has a vested interest and a prerogative to ensure school accountability. But this public accountability need not be determined, as it has been, only through forms of external auditing. There are credible ways to include the judgments of education professionals and use internal as well as external sources of evidence for school accountability. Indeed, if we were more trusting of our teachers and school administrators, this would be the case, as it is in many other places around the world. A number of years ago, I was telling the superintendent of a Canadian school district about the high-stakes accountability system that had been devised in Kentucky. She listened carefully and then quietly commented, "You Americans just don't trust each other, do you?"

In fact, mistrust may be a general hallmark of our society, not just something that turns up in our thinking about teachers and schools. One does not have to scratch very deeply in this country to uncover the injustices, racism, classism, unbridled capitalism, and other forms of exploitation that destroy trust. In this respect, as in so many others, our schools are simply a microcosm of the larger society.

Finally, let us acknowledge another reason that the current system of school accountability does not change. It actually benefits certain elements of our society—the privileged and the powerful. Despite its name, the No Child Left Behind Act (NCLB), by relying so strictly on test-based accountability, serves those who have always tested well and discriminates against those who have not. We have known for many years that those who most succeed on standardized tests, with some notable exceptions, are middle- and upper-class whites. If this is the only means of holding schools accountable, we can predict, almost by zip code, which schools will turn up as failing schools: inner-city schools, poor rural schools, and those with high concentrations of students who speak English as a second language. If these are the schools from which resources are withheld because of poor test results, how can we say we are leaving no children behind? How can we claim that this approach fosters equity? If we purport to give all students a fair chance at success, this is not the way. The current law and school accountability approach is undemocratic in design if not intent.

What can we do to revise this law so that it can live up to its name? The key is to reconceptualize what it means for a school to be accountable. Further, we must not just hold schools accountable, but must enact a system of reciprocal accountability that holds all levels of government—local, state, and national—responsible for our schools. At the heart of this redesign must be some new propositions, based on underlying democratic values. The propositions I describe below have been underlying currents throughout the chapters of this book. Let us now make them explicit.

PROPOSITIONS FOR A DEMOCRATIC SYSTEM OF SCHOOL ACCOUNTABILITY

In chapter 1 of this book, I present some specifics about what schools should be accountable for and to whom they should be accountable. Then I lay out a four-component model for school accountability, derived from a quality-oriented business model. Throughout this book, my coauthors have fleshed out what is meant by these components and how they can be realized in practice. It isn't that these components are new to the thinking of those already involved with improving and renewing schools; it is that they haven't been joined together to articulate a bona fide school accountability model with a coherent strategy for action. In what follows, I attempt to move from model to action. Let us first examine three propositions that support the proposed actions.

All Students Should Be Engaged, Supported, and Challenged

Jean Whitney in chapter 3 helps us to understand the implications of the sometimes fuzzy concept called *opportunity to learn*. She not only describes the issue as it has been discussed in the literature and negotiated in court cases, ranging from adequate school financing to issues of access, but also makes a strong case that students are not given legitimate opportunities to learn until they are engaged and supported in meaningful work. It is not enough to simply provide access. In my work with practicing teachers, I can confirm that many teachers are aware of this need and are continuously trying to understand how best to engage their students. They know this is the problem that must be solved if we are to raise student learning to higher standards.

But the challenge is great and complex. The simple fact is that learning cannot be done for someone else. Teachers cannot *cause* learning to happen for their students. They can organize things, creating physical, emotional, and cognitive conditions that help students to make connections to subject matter. They can foster human relationships that enable students to feel at ease and learn in social contexts, as emphasized by many learning theorists. They can approach teaching in the classroom with an expertise that uses clear expectations, ongoing feedback, modeling, and a host of well-known pedagogical practices. All of these can be thought of as providing opportunities for students to learn, with the underlying purpose of engaging students so that they will, in fact, learn.

But can teachers absolutely guarantee that all students will learn a given curriculum to a given level by a given date as measured by a given test? Not very likely, especially given the many variables that go into the learning process, ranging from students' backgrounds to their interests and types of intelligence, to their present life circumstances. This is why testing alone is not enough to understand the whole story of whether teachers and schools are behaving accountably. Understanding what teachers and schools are doing to address their own specific context is crucial to making an accountability determination. Would we say that a privileged suburban school whose students score well on state tests is acting accountably if their students are spending most of their time on a drill-and-practice curriculum? Would we say that a poor rural school whose students test poorly on state tests is not acting accountably if their students are engaged in real-life investigations that use important subject-matter content and processes? Tests simply do not provide the information needed to understand how a school is or is not engaging and supporting its students in challenging and engaging work.

It is important to realize that engaging students with meaningful opportunities to learn is a schoolwide responsibility, not just the province of individual teachers. Further, this is something that should be a shared responsibility with districts and states. Schools should work on organizational capacity, as described by Melody Shank in chapter 5, in order to increase the opportunities for students to learn. Districts should provide direction and leadership (chapter 8), attend to teacher quality through their hiring, professional development, evaluation practices, and climate of teacher professionalism, as seen in Denver, for example (chapter 4), and find ways to engage the local community (chapters 6 and 8). States should monitor local systems and provide adequate resources and guidance (chapter 9).

At the school level, how do we measure whether students are being engaged, supported, and challenged? The most obvious way is to ask the students, of course. An interesting approach to this is the online report-card system for schools developed by UCLA.[4] Here, students and parents respond to surveys, "grading" their own schools in public on categories such as learning materials used, democracy in the classroom, teacher quality, access, engagement, safety, and student learning. Another important data source would be to evaluate students' successful transition to postsecondary experiences. Did the school or district provide the opportunities that enabled students to succeed in college, work, or other life choices?

Katharine Pence in chapter 7 shows us how a standards-based system of school accreditation includes a focus on student engagement and opportunities to learn, especially through the lenses of the curriculum and instruction standards. Knowing whether schools are engaging students must be done through school visitations, not through the proxy of testing. Direct observation of classrooms and student work is needed, along with interviews with teachers, administrators, students, and parents, and other qualitative methods of data collection. Shadowing students as they go from one class to the next throughout the day can provide powerful insights into how students are or are not being engaged by their teachers. The NEASC accreditation system that Pence describes is not one of a kind. In fact, it was adapted from the British Inspectorate system, which has had a long history of using such visits as a form of school accountability.

Tom Wilson worked with NEASC to revise its accreditation process in 1998 and designed the Rhode Island system of school visitations that is currently used in its School Accountability for Learning and Teaching (SALT) system.[5] He has developed a research methodology for visitations that includes training in the use of professional judgment, evidence, and team consensus. He describes the crucial role of professional judgment in the process:

> It is commonly believed that the evaluation of school performance must be "objective," usually meaning that judgment must be excluded from the evaluation process as much as possible. It is commonly believed that in order for the measurement of one school to be fair, it must be as consistent as possible with how every other school is measured. Most educational inquiry procedures try to minimize the use of judgment in service of the belief that research methodology should ensure objectivity and consistency. Thus, the explicit use of judgment in the visit seems strange at first. . . .
>
> Professional judgment is essential in our courts and legal systems, which most would agree are our most important and effective systems of public accountability. The judgment of a jury is not only central to executing justice, but also to developing case law. Our legal system assumes that professional judgment is legitimate. . . .
>
> In the school visit, the explicit use of professional judgment not only makes the findings valuable, but it also makes the team's inquiry possible. Other research methodologies are not designed to do that. Professional judgment makes it possible for the team to consider the complex, real life of a school in real time, to make sense of the school within the severe limitations of the school visit, and to build conclusions about how well the school is performing that are both legitimate and constructive for the school. . . .
>
> Individual judgment that is not tested or challenged—that sees only what it knows—holds little value for an inquiry. The collection of evidence, the team's deliberations, and the requirement for deliberate consensus agreement all refine and check the team's judgment.[6]

Wilson also discusses the role of standards in a school visitation. While they are important and useful, he says, they must not be the driver of the process:

> Standards can provide useful clear areas of focus for the team. But when in the name of precision or objectivity they become the framework for what the team is supposed to see, this controls or circumscribes the judgment of the team. When the team is asked to set aside or distort its own judgment and see the school only from the vantage point of the standard,

> rather than from how well the school's actual standards are functioning, this limits the potential value of the visit as a method.
>
> Requiring a team to respond to too many standards (or parts of standards) can result in limiting the legitimacy of the visit by forcing the team to sort out the standards, rather than to sort out the school.
>
> In the words of a wise English inspector, a team member should "know what he sees, rather than see what he knows."[7]

Wilson's emphasis of practitioner judgment is a critically missing piece in our current accountability system. If we want to engage, support, and challenge students, we must clearly do the same for teachers. And who better to do that than teachers themselves?

The Teaching Profession Should Be Strengthened

The current accountability approach weakens the teaching profession rather than strengthens it. Not that the emphasis on content knowledge in NCLB defining the highly qualified teacher is ill conceived. It isn't. Improvement in content knowledge can only help teachers do their jobs better. As can improvement in instructional technique, better understanding of students, greater facility in developing engaging work for students, greater assessment literacy, better methods of teacher evaluation and support, and better ways of collaborating with each other and with parents and community members. There should be no doubt that teaching in public schools is a very demanding and complex task. The need to invest in the ongoing, job-embedded professional development of our teachers cannot be overstated.

If we are serious about improving and renewing our schools, we must begin with upgrading the teaching profession. As Barnett Berry says in chapter 4, this means not just improving salaries and working conditions but giving voice to teacher perspectives, acknowledging teacher expertise, and empowering teachers to make important decisions about what happens in schools and classrooms. With the present form of accountability, teachers are often treated as technicians following the prerequisites of state testing and standards rather than as leaders making important decisions about teaching and learning.

Back to trust. Can teachers be trusted to make such crucial decisions when such important changes in schooling are called for? The answer is twofold: there is no effective alternative if we want classroom life to actually change for students; and we need not rely on trust alone—we can build school capacity for supporting and holding teachers accountable.

On the first point, let us be mindful of the reality that in any given classroom, the teacher is the leader of the students. The question is what kind of a leader do we need in the room in order to develop the skills in our students that we deem critical for a democratic society? Do we want a teacher who follows orders from above and demands the same of her students? Or one who can make informed decisions on behalf of her students? One who is compelled to move all students through a prescribed curriculum on a given timetable or one who is skilled in working with the enormous diversity of students in a way that honors who and where they are and how they learn? One who must rely on outside experts to tell her how well her students are learning or one who knows how to assess learning and adjust instruction accordingly within her own classroom? If we want students who are learning how to acquire knowledge deeply, are capable of thinking well, and can make well-informed decisions, then what alternative is there other than to provide teachers who can do things themselves? We cannot treat teachers as if they are obedient troops in an army unless the purpose of schools is to create good soldiers. Democratic schools need highly professional teachers.

Secondly, let us agree that trust must always be balanced with systems of support, feedback, and evaluation. In this book, we have seen some excellent examples of these kinds of systems. Melody Shank in chapter 5 describes in great detail the culture and structure in schools that develop the capacity for change, including a teacher-led system of salary review. She helps us understand that collaborative learning organizations can provide the means for teachers to deliver instruction that is standards based and full of equitable opportunities to learn. Delwyn Harnisch and his teacher colleagues in chapter 2 show that a teacher network focused on developing professional learning communities can be transformative to teachers and administrators alike. Barnett Berry in chapter 4 illustrates how teacher evaluation in Denver provides a means for holding teachers accountable for addressing new goals and objectives for student learning.

On the larger scale, a promising development is that many teacher unions have made great strides in fostering responsible professionalism on the part of teachers. The Teacher Union Reform Network (TURN), consisting of twenty-one local affiliates of both NEA and AFT, has been a leader in redefining the role of the teacher union so that it sees itself as responsible not just for the bread-and-butter issues of salaries and working conditions of teachers but also for student learning and the collective stewardship of schools. TURN describes itself in the following way:

> the past adversarial relationship among union leaders, teachers, and administrators must be replaced with a compact that says, "We are all in this together." Everyone recognizes that this will be difficult, but succeeding in this new and unpredictable environment can only be assured by the mutual effort of administrators, union leaders and teachers, and the creation of a new social framework to hold it together.[8]

One way that a number of teacher unions in TURN have improved teacher accountability is through establishing systems of peer review. Dal Lawrence, longtime president of the Toledo Federation of Teachers, member of TURN, and developer of a seminal peer review system of teacher evaluation, has this to say about the beneficial effects of giving teachers the professional responsibility of conducting peer evaluations:

> It should be obvious that without teacher ownership there will be no buy-in to standards. The isolated world in which teachers perform fits nicely with the top-down model of school governance. When Mrs. Wright has problems down the hall, it's always the principal's responsibility. Contrast that to medicine or other professions where a sense of concern for competence exists within an entire professional community.
>
> By transferring responsibility for instructional competence to teachers, the Toledo Plan created a professional model where all teachers have an interest in teaching success. That is a mighty blow at teacher isolation with its fragmented sense of responsibility for effective work that dominates our schools today.[9]

The proposition here is not that teachers should be left to their own judgments in a laissez-faire type of teacher professionalism. There are well-established standards for what constitutes a professional teacher, including those developed for beginning teachers under the Interstate New Teacher Assessment and Support Consortium (INTASC), used by many teacher education and state certification programs, and those developed by National Board for Professional Teaching Standards (NBPTS) for experienced teachers.[10] These standards can and should be used as a means for guiding teacher decision making and supporting meaningful evaluation practices.

School Accountability Should Be Primarily Local

This proposition gets at the heart of the power issue involved in school accountability. A key component in the model proposed in this book is that students, parents, and the community are the primary clients of the school and therefore should be the primary "customer," as George Entwistle would put it, for an accountability system. With the current system of school accountability, schools are being held accountable to the state and federal governments. Control has been wrested from local boards to the more remote arena of legislators and state department officials. It is critical that this trend be reversed if we mean to ensure a democratic role for schools. Centralized bureaucratic control may be common in the corporate and governmental world, but for schools this will not provide the local empowerment that is needed to ensure that students are engaged in meaningful work and that parents' desires and hopes for their children are honored. Certainly top-down command systems of governance do not fit the need for schools that meet the needs of increasingly diverse communities, nor do they fit the quality management principle that those closest to the work should be responsible for making decisions. In the case of schools, the important decisions are not just about instructional means toward prescribed ends, but about the interpretations of the ends themselves. As Norm Fruchter and Kavitha Mediratta show in chapter 6, these decisions can and should include community representatives and organizations.

One step in the right direction toward reversing the centralization trend prevalent in school accountability may be seen in Nebraska and Maine, where local assessment systems have been developed, in lieu of high-stakes statewide tests. The local assessment systems in both states have been designed to show student proficiency in meeting state standards. While very labor intensive on the part of teachers, these systems allow local contexts and teacher judgments to be used in assessing student learning. Assessments are created for and embedded in local curricula, rather than adjusting local curricula to meet the requirements of an external state test. As shown in chapter 2, teacher professional development in this context can focus clearly and intensely on matters of teaching and learning. Moreover, the validity of inferences about student learning is greatly enhanced by having multiple assessments given over a period of time in a variety of modalities, including performance-based assessments designed to measure thinking and communication skills.

What about the validity and reliability of such local assessment systems? Are they up to par? One again we return to trustworthiness questions—of objectivity vs. subjectivity and external vs. internal measures. In Nebraska, a state panel is convened yearly to review assessments and the assessment processes in each local school district. This technical review panel consists of respected measurement specialists throughout the country. School accountability is determined not only by this expert panel's review of the quality of the district assessment process but also by the students' performance on the standards. Both evaluative processes, the assessment quality review and the student performance review, are reported to the public annually. In Maine, a process of school visitations aimed at evaluating local assessment systems has just been piloted, as described in chapter 9.

In addition to local assessment system, there must also be a local accountability system that serves as the primary determinant of whether schools are operating responsibly. Otherwise, conflicting demands from different levels of government make for an incoherent and conflicting system. Assessment information, validated by the state, should be reviewed by a local entity, whether it be the school board, a local council such as the one described by Phil Schelchty in chapter 1, or a representative group of community organizations, as described in chapter 6. It is this local group that should then decide how accountably a given school is behaving and what next steps should be taken for the sake of improvement and renewal. This group should also look at data provided by school visitations. Such a local accountability process would utilize human judgment about school successes and failures rather than decisions made automatically by numerical systems of Annual Yearly Progress (AYP). As in medicine and other professional arenas, and as Tom Wilson points out, data should inform decisions, not make them.

What about checks and balances to ensure that local assessment and accountability systems hold true to established state standards and concerns related to a new model for school accountability? How will we ensure that schools and districts, for example, are demonstrating accountability with respect to student learning, opportunities to learn, responsiveness to students, parents, and community, and organizational capacity? This is a role for the state to play.

More and more the state has assumed the role of rule-maker and enforcer for a centralized form of school accountability. As local forms of accountability take on more of a leading role, the state should focus less on regulatory control and instead provide more guidance, support, and monitoring. Local boards and councils—indeed, teachers and administrators as well—will need to understand the new terms of accountability. They will need to be convened and networked to discuss guidelines concerning the components of a new school accountability model. It was just such state leadership in Maine, with the convening of the Rethinking Accountability meetings, that helped George Entwistle's district to reframe its local accountability efforts described in chapter 8.

Districts and schools will also need to be supported with on-site technical assistance, and perhaps coaching, upon request. And they will need to be monitored to ensure that attention is focused on accountability components and progress is being made. Wilson explains that school visitations can and should fulfill both support and monitoring functions:

> It is critical to maintain both monitoring and supporting in a visit protocol. This will strengthen the team's ability to generate significant knowledge about how well the school works. Maintaining an effective tension between these will require a shift in the common belief that monitoring and support are by their very nature separate. Americans tend to believe that external information is necessary for external monitoring and that supporting the internal life of a school requires manipulation of its internal process. The visit methodology posits that it is most effective and efficient to do both at the same time. Good information and knowledge about a school makes that possible.[11]

But where will the accountability guidelines come from in the first place? In chapter 1, I made the point that defining what school accountability means has never been fully discussed in a public forum. The essential questions have not been posed for all to consider: For what should schools be held accountable? To whom? By what means? It should be the role of the state to create public forums that address these questions—face-to-face, on TV and radio, through Web-based surveys, and whatever other means are needed to include all in the conversation. Such a series of events and outreach efforts could provide the information, engagement, and ownership needed for the public support of a new system of school accountability.

It is interesting to speculate about the continued role of the federal government in all of this. Since NCLB is now in statute and regulation, it appears that the federal role will forevermore be an active one, no longer leaving states to their own prerogatives regarding public education. Perhaps establishing a new way of funding education that overcomes the inequities of the property tax system now in place would be a proper role for this level of government. In addition, it would make sense that there would be an information, support, and monitoring function at this level relative to state efforts, just as states would provide this for local schools and districts. What should not be the case is that the federal government should preempt local accountability decisions through prescribed system components, assessment or accountability methodologies, curricula, or instructional approaches. Support for research would be most appropriate at the federal level, provided this research is also not prescribed in ways that narrow the flow of information, undermine local approaches, or limit methodologies to the quantitative or experimental forms that are associated with the hard sciences, but not always appropriate for human endeavors such as education.

SOME ACTION STEPS

Where do we go from here? As Patrick Phillips suggests in chapter 9, we should first make sure we are doing no harm. Then we should seek to create balance where the present system is badly out of balance. Then, I would add, for the sake of building a new, dynamic form of school accountability designed for improving and renewing schools for the future, we must move forward with new and better ways of working together across levels of government, institutions, and constituencies. We must rely more on partnerships and less on mistrust.

Doing No Harm

I recognize that the legislators who have enacted NCLB and various state versions of high-stakes testing may be loath to admit the severe problems the current accountability approach has created. We often hear the argument about giving this new experiment adequate time, staying the course, and not giving in to "soft bigotry of low standards." But we must insist that an honest look be taken—and made quite public—at the consequences of these policies, especially for the disadvantaged and underserved of our society, the very people such an approach claims to assist. We must hear the voices of students and teachers and respect their viewpoints. We must stop blaming the victims of our damaging policies.

We can first stop doing harm by immediately removing high-stakes consequences from all the testing that is going on. No more rewards and sanctions for schools and districts, threats of withheld funds, or support for parent abandonment of public schools based on testing. No more threats to students of not receiving a diploma based on external standardized testing or to teachers of losing their jobs or having their school reconstituted, based on testing. No more declarations of failing schools. The laws must be changed as soon as possible to remove the real damage being done to our schools every day.

The second thing we can do to stop doing harm is to reallocate and provide more resources to our schools, students, and educators. Stop siphoning so much needed educational funding into testing and tutoring corporations. Invest instead in the professional development of teachers and administrators, enabling them to hone their crafts so that schooling is more engaging and productive for students and local assessments are valid and reliable. More funds are needed to ensure that students have adequate and equitable opportunities to learn, especially given the higher standards for learning that we envision. Certainly more funds are needed to support the strengthening of the teaching profession.

At present, schools are living and working with enormously unfair expectations, given the amount of resources that are provided. We have created a recipe for failure by combining ever-rising expectations for test results on an arbitrary timetable with a lack of support for the enormous job being asked.

Finding Balance

The current approach to school accountability is unbalanced. It looks only at outcomes, not processes. It gives credibility only to quantifiable data, and dismisses the information that could be gained through qualitative methods. It privileges an external source of assessment and accountability over an internal one. It favors putative objective and scientific means over professional and community judgments.

The single, most important change we can make to achieve balance in evaluating school accountability is to implement systems of school visitations. These systems must be done collaboratively with school practitioners, not as a policing action from above. Otherwise they will become one more top-down accountability mechanism, bound to elicit gamesmanship rather than true portrayals of schools. The SALT system presently at work in Rhode Island might serve as a model for other state efforts. Here, the state contracts with an organization outside the line of bureaucratic authority to train teachers and administrators to conduct visits and write reports about the status of the school. Akin to the NEASC review described in chapter 7, such visits not only provide important information to outside audiences but also serve as a vital form of professional development for practitioners. In a recent survey of those conducting SALT reviews, 80 percent of the teachers and 74 percent of the administrators reported that the experience was "the most powerful professional development experience they have ever had."[12] Thus, this process can serve to broaden the base of information about school accountability as well as contribute to the professionalization of teaching.

School visitations are critical in order to gauge the opportunities to learn that are being provided to students. Testing simply cannot serve as a proxy for the empirical understanding provided by direct observation and inquiry.[13] They can also be instrumental, as Katharine Pence explains in chapter 7, in developing the organizational capacity of a school.

How else might one know if a school has developed the capacity and habit for "double looping" deemed by Melody Shank in chapter 5 to be crucial to a collaborative learning organization? Recall her definition: "Double-loop learning is an examination of not only what worked to achieve intended outcomes, but of the assumptions and consequences of actions and additional possibilities." It is this kind of professional accountability for which we should be striving. Indeed, without this kind of internal accountability, it is very unlikely that any form of external accountability will have an effect.[14]

A workable model for a balanced system of accountability that includes a school visitation process has been proposed by the Massachusetts-based Coalition for Authentic Reform in Education (CARE).[15] It calls for four operational components:

- Local authentic assessments that are gateways to graduation, approved by regional boards and based on the Common Core of Learning and a streamlined set of competencies;
- A school quality review model to assess the effectiveness of school practices, based on models in Britain, Boston's Pilot Schools, Rhode Island, and Massachusetts's charter schools;
- Standardized testing solely in literacy and numeracy, to provide one method for tracking progress of schools from year to year; and
- Annual reporting by schools to their communities, using defined indicators that focus on equal opportunity and access to knowledge for all students.

Moving Forward

We must initiate and follow through with efforts to build a more comprehensive, coherent, and democratic system of school accountability. States need to transform their present regulatory roles into collaborative ones and convene the public to inform and gather information for developing the new system. Districts and schools need to develop internal accountability cultures and structures that can provide a firm foundation for a localized system of school accountability. Parent and community organizations need to be included in local school accountability systems. Local and classroom assessment systems need to be developed and implemented. Teacher organizations need to continue reforming themselves to engage more fully with professionalization efforts, including mentoring, peer review, and advancement within the ranks based on performance.

Work of this magnitude speaks of the need for leadership at all levels. One can only imagine what might happen if the president of this country and the governors of our states devoted themselves and our tax dollars as much to a better model of school accountability as they have to the one that is now proving to be so debilitating. Of course it will take more commitment than that.

A HUMAN ENTERPRISE

Schools cannot be separated from the larger society. They reflect what society is, even as they are asked to change it. Reflecting on this truth, it seems important to think about the values of our society that lie beneath the current system of school accountability. Are they the kinds of values held by the majority of Americans? Do they spring from democratic beliefs? To me, the way we now hold schools accountable reflects a fundamentalist kind of "family values," not the kind of family values held by those I know and love. When we think about the children and adolescents in our schools, do we think they need care and support to grow into healthy, bright, and independent adults or do we think they need more discipline and "rigor?"[16] When we disempower teachers, mostly women, do we exercise a form of male dominance? Does our strict adherence to the black-and-white world of test scores reflect an affinity for absolutism? Do we think of struggling public schools as "bad" or shameful? I do not believe these perspectives on schools are shared by the majority of families in this country—but I do think they are behind the current way of holding schools accountable.

Thinking about schooling in terms of families and parenting brings the students to the fore. I work with preservice teacher candidates, including many graduate students changing careers in midlife. As they try to develop a set of educational perspectives and values that may serve as compass points in their new careers, I encourage them to ask themselves what they would want for their own children. Too often, I think, we think of schooling in terms of abstracts—curricula, pedagogy, assessments, and so on. What we need to do is to put a child's face in the picture—to see, if we can, through the eyes of our children. And think of these children as our own, not just other people's children.[17]

A few years ago, Anne Wheelock, Damian Bebell, and Walt Haney conducted a most remarkable study on student perceptions about the high-stakes Massachusetts Comprehensive Assessment System (MCAS) that used children's drawings as the source of data. The researchers asked students in fourth, eighth, and tenth grades to "draw a picture of yourself taking the MCAS." They coded 411 drawings according to emerging categories and analyzed the findings. Among the positive affective responses were depictions of diligence and persistence (21.5 percent of the fourth graders compared to 8.3 percent of the eighth and tenth graders), thinking and problem solving (7.3 percent of the drawings), and confidence (5.4 percent of the drawings). On the negative side were depictions of anxiety (13.4 percent of the drawings), anger and hostility (10 percent of the drawings), boredom (4.9 percent of the drawings), sadness, disappointment, and pessimism (2.7 percent of the drawings), and loss of motivation and withdrawal from testing (5.3 percent of the drawings). From this study, the researchers concluded:

> MCAS drawings suggest that high-stakes testing in Massachusetts does not motivate all students in the same way. While some students may respond to the knowledge that their future life chances depend on their "passing" MCAS by mobilizing their resources and persisting to the end, others may simply give up. Older students and urban students appear to be especially vulnerable to these feelings, perhaps because, anticipating failure for themselves or their friends, they view MCAS less as a challenge than a source of intimidation and humiliation.[18]

Intimidation and humiliation. Certainly not what I want for my dear child, nor would most parents want this for their children. And yet we hear stories over and over about young children getting sick, breaking down in tears, buckling from the pressure we have put on them with these tests. Older students are more likely to simply drop out. A high school teacher in an Alaskan rural village told me a couple of years ago how the state exit exam was affecting his native students:

> A student told me that the test was just "another way for white people to tell us we're stupid." Some students view almost any assessment by white teachers as a put-down. More testing increases the frequency with which we insult these students, and high-stakes testing increases the anger they feel when they fail. On their first day of high school, three of our students who were in the second class that was supposed to have to pass the exit exam asked, "Why should we come to school when we can never graduate?" They did not believe that they would ever be able to pass the test. Instead of inspiring students to learn as much as they can, the test is inspiring some of them to give up.[19]

I am sick of these kinds of effects on our children and young adults. I don't accept the reasoning that says we must have such bitter medicine to fix our ailing schools. The whole fear-inducing argument that we must bear down on our schools because we are in this life-and-death economic struggle with the rest of the world strikes me as disingenuous and degrading. We know that schools are not the primary factor in a nation's economic prosperity.[20] The appeal to parents that our children will not be able to make a living unless we have this testing regimen is a straw man. Of course we all want schooling that helps our children live the good life. How can intimidating and humiliating them be the way to do that? How can simply subjecting them to more and more standardized testing without improving their opportunities to learn help them attain their goals or guide them in becoming productive members of a democratic society?

I am also sick of the discriminatory nature of the current accountability approach, especially in light of its rhetoric about leaving no child behind. We know that the ill effects of the current system of high-stakes testing impact minorities and the poor the most.[21] There must be a better way to create justice in our schooling.

In fact, we know it is not just schooling that is at issue here and that the problems of schooling cannot be isolated from those that exist in the larger society. The poor are so badly treated in our rich country that it is absurd to think that schooling can act alone to improve their chances in life. In his recent keynote address to the American Education Research

ABOUT THE CONTRIBUTORS

Barnett Berry is the founder and president of the Center for Teaching Quality, Inc., based in Chapel Hill, North Carolina. Dr. Berry's career includes teaching in an urban high school, working as a social scientist at the RAND Corporation, serving as a senior executive with the South Carolina State Department of Education, and directing an education policy center while he was a professor at the University of South Carolina. In the mid- to late 1990s, Dr. Berry played a major role in developing the blue ribbon report of the National Commission on Teaching and America's Future, and then later leading its state policy and partnership efforts. Dr. Berry earned his PhD in educational policy from the University of North Carolina at Chapel Hill, is the author of over one hundred journal articles, book chapters, and commissioned reports on school reform, accountability, and the teaching profession, and serves on boards and in an advisory capacity to a number of organizations dedicated to educational equity and social justice.

George H. Entwistle is currently the superintendent of schools in a growing coastal community outside Portland, Maine. He is passionate in his belief that human resource and organizational development competencies are essential to the effectiveness of public school leaders. In his leadership role as superintendent, he is currently engaged in developing a systems model of local accountability and facilitating organizational planning that is clearly responsiveness to local requirements. His teaching, writing, and research are concentrated in the areas of human resources development, organizational planning strategies, and the creation of truly high-performing organizations. Dr. Entwistle is a faculty member at Boston University's School of Education.

In the past, Dr. Entwistle has held clinical, leadership, and executive positions both in private and public organizations associated with the manufacturing, engineering, public education, higher education, and mental health sectors. He is a member of the Academy of Management and the Association for Supervision and Curriculum Development and sits on the board of directors for the New England School Development Council (NESDEC).

Norm Fruchter is the director of the NYU Institute for Education and Social Policy and Clinical Professor of Education Policy at NYU. For ten years he was the program advisor for education at the Aaron Diamond Foundation. His publications include *Hard Lessons: Public School and Privatization*, *New Directions in Parent Involvement*, and *Choosing Equity: The Case for Democratic Schooling*, as well as two novels, *Coat upon a Stick* and *Single File*.

Fruchter has worked as a senior consultant with the Academy for Educational Development and Advocates for Children of New York, and directed the Institute for Citizen Involvement in Education in New Jersey. He was the cofounder and codirector of Independence High School in Newark, an alternative high school for dropouts, and, for ten years, served as an elected school board member in Brooklyn's District 15.

Michael Fryda received a bachelor of science degree in zoology from the University of Wisconsin in Madison and a master's of secondary teaching and his teaching certification with an endorsement in Biology at the University of Nebraska in Lincoln. He most recently received a second endorsement in assessment through his work with the Nebraska Assessment Cohort. He is in his third year as an educator, teaching general physical science at Westside High School in Omaha, Nebraska. He is active in his department's state assessment writing procedures. The weekly game club that he runs at his school has over fifty active members. The goal of the club is to provide a positive after-school environment for students while expanding critical thinking skills. Michael resides in Lincoln, Nebraska, with his wonderful wife and two cats. He can be reached at mfryda@westside66.org.

Delwyn L. Harnisch is a professor of educational psychology at the University of Nebraska Lincoln (UNL). He is currently a coprincipal investigator of a grant project focused on supporting teacher learning in science and technology and an external program evaluator for an NSF sponsored project. His background and expertise is in measurement, assessment, and program evaluation. At UNL, Dr. Harnisch is currently a senior research scientist for a technology-supported assessment program. Prior to UNL, he spent twenty-five years at University of Illinois at Urbana-Champaign focusing on the integration of technology into the teaching and learning process. He has just completed a five-year term as the editor for the National Council on Measurement in Education (NCME) and developed and directed the NCME website (ncme.org). Dr. Harnisch has authored over 150 research articles and five books.

Mitzi Hoback is director of staff development at Educational Service Unit (ESU) 4 in Auburn, Nebraska. The ESU serves schools in a five-county area in southeast Nebraska. Mitzi has been an educator for thirty years. She was K–12 coordinator for high ability learners for Conestoga Public Schools in Murray and Nehawka, Nebraska, and also taught elementary grades for Conestoga and Weeping Water Public Schools. Mitzi holds a master's degree from Peru State College and endorsements in assessment and gifted education from the University of Nebraska in Lincoln. She is a graduate of the second Nebraska Assessment Cohort (NAC) Program.

Ken Jones is an associate professor and the director of teacher education at the University of Southern Maine. In his career, he has been a middle school teacher, the director of a school-university partnership, an urban district mathematics specialist, and an assistant professor of mathematics education. He was closely involved in the implementation and study of the Kentucky Education Reform Act in the 1990s. His teaching and scholarly interests include school accountability, classroom assessment, mathematics education, teacher education, and professional development. He can be contacted at kjones@usm.maine.edu.

Darin Kelberlau is currently a curriculum specialist for data and technology support in the Elkhorn Public Schools district in Nebraska. Prior to his current position, he spent ten years in the classroom teaching mathematics. He obtained a bachelor of arts degree in mathematics from the University of Nebraska at Lincoln in 1993 and a master's of science degree in curriculum and instruction, specializing in instructional technology, from Peru State College in 2002. Presently he is a doctoral student at the University of Nebraska at Lincoln in the Educational psychology department studying Qualitative and Quantitative Methods in Education. He was a member of the Nebraska Assessment Cohort (NAC) 2002 and remains active with the NAC and Nebraska Leadership for Learning cohorts as a graduate assistant.

Kavitha Mediratta is a senior research scientist at the New York University Institute for Education and Social Policy. She initiated the institute's Community Involvement Program (CIP) in 1995, and was instrumental in developing CIP's dual strategy of building community-driven education policy reform coalitions and expanding the capacity of community organizations to lead effective local school improvement organizing campaigns in New York City. As CIP's director of research, she was the primary author of several recent institute studies, including *Constituents of Change, Community Organizations and Public Education Reform, Parent Power and Urban School Reform, The Story of Mothers on the Move, From Governance to Accountability, Building Relationships That Make Schools Work*, and *Community Organizing for School Reform: How Communities Are Finding Their Voice and Reclaiming Their Public Schools*. Before coming to the institute, Mediratta served as a Warren Weaver Fellow at the Rockefeller Foundation, where she researched community-building approaches to community development, and helped develop a school reform constituency-building funding initiative in New York City. She has also worked as a staff developer in the New York City public schools, and taught upper elementary and middle school science in southern India and in U.S. urban public and private schools.

Monty Neill is currently director of the National Center for Fair and Open Testing (FairTest). He has led FairTest's work on testing in the public schools since 1987. He has initiated national and state coalitions of education, civil rights, and parent organizations to work toward fundamental change in the assessment of students and in accountability. He currently chairs an alliance of dozens of groups working to develop alternatives for use in overhauling federal education law (the No Child Left Behind Act, in particular). He earned a doctorate at Harvard University with his dissertation *The Struggle of Boston's Black Community for Quality and Equality in Education: 1960–1985*. He has taught and been an administrator in preschool, high school, and college.

Among many publications, he is coauthor of *Failing Our Children*, a report analyzing the federal No Child Left Behind Act and providing guidance toward new, helpful accountability systems. He led the National Forum on Assessment in developing *Principles and Indicators for Student Assessment Systems*, signed by over eighty national and regional education and civil rights organizations. He also authored *Implementing Performance Assessments: A Guide to Classroom School and System Reform*, and *Testing Our Children: A Report Card on State Assessment Systems*, the first comprehensive evaluation of all fifty state testing programs.

Katharine Pence obtained a bachelor of arts degree in early childhood education and a master's of arts degree in special education from Saint Joseph College in West Hartford, Connecticut. She also holds an administrative certificate from the University of Southern Maine in Gorham, Maine. Katharine has thirty-two years experience in education, including seventeen years as an elementary principal at Kennebunkport Consolidated School in Kennebunkport, Maine.

During her tenure in Maine School Administrative District #71, Katharine has been actively involved at both the regional and national levels. As a special educator, Katharine served as a facilitator for the special education review system in Maine and she was appointed by then-governor John McKernan to serve as a representative from Maine to the Education Commission of the States. Katharine has been actively involved with the New England Association of Schools and Colleges (NEASC) and routinely facilitates accreditation visits throughout the six-state region. Currently she is a member of the NEASC board of trustees and serves as the chair of the Commission on Public Elementary and Middle Schools.

Patrick Phillips currently serves as the deputy commissioner of the Maine Department of Education. Prior to his current position, Mr. Phillips served as assistant superintendent for MSAD #28 in Camden, Maine, and previously as assistant superintendent in Windham, also in Maine. From 1993–1999, Mr. Phillips served as the principal of the Blue Hill Consolidated School in Blue Hill, Maine. His teaching career spans three decades from the 1970s to the 1990s, in schools from Denver, Colorado, to Easton, Maryland. Across all these roles, Mr. Phillips has sought to develop and promote educational systems that maximize individualization and equitable outcomes. Mr. Phillips makes his home in Camden, Maine.

Melody J. Shank is an associate professor of teacher education at the University of Southern Maine. She has been involved in school reform since 1990, when she began serving as a coach for the Coalition of Essential Schools initiative in Indiana. Her research focuses on the reform of high schools and collaborative teacher learning, especially related to the ways schools can support teacher learning as part of everyday work. As co-investigator for the Strengthening and Sustaining Teachers project in Portland (a project bringing the university, the school district, and the teachers association together to create a continuum of support for teacher development), she focused on the development of mentoring relationships and school structures that support both new teachers and their mentors. Her recent *Educational Leadership* article "Common Time, Common Space, Common Work" highlights the cultural and structural aspects of a collaborative high school that support new teachers.

Dr. Shank also works with secondary teaching interns and partner schools as a site coordinator in the University of Southern Maine's graduate-level teacher education program, the Extended Teacher Education Program (ETEP). Her most recent teacher education initiative is the establishment of a secondary unified general and special education teacher education program, through which candidates will simultaneously pursue preparation as both a special education teacher and content specialist.

Ronald Shope is an associate research professor at the University of Nebraska, Lincoln. He teaches both distance and face-to-face classes in research methods, including foundations of educational research, qualitative research, and survey research. He is a research associate in the Office of Qualitative and Mixed Methods Research at the University of Nebraska, Lincoln, and the director of the Assessment and Institutional Research at Grace University in Omaha. He holds a PhD in speech communication from Pennsylvania State University (1995). Dr. Shope specializes in grounded theory and case study designs and has worked on mixed methods research projects. He has coauthored an instructor's manual for a research text and cowritten conference papers dealing with technology in teacher education and mixed methods research in mass communication.

Jean Whitney is currently assistant professor of special education at the University of Southern Maine, where she teaches research methods, action research, a course on transitions for elementary and secondary students, and supervises and co-coordinates a unified secondary, special education and content certification master's degree program. Prior to her work at USM, Whitney coordinated a doctoral-level program in educational leadership education and disability policy at UMASS Boston. In 1998 she was awarded a Switzer Fellowship from the National Institute for Disability and Rehabilitation Research, which funded research on the school-to-adult life experiences of students with and without disabilities in a Massachusetts High School. Her current research agenda involves capturing the voices, impressions, and firsthand accounts of education from a diverse array of students and teachers in today's schools. She works with students who have significant disabilities in research that uncovers their perspectives with authenticity and clarity. One strategy to accomplish this is called Photovoice, a participatory action approach to helping disenfranchised groups use cameras, write about their pictures, and share the pictures and words with policymakers. Using more traditional research methods, Whitney's research focuses on diverse, urban, high school students' reports of the barriers and factors that stand in the way of their pursuit of their choice of careers. In addition to this professional work with high school students and preservice teachers, Whitney keeps busy with two children of her own.